NOMMO

NOMMO

A Literary Legacy of Black Chicago (1967-1987)

An Anthology of the OBAC
Writers' Workshop
Edited by Carole A. Parks

OBAhouse

The OBAC Writers' Workshop, Chicago, Illinois
OBAhouse
Copyright © 1987 by The Organization of Black American
Culture (OBAC) Writers' Workshop
All rights reserved. Published in 1987

Printed in the United States of America

Acknowledgments: This project is partially
supported by a grant from the Illinois Arts
Council, a state agency; by a grant from the
Chicago Office of Fine Arts/City Arts I, made
possible by the Illinois Arts Council, the John D.
and Catherine T. MacArthur Foundation and the
Woods Charitable Trust; and by the generous
patronage of Dorothy Abbott and Soyini Madison.

Library of Congress Catalog Number: 0-933653-02-6

Dedicated to
Hoyt Williams Fuller

Contents

I. Essays
The OBAC Tradition

Literary and Social Commentary

II. Poetry
1967 - 1976

III. Creative Prose
(Fiction/Drama)

IV. Poetry
1977 - 1987

V. Guest Contributions:
Remembering Hoyt W. Fuller

Preface

Nommo.

Have you ever beheld a blackberry? I mean, carefully, thoughtfully examined it? The flesh as sweet as sun, translucent and blueblack. Tender. Its surface a study in bumpy hills and deep valleys. It is a fruit of many seeds, capable of reproducing itself a thousand times over.

Nommo.

If words were fruit, then this volume would burst with its own blackberry ripeness. The sweeter the juice.

Nommo.

The power of the word. The exquisite blueblack flesh. The fruit of many seeds. Our voices, vineripened and ready. For the most potent wine. The deepest cobbler. The sweetest jam.

Nommo is the journal of the OBAC (Organization of Black American Culture) Writers' Workshop. (*Nommo* is of Bantu origin and means the magical power of the word to make material change.) And this volume is indeed a special one. We have departed from the normal periodical format and created an anthology as rich, we hope, as the twenty-year history we celebrate herein.

OBAC Writers' Workshop, 20 years old in 1987, is indeed the oldest organization of its kind in the country. But it is not just age we celebrate here. We celebrate the deliberate seasoning that makes this one wine, that one vinegar.

We celebrate the lifeline that brought us here; the tradition of Black Chicago literature that extends back to the Thirties and Forties and the era of Langston Hughes, Richard Wright, Arna Bontemps, Margaret Walker. We celebrate our bridges. Gwendolyn Brooks, whose literary width and breadth span the generations from the Forties to the Eighties. And beyond.

We celebrate, we recognize and acknowledge the history that coils itself around us, the rings of the great oak. We celebrate our roots and our branches.

OBAC Writers' Workshop is an integral part of the literary tradition of Black Chicago, which in turn is integral to a Renaissance of Black Arts nationally and internationally. The founding writers of the workshop, as you shall later read, articulated the concerns and issues of our reality—race and culture, politics and power. They, like OBAC's early visual arts workshop which created the Wall of Respect, espoused a public approach to art. They took it out of the ivory towers and into the streets, parks, taverns, churches.

This is the founding spirit of OBAC, and though the group has been through countless transformations since 1967, this remains the guiding philosophy; to develop Black writers and critics, and an aesthetic by which they both must be measured.

OBAC writers have represented every walk of life, from cab drivers to college professors. Among their ranks include some of the most well-known and respected writers in the nation. Many of them have earned the accolades of the literary world: National Endowment Fellowship, Carl Sandburg Award, American Book Award, General Electric Foundation Award for Younger Writers, Illinois Arts Council Fellowship, among others. They have been the celebrated and the unsung, the famous and the ordinary. And all that falls in between.

This fat, ripe volume of poetry, prose, and plays represents the evolution of the writers and writings that have come out of OBAC over the past 20 years. It is also blessed to have within its heart a crisp collection of works dedicated to OBAC's co-founder, longtime advisor, and guiding spirit, the late editor and scholar, Hoyt W. Fuller.

This is the blackberry and its seeds are many. Take them. Taste them. And let them grow within you.

Sandra Jackson-Opoku
President
OBAC Writers' Workshop
September 1987

Introduction

In traditional life, the individual . . . owes his existence to other people, including those of past generations and his contemporaries. . . . Just as God made the first man, as God's man, so now man himself makes the individual who becomes the corporate or social man. It is a deeply religious transaction. Only in terms of other people does the individual become conscious of his own being, his own duties, his privileges and responsibilities towards himself and towards other people. . . . The individual can only say: 'I am, because we are; and since we are, therefore I am.' This is a cardinal point in the understanding of the African view of man.

Space and time are closely linked, and often the same word is used for both. As with time, it is the content which defines space. . . . The land provides [Africans] with the roots of existence, as well as binding them mystically to their departed. People walk on the graves of their forefathers, and it is feared that anything separating them from these ties will bring disaster to family and community life. To remove Africans by force from their land is an act of such great injustice that no foreigner can fathom it.
—John S. Mbiti
  African Religions and Philosophy

Now like my sister's embrace
Across the treacherous waters and centuries
I want to put my mouth on paper
The poet in me wants to carve
A monument in song
A simple song
Stronger than any granite wall
A song that says
Kate Molale is the people

But the poem won't come
—from "My Sister," by Keorapetse Kgositsile, in
  Somehow We Survive, *edited by Sterling Plumpp*

Experience this anthology as a family album: as pictures of how we are, once were and promise to be; as a record that sings of our daily triumphs and tragedies. For there is a Spirit in this place, greater than form. Sometimes it growls and grabs us, rattling bones in the closets of our consciousness. Sometimes it insinuates itself in, subtly or sensuously reading the mind like the life lines of our palms. And, sometimes, it takes us so high that we can touch the heavens of our own hem.

Can I get a witness? Will you be a witness to the Spirit of the African family? Because this album is for us. For our eyes. No retouching. For our ears. No synthesizing raw energy into background music for somebody else's lives. As Toni Morrison said recently, referring to a woman in her novel, *Beloved,* "I imagine Sethe in the room. If I read to her what I've written, will she say I'm telling the truth? . . . If I'm specific, and I don't overexplain, then anybody can overhear me."

So everybody is here—not separately labeled away behind "Gucci" or "underclass"; instead, a Kwanzaa kaleidoscope of dashikis trimmed in liberation colors, designer sequins from Knew Yohk, corner-store burgundy suits, Army fatigues, and resplendent redyellowgreen prints from the Motherland. Nobody discarded onto park benches, into paper bags under the "L," or behind walls with no exit because they might ruin the mood. How could we leave anyone out, when the Spirit is so expansive it infused the first human ever born, and at this moment embraces a new infant in every part of the world?

The Organization of Black American Culture (OBAC) Writers' Workshop was born of this Spirit. OBAC, too, is grounded but still becoming. Its workshop mirrors the contradictions and consistencies of a gathering place truly open to the community. Where someone who has just discovered the power of words sits next to an accomplished writer familiar with nearly every masterpiece of world literature. Where the craftsperson debates someone who "just lets it flow." Where language is as personal and many splendored as the different backgrounds and perspectives that shape it.

Yes, OBAC writers are more "political" than others. But only to the extent that they make clear where they are coming from, and precisely because they understand that "nonpolitical" writers in fact support a very specific, static Western aesthetic. One which pretends, indeed seeks, to divorce form from content, action from consequence; which extolls beauty, time, land or words as Things apart from spirit or function; Things to be possessed for their own sake; property that can be stolen, hoarded, fenced, subjugated, gutted—"civilized," like slaves, for the collector's private enjoyment.

OBAC members seek to be a part of—not apart from—their community. They absorb, reflect, recall, evaluate, interpret, illuminate, divine *vis-à-vis* that community. They are also concerned with aesthetics, but in order to free, not to shackle. Their standards of excellence emphasize truth, growth, purpose and responsibility. Their craft serves not to escape or distort reality, but to communicate it in ways it can be brought home and handled.

Do not misunderstand: of course, OBAC writers strive to say something well; they simply believe it even more important that they have something to say. Something that affirms our worth as a people, our connectedness to the human and natural world; that negates predominate political messages which would persuade us of the opposite (*e.g.*, that hair can be "good" or "bad"; that those who run it "misspeak" and "mismanage," while others lie and steal; that CIA thugs are "freedom fighters," but dispossessed Africans, "rebels"). OBAC's aesthetic respects the contributions of other cultures, serves as a bridge to worlds both internal and beyond. And in its focus on the struggles of the human spirit, their work strikes a far more universal chord than their detractors dare admit.

The challenge of this journal/book is that we are dealing with something organic, oral and aural, which, of course, the printed page is not. We're dealing with an aesthetic that continues to evolve from—indeed, *after*—the very work it seeks to describe. Scholar-musician Max Roach once alluded to this characteristic in *Black World* magazine (11/73) when explaining why our tradition focuses on personal interpretation, why "our culture . . . allows us the luxury of being an individual." Europeans, he said, promote the "colonial psyche" that you can standardize greatness because *they already produced it,* centuries ago, through Shakespeare, Bach, Michelangelo, *et al.* "I believe there's greater and greater and greater," he continued. "And this is why I say our culture is fluid, that each generation . . . we just keep growing and growing and we grow out of each other, just like . . . an endless book."

In other words, we did not approach this volume as some Super-BowlWorldHeavyweightMissAmericaPageant of the Universe's Greatest Writers Who Ever Lived. We began by inviting everyone who has been an OBAC member to submit some of their favorite and/or most representative work, old as well as new. If we couldn't locate someone, we tried to get samples of their work from OBAC publications and other sources. We had a number of ambitious goals: to show the level of excellence the organization has sustained for over 20 years; to show the range of its various members; to show lesser known and new writers; and to show how OBAC alumni have developed over the years.

As editor, I had only two major concerns: 1. Focus on the all-inclusive Spirit of OBAC. (Members don't always agree with each other, but their procedure is that they still have to listen.) 2. Try to be faithful to the individual writer's logic. (Even if it looks broke, it don't necessarily need fixing.) Most of the writers experiment with punctuation, spelling, capitalization, and form to create a personal style, authentic voice and/or unusual perspective the reader can usually appreciate. When I couldn't tell (or ask about) the writer's design, I left the work alone. These cases generally involved spelling (*e.g.*, a possibly unintended *double entendre*) or inconsistencies in usage that is standard in the community and does not detract from the writer's message.

We divided the largest body of work—poetry—into pre-1977 and after, since the latter period saw OBAC serving a new generation of poets without benefit of its eminent founder-mentor, Hoyt W. Fuller. The only real liberty I took resulted from OBAC members' rather cruel request that I not organize the pieces along the usual alphabetical lines. So, particularly with the poetry, I tried to suggest the kind of dialogue, versatility and on-going development that characterize OBAC. (Not to worry; there's an index to the writers if you're one of the thousands who doesn't read anthology pages in sequence.)

I am especially gratified that we could include the special section on Hoyt Fuller. Having agreed to edit a commemorative issue of *First World* magazine following Hoyt's death in 1981, I felt compelled to carry around the scheduled contents when we had problems getting the issue published. How fitting that his "children" reserved his place in this album of their family reunion.

A special thanks to Angela Jackson, Sandra Jackson-Opoku, Judy Massey, Sterling Plumpp, and Collette Armstead for their assistance, particularly in compiling the OBAC biographical notes. (Though we could not get updated information on all the members, plans are to rectify this in a forthcoming companion volume.)

Finally, I'd like to remember all those who, without fanfare, keep on keeping on, who provide the inspiration for the following portraits and songs. As South African poet "Willie" Kgositsile suggests in his poem, "Sisters," words (especially English ones) replace neither the unfettered purity of music nor the muscle needed to carve freedom out of granite walls. Nevertheless, words do have power. *Nommo*, as incantation, is the re-calling and sharing of our Spirit that is source as well as destiny.

ever wonder where the circle came from
or who were the first people to use the triangle?
who were the original cultivators of the earth, who used
water of the nile to power minds and machines? what people
created music from instrument and voice and viewed the
building of cities as art and science? who were the
first to love because love contained the secrets of tomorrow?
look at yourselves.
—from "Seeking Ancestors," in *Killing Memory, Seeking Ancestors*, by Haki R. Madhubuti

Carole A. Parks
September 1987

ESSAYS

1

■ ■

The OBAC Tradition: Don L. Lee, Carolyn Rodgers and The Early Years

Maria K. Mootry
Guest Contributor

In the 1960's, almost every Black Chicago poet who wrote a poem also penned an essay, clarified issues, took a stand. At the risk of oversimplification, their socio-artistic ideology may best be described as one based on a dialectic between oppositional and consolidationist modes or ideas. The oppositional modes of thought were directed outward to attack global and national racism, and inward against various perceived betrayers, *i.e.*, primarily middle-class assimilationist Negro Americans. The consolidationist modes were directed outward to promote unity with the international Third World and Afro-World populations, and inward toward community solidarity, often focusing on building unity between the sexes.

The dialectic also involved a selective historical consciousness that tended to validate the present and future at the expense of the past. Thus, names of contemporary places, people, organizations, and publications dominate the Sixties' cultural ambiance. Chicago poets lived in a continuous present, inspired by happenings at the South Side Community Art Center, the DuSable Museum of Afro-American History, Phil Cohran's Afro-Arts Theatre, and Ellis Bookstores. For organizations, they turned to Val Gray Ward's Kuumba Workshop or Don L. Lee's [Haki R. Madhubuti] Institute of Positive Education. For alternative political and lifestyle ideas there were the powerful persuasions of the Nation of Islam's *Muhammad Speaks* newspaper. For publishing new Black poets' poems, essays and pictures, there were Don L. Lee's Third World Press and Johnson Publishing Company's *Negro Digest* (later *Black World*).

For their artistic practice, they turned to the Organization of Black American Culture. OBAC was founded in 1967 by a group of writers, musicians, and painters including persons as varied as David Llorens and Gerald (Abdul) McWorter. The organization's major mentors were two older, established Chicago intellectuals, the Pulitzer Prize winning poet Gwendolyn Brooks and Hoyt Fuller, critic-editor and fiction writer, who was then managing editor of Johnson's *Negro Digest*. For an overview of OBAC's many members, see Eugene Redmond's handy poetry survey, *Drumvoices*[1] (pp. 386-388). Our focus here will be on Don L. Lee and Carolyn Rodgers, who were OBAC's most productive writers, both in terms of poetry and poetic theory. During OBAC's salad days, Lee published four key volumes: *Think Black!* (1967); *Black Pride* (1968); *Don't Cry, Scream* (1969), and *We Walk the Way of the New World* (1970). In addition to several essays, Rodgers' poetry includes *Paper Soul* (1968), *Songs of A Blackbird* (1969), *2 Love Raps* (1969), and the collection, *How I Got Ovah* (1975). In the interest of time and space, these two writers will be used here to point up some key issues and practices of OBAC's early history.

Just as the Harlem Renaissance poets of the 1920's turned their backs on the Dunbarian dialect plantation tradition, the poets of Chicago's Black Renaissance, many of them members of OBAC, turned their backs on their integrationist-modernist predecessors. Rightly or not, they perceived the precise, intricate poetry of Black Modernists to be a capitulation to white elitist cultural hegemony. Consolidation, or racial solidarity was the ruling consensus, and at the heart of that consensus was the issue of the very language a poet should use. For instance, Carolyn Rodgers, one of the more successful and prolific members of OBAC, articulated her artistic ideology in several essays. In 1970, she denounced "White English" in her essay, "The Literature of Black"[2] when she wrote;

> "Black writers must not use the colonizer language as it exists. Correctness, learnedness, is intensified oppression, better oppression." (Rodgers, p. 10)

Possibly following Frantz Fanon's remarks on the role of language in Afro-World oppression, Rodgers denounces not only "correct" pronunciation of English, but "correct" spelling, "correct" punctuation, and "correct" typography. Calling for a new order, she warns:

> "To start sentences with capitals, to end sentences with periods, to use commas, etc., etc., etc., reeks of a higher subtler more destructive order. Which we seek to destroy in Black minds for example. . . ." (Rodgers, p. 10)

Thus, Rodgers, even in her *prose* tries to defy what she considers language-oppression. Writing "Black" for Carolyn Rodgers and for other OBAC members, meant creating a new linguistic order: "call it flat rappin or round or rhyme rappin, dig it. . . ." (Rodgers, p. 11). Rising to an almost mystical conclusion, Rodgers cites Coltrane's and Sun-Ra's non-European sound patterns as the basis for limitless forms—whether in poetry or the plastic arts. Painters, she suggests, should forget canvases and paint "on anything, everything." Musicians, she exhorts, should use "2-sharp y-minus x-nothing every sound nonsense sound inner liberating sound." (Rodgers, p. 11).

Rodgers' concept of art embraces style as a weapon. For Rodgers, the artistic rebel must constantly seek alternatives to the majority media. Rodgers' corollary assumption was that aesthetic reordering would disrupt oppression. Or, as she explains:

> The very order of words on paper becomes
> questionable . . .
> symptoms of the honkie's ORDER,
> like where
> you put stamps on letters
> how a man and woman walk down the street
> what fingers you wear rings on when married
> what time the world goes to work (9) and
> lunch 12-1 and gets off (5) . . .
> Perhaps what is needed is nonsense to create
> newsense. Liberating sense, Sense that has no
> oppressive tradition. Check. The very
> sentence,
> *John walked,*
> is totally different from
> John split,
> John made it,
> John spaced.
> (Rodgers, p. 10)

Don L. Lee (Haki Madhubuti), however, seemed to perceive literary art less as a revolutionary end than as the means to a revolution beyond the art itself, *i.e.*, beyond the mere reordering of majority forms. In his *Jump Bad* essay, "Black Writing,"[3] for instance, Lee describes the "shadowiness" of the Harlem Renaissance and the "restrictiveness" of the Negritude Movement to emphasize the *functional* aspect of the new Black art: "The poet of the Sixties and Seventies moves beyond mere rage and 'black is beautiful' to bring together a new set of values, emotions, historical perspectives and futuristic direction—a transformation from the lifestyle of the *sayer* to that of the doer." (*Jump Bad*, p. 37)

Later, in the same essay, interestingly, Lee cautions that it is impossible to define the Black aesthetic. For him, Black art is subject to constant innovation and advancement, altering each time a new artist appears (*Jump Bad*, p. 38). Thus, Rodger's and Lee's aesthetic theories demonstrate the complexity of Black Arts Movement theory in general.

If the theoretical positions among Chicago OBAC poets are complex, the question of interconnected poetic practice is equally challenging. This is true for a number of reasons. Two salient ones are (a) the poets themselves practiced a much wider range of theme and technique than they espoused, and (b) the innovations they sought ironically had roots both in the modernist defiance of conventional prosody and the Beat (1950's) emphasis on linkages between poetry and contemporary music, particularly progressive jazz.

To illustrate these points, it may be useful to take a closer look at one of Lee's earliest statements on his Black Arts philosophy and his poetic theory. In his Introduction to *Think Black!* (1967),[4] Don L. Lee opposes Harlem Renaissance poets like Countee Cullen who insisted on being writers first, Negro writers second. "Black poet am I," Lee declares defiantly. Then he goes on to explain where Black art comes from ("created from black forces that live within the body"); which Black writers had lost their creativity (Louis Lomax, Frank Yerby and Ralph Ellison); and what Black Art should do ("Elevate and enlighten our people and lead them toward an awareness of self, *i.e.*, their blackness"). For Lee, as for Carolyn Rodgers, the Black writer was to maintain close contact with the Black masses: "The Black writer learns from his people and . . . is able to give back his knowledge to the people . . . Black artists are culture stabilizers, bringing back old values, and introducing new ones." (*Think Black!*, p.6) Yet Lee's defense of the Black "masses" is not as racially ethnocentric as it seems. A closer look at the introduction and Lee's poetry shows not only a man who proclaims defiantly, "Black poet am I," but a latter day prophet whose prose and poetry continually remind Euro-America of its sins against *all* the colored peoples of the world. For instance, in the same introduction mentioned, Lee places his birthday not in the context of Black history, but in the context of America's incarceration of its Japanese citizens. Giving his birthdate as February 1942, Lee proceeds to explain:

> In the spring of that same year 110,000 persons of Japanese descent were placed in protective custody by the white people of the United States. Two out of every three of these were American citizens by birth; the other third were aliens forbidden by law to be citizens. No charges had been filed against these people nor had any hearing been held. The removal of these people was on racial or ancestral grounds only. World War II, the war against racism; yet no Germans or other enemy agents were placed in protective custody. There should have been Japanese writers directing their writings toward Japanese audiences. (*Think Black!*, p. 6)

Later, in an anti-Vietnam War poem, "The Long Reality," Lee decries Napalm bombings and expresses solidarity with his "Viet-brothers," calling upon them in these lines:

> Viet-brother come give us a hand
> we fight for freedom,
> we fight for land. . . .

Therefore, Lee's definition of a "Black poet" seems to include a Third World consciousness much broader than the Afro-American racial nationalism usually associated with proponents of a "Black aesthetic."

Rodgers exhibits a different type of "deviation" when the total corpus of her Black Arts work is reviewed. Although she demands a specific aesthetic, as cited above in her "Literature of Black" essay, and although much of her poetry is an attempt to meet this aesthetic, a sizeable portion of her poetry is actively "mainstream" in idea and form. In "One" from *Paper Soul* (1968), a fine poem reprinted several times, Rodgers addresses a recurring theme in her writings, *i.e.*, loneliness. Not only the theme, but her word choice is reminiscent of some of Gwendolyn Brooks' own early "modernist" poetry. The opening paragraph offers a good example:

> People die from loneliness
> Life becomes an incurable disease,
> a job, an excuse—an operation
> of sloppy directions.

The poem's alienation theme, its use of metaphor and its diction remind the reader of modernist Gwendolyn Brooks' portrait, written almost 30 years earlier, of a lonely, isolated couple locked in a meaningless marriage:

> Clogged and soft and sloppy eyes
> Have lost the light that bites or terrifies.
> There are no swans and swallows anymore.[5]

Rodgers' last line is no Black effusive affirmation, but is as starkly stoical as much of Brooks' early poetry. "I am the stray one,"[6] Rodgers concludes, accepting life's diminution as simply as Brooks' resigned residents accepted the disappearance of "swans and swallows."

The use of wit, oddly enough, is another unifying thread among OBAC poets—wit and satire, of course, often being good literary weapons. The wit varies however. Rodgers' humor is broader, more simply comic, while Lee's humor is often satiric and, true to his functional view of art, used to expose an enemy target's self-delusions. Rodgers, for instance, in "Now Ain't That Love," offers a slapstick comic view of herself hopelessly in love with her man:

> when i'm near him
> i am a skinny, dumb, knocked-kneed
> lackey, drooling on the words of
> my maharajah . . . *(Paper Soul)*

Lee uses humor and satire more often than most OBAC writers, which explains in part his extreme popularity as a reader of his poetry. Lee's wit is satirical, reflective of the Black vernacular tradition of signifying and making fun of grim situations (Langston Hughes called it "laughing to keep from crying"). In "A Poem for Black Women," Lee offers this candid aside:

> i mean
> that woman moved
> me
> (i even hit on her a couple of times)
> *(Think Black!*, p. 10)

Yet the over-all poem is a "consolidationist" theme of unity between Black men and women. In a more somber poem about his faulty upbringing, entitled, "Education," Lee injects a bittersweet, cutting wit, primarily through oxymoronic patterns. The opening stanza is a good example of this use of tragic satire:

"I had a good teacher
He taught me everything I know;
how to lie,
cheat,
and how to strike the softest blow.
(*Think Black!*, p. 11)

Lee's teacher, he goes on, taught him how "to be inferior without hate," how to "pray, smile and how not to fight," how to "accept most things against my will." The irony and satire are effective, even devastating. The mode, of course, is oppositional toward the Black bourgeoisie. At times, Lee's humor spreads to farce, as when he admits in "In a Period of Growth" that he would have reacted badly to anyone calling him Black before his "conversion":

i wd've
broke his right eye out,
jumped into his chest,
talked about his momma,
lied on his sister,
and dared him to say it again.
all in one breath.
(*Think Black!*, p. 19)

Lee's "taxes" is reminiscent of Langston Hughes' lighter poetry in its simplicity; it also demonstrates Lee's capacity for building up to a surprise ending with a clever play on words, even as he makes his social statement:

Income taxes
every year due,
Sales taxes,
I pay these too.
Luxury taxes,
maybe one or two,
Black taxes,
on everything I do.
(*Think Black!*, p. 19)

The use of innovative typography is another common bond among OBAC poets. For Lee, the innovative typography is often a way at getting to the ideas Rodgers articulated in "The Literature of Black"—

that is, a new sense of language and idea; the effect is often considerable, leading to aural as well as visual wit. The concluding poem of *Think Black!* is only one of many examples:

BLACK PEOPLE   THINK
PEOPLE   BLACK PEOPLE
THINK PEOPLE   THINK
BLACK PEOPLE   THINK—
THINK BLACK.
(*Think Black!*, p. 24)

The poem is almost a "concrete poem," which can be read horizontally as well as vertically. An even more complicated example, reflecting possible jazz influences, is found in Lee's "Mwilu/or Poem for the Living (for Charles and LaTanya)." The poem opens with this spacing:

jump bigness upward
like u jump clean   make everyday the weekend
& work like u party.
(*Jump Bad*, p. 40)

The single line "work like u party" is typical Lee wit and "spoken" cadence full of double entendres. The next excerpt from the poem, however, is more complex, more visually exciting and probably even more exciting aurally:

never   Muslim eating pig sandwiches   never
never   listerine breath even cuss proper   never
never   u ignorant because *smart* was yr teacher   never
never   wander under wonder fan-like avenues   never
never   *will be never* as long as never teaches   never.
(*Jump Bad*, p. 41)

In these lines, social criticism mingles with Black vernacular and postmodernist concretism. True to Rodgers' dictum, Lee defies "correctness" to make a unique poetic statement through form.

In "Somebody Call (for help)," a poem about a man/woman fight in the ghetto, Rodgers herself uses innovative typography to stress innercity hysteria. In the poem's final lines, Rodgers builds to a climactic use of capital letters and "s" sounds to suggest simultaneously running blood on the walls and the bewilderment of ghetto residents:

BLOODSsss
RUNNINGRUNNINGRUNNING
against the walls
. . . .
somebody   (pleeease)
CALL
for help

The phrase "against the wall" relays the sense of entrapment; the desperate need for deliverance. The word "Bloods" is a pun, referring to Black people as well as to blood itself. Again, social protest and artform are one; the message becomes one with its medium.

Did Rodgers or Lee or any of the Black poets learn any of these poetic techniques from Beat poets or Modernists? Certainly as early as 1960, Gwendolyn Brooks had played with Black English and visual spacing to great effect in her famous poem, "We Real Cool." The opening lines from the poem establish its uniqueness and its breathtaking use of enjambment:

> We real cool.   We
> left school.   We

Also, throughout her poetic career, Brooks and her Black modernist contemporaries, Robert Hayden and Melvin Tolson, were known for their innovation and their capacity to shift from classical to vernacular diction and forms. However, the OBAC poets seemed more responsive to the counterculture and street culture that surrounded them. Certainly the poets of Chicago felt freer to use "profane" words and street language in a way that makes Brooks' use of the vernacular tame in comparison. Rodgers could begin a poem with the lines "I mah/kick yo ass-ss/" without blinking. Lee could report his girlfriend's opinion of men ("blackmen ain't shit") with similar lack of compunction. The fact is, the Sixties were a *different* time than the Twenties or the Forties, not only for Black cultural nationalists but for all counterculture activists. And the best OBAC writers, including Lee and Rodgers, wrote out of their own place and time, with the approbation of flexible mentors like Gwendolyn Brooks.

Notes

[1] Eugene B. Redmond, *Drumvoices: The Mission of Afro-American Poetry: A Critical History* (New York: Anchor Press, 1976).

[2] Carolyn Rodgers, "The Literature of Black," *Black World* (June, 1970), pp. 5-11). Hereafter cited in the text as "Rodgers."

[3] Don L. Lee, "Black Writing," in *Jump Bad,* ed. by Gwendolyn Brooks (Detroit: Broadside Press, 1971), pp. 37-39. Hereafter cited in the text as *Jump Bad.*

[4] Don L. Lee, Introduction, *Think Black!* (Detroit: Broadside Press, 1967). Hereafter cited in the text as *Think Black!*

[5] Gwendolyn Brooks, "the parents," *The World of Gwendolyn Brooks* (New York: Harper, 1971), p. 70.

[6] Carolyn Rodgers, "One," *Paper Soul* (Chicago: Third World Press, 1968). No pagination. Hereafter cited in the text as *Paper Soul.*

Editor's Note: The following Statement of Purpose and commentary by Abdul Alkalimat, Haki Madhubuti, Hoyt Fuller, Sterling Plumpp, and Angela Jackson were originally published in OBAC's periodicals, NOMMO and Cumbaya. They provide a brief overview of the organization's philosophy, founding and development.

Statement of Purposes

To work toward the development and definition of a Black Aesthetic

To encourage the highest quality of literary expression reflecting the Black Experience

To establish and define the standards by which that creative writing which reflects the Black Experience is to be judged and evaluated

To encourage the growth and development of Black critics who are fully qualified to evaluate and judge Black literature on its own merits while, at the same time, cognizant of the traditional values and standards of Western literature and fully able to articulate the differences between the two literatures

To encourage an atmosphere of brotherhood and tolerance within the workshop, so that criticism can be both given and accepted as being constructive in intent

To work toward the establishment of a regular publication—in the form of newsletter, journal or newspaper, or in whatever form the workshop members choose—which will make available to the Black community the creative products from the workshop, ideas relative to Black Experientialism and OBAC, and news and announcements

To work toward the periodical publication of books and anthologies containing the literary work of workshop members, plus, if desirable, creative work from other OBAC workshops

To provide a forum and a community of hospitality for local and visiting writers

■■■■■■■■■■■■■■■■■■■■■■■■■

OBAC Position Paper:
Some Ideological Considerations

Gerald A. McWorter (Abdul Alkalimat)
(April 1967)

The purpose of this policy paper is to state some of the notions relevant to my thinking about OBAC. I hope to address myself to the following questions: 1) In general terms, what is the fundamental posture of OBAC? 2) What are the goals of OBAC? and 3) What programmatic directions are implicit in our goals?

There are two sides to our general approach, the realities of the everyday cultural life of Black People, as well as the development of a special set of standards with which to interpret and evaluate. On the one hand, we are saying it is necessary to establish a new positive acceptance of our cultural resources, our treasures. The boo-ga-loo might thus be understood for men as a warrior's dance, arrogant, strong, and Black, and for women as an uninhibiting form for the portrayal of Black sensuality. We join W. E. B. Du Bois in saying (1900): "Especially do I believe in the Negro race: in the beauty of its genius, the sweetness of its soul." However, we are not saying that whatever is Black (*i.e.*, found among Black People) is good. We must develop standards which establish our self-conscious control over our own culture. Consider for a moment the disc jockey and the art museum curator. The DJ is most sensitive to mass reactions, while the curator is most sensitive to a small élite of art critics. We must find/discover the dynamic of synthesis, and hopefully not be forced to choose between the mass approach and the élite approach.

A primary fact about the life-style of Black People is the intensity of the "now." We must incorporate this into OBAC and avoid being static in the current context of Black life. This is relevant in a number of ways: 1) A shortcoming of many groups dealing with knowledge about Black People is the indiscriminate concern for chronicle and "facts." OBAC must have as criteria for its substance "the now possibility" of it; so, rather than chronicle and facts, our concern is with living legend and myth. As a social scientist once wrote, "Whatever men define as real to themselves, is real in its consequence." 2) Remember the British man having formal tea in the bush of Africa. We must not inadvertently allow OBAC to generate such conflict and farce. We must not superimpose one thing on another. Ours must be a new, *now*timed Black dialectic. We have as a given the Black community in all its complexity and splendor, and we have a developing set of ideas, ideals, and visions of the good. In being responsible to

11

both, new forms, new content, new programs must be projected as our only legitimate future.

What of our goals? We have to be concerned with an end result which includes the art produced, the artists involved, the people involved, and the context within which everything happens. While no definitive statement can be made at this point, let us consider a few tentative notions. Recognize that in beginning something new, we must inspect and consider everything, even the familiar. Our goal in art is to develop and project new themes, heroes, and attitudes. This content must stand the test of being contemporary, authentically related to Black People's experiences, and consistent with the ideas and values developed as the overall ideology of OBAC.

The People. We must develop a critical audience, an audience which is at once receptive and demanding. We must recruit those Black artists robbed of creative expression. We must mold our audience and young artists, not into some ambiguous undifferentiated mass public, but into a self-conscious brotherhood moving with a purpose and a method.

This, then, is the job ahead. It is the job of building OBAC into an organization deeply grounded in the Black community, all inclusive of both the people and their artists. It is the job of building an organization which far transcends individual differences, the job of building a movement so people will have faith in themselves and the strength of self confidence. ART CAN BE REVOLUTIONARY, AND SO IT MUST BE WITH OBAC.

We must remember that among the most denigrating aspects of what happened to our people in America is the systematic attempt to deny them history, a link with a past of proud kingdoms, whereby symbols, images, and sounds express the spiritual truth of a people.

OBAC must ring fear and terror into the ears of those who are guilty.

OBAC must be celebrated with joy among Black People, "soul clap hands and sing."

Black Poetics/for
the many to come

Don L. Lee (Haki R. Madhubuti)
(1968)

The most significant factor about the poems/poetry you will be reading is the *idea*. The *idea* is not the manner in which a poem is conceived but the conception itself. From the *idea* we move toward development & direction (direction: the focusing of yr/idea in a positive or negative manner; depending on the poet's orientation). Poetic form is synonymous with poetic structure and is the guide used in developing yr/idea.

What u will be reading is blackpoetry. Blackpoetry is written for/to/about & around the lives/spiritactions/humanism & total existence of blackpeople. Blackpoetry in form/sound/word usage/intonation/rhythm/repetition/definition/direction & beauty is opposed to that which is now (& yesterday) considered poetry, i.e., whi-te poetry. Blackpoetry in its purest form is diametrically opposed to whi-te poetry. Whereas, blackpoets deal in the concrete rather than the abstract (concrete: art for people's sake; black language or Afro-american language in contrast to standard english, &c.). Blackpoetry moves to define and legitimize blackpeople's reality (*that* which is real to us). Those in power (the unpeople) control and legitimize the negroes' (the realpeople's) reality out of that which they, the unpeople, consider real. That is, to the unpeople the television programs *Julia* and *The Mod Squad* reflect their vision of what they feel the blackman *is* about or *should* be about. So, in effect, blackpoetry is out to negate the negative influences of the mass media; whether it be TV, newspaper, magazines or some whi-te boy standing on a stage saying he's a "blue eyed soul brother."

Blackpeople must move to where all confrontations with the unpeople are meaningful and constructive. That means that most, if not all, blackpoetry will be *political*. I've often come across black artists (poets, painters, actors, writers, &c.) who feel that they and their work should be apolitical; not realizing that to be apolitical is *to be* political in a negative way for blackfolks. There is *no* neutral blackart; either it *is* or it *isn't*, period. To say that one is not political is as dangerous as saying, "by any means necessary," it's an "intellectual" cop-out, & niggers are copping-out as regularly as blades of grass in a New England suburb. Being political is also why the black artist is considered dangerous by those who rule, the unpeople. The black artist by defining and legitimizing his own reality becomes a positive force in the black community (just think of the results of Le Roi Jones [Imamu Amiri Baraka] writing the lyrics for the music of James Brown). You see, *black* for the blackpoet is a way of life. And, his totalactions will reflect that blackness & he will be an example for his community rather than another contradictor.

Blackpoetry will continue to define what *is* and what isn't. Will tell what it *to be* & how to *be* it (or bes it). Blackpoetry *is* and will continue to be an important factor in culture building. I believe Robert Hayden had culture building in mind when he wrote these lines in an early poem:

> It is time to call the children
> Into the evening quiet of the living-room
> And teach them the legends of their blood.

Blackpoetry is excellence & truth and will continue to seek such. Blackpoetry will move to expose & wipe-out that which is not necessary for our existence as a people. *As a people* is the only way we can endure and blacknation building must accelerate at top speed. Blackpoetry is Ornette Coleman teaching violin & the Supremes being black again. Blackpoetry is like a razor, it's sharp & will cut deep, not out to wound but to kill the inactive blackmind. Like, my oldman used to pickup numbers and he seldom got caught & I'm faster than him; this is a fight with well defined borders & I know the side I'm ON. See u. Go head, now.

—As-Salaam Alaikum

Introduction Toward The Black Aesthetic

Hoyt W. Fuller,
Advisor, OBAC Writers' Workshop
(1972)

What the writers of the Organization of Black American Culture (OBAC) are seeking to do is both quite simple and very profound. On the one hand, their aim is no more radical than the clear, imaginative representation of their experiences; but that, on the other hand, also happens to be revolutionary.

If there exists a paradox here, it flows from our history. It was never intended by the Europeans who seized this land from the Indians and who brought our ancestors here to labor for them that black men would ever stand free and proud. The slavers systematically set out to destroy those cultural links through which black people would have preserved their heritage, and Africa, the homeland, was deliberately defined as a "dark" and "savage" place where civilization did not exist until white men brought it. The black past, then, held no value or dignity; the only heritage worth owning, for the American children of Africa, was the heritage of the enslaver.

Generations of black Americans have lived out their lives seeing themselves through the eyes of white men. Even today, millions of black Americans evaluate their worthiness according to their approximation—in skin color, in morals, in outlook, in ambitions—of white standards. What they say to themselves, in effect, is this: I approach wholeness as a human being to the degree that I look and think and behave like white people.

Naturally, if the founders of the American republic never envisioned black people as free citizens, these great and good men never imagined that a black literature was possible. The American experience was the "universal" experience, and the literature which developed from this experience could be defined in its dimensions by those writers and critics whose task it was to reflect and authenticate it.

But black Americans did not remain slaves, and they did not remain shorn of their heritage. And, long before slavery was legally abolished in the land, black people were about the business of creating a literature which reflected their own experience. This literature, in its inherent statements, contradicts the credos and the postures of the American republic and, by inference, assigns evil and inhumanity to the American experience. Black literature accuses America. Black literature says to America: "You live a lie."

15

In its thrust to deny this assignment of guilt, the American Literary Establishment has sought to invalidate black literature. The literature which has dealt honestly with the black experience has been characterized as "protest" and, when possible, dismissed. Black writers have been advised to abandon their natural subjects and to select "universal" subjects, meaning, of course, those subjects which do not point the direct finger of accusation at white America; and those black writers who have obliged have been suitably rewarded with the esteem and fame which only the Literary Establishment can provide.

What the writers of the OBAC Writers' Workshop are attempting, simply, is to write naturally and honestly out of their own experiences, rejecting the counsel of the critics and the university professors that they concern themselves with "universals." And, in doing this, they are—wittingly or unwittingly, it does not matter—moving toward a black aesthetic.

And this is revolutionary. It is revolutionary because it represents, finally, an affirmation and validation of the black experience as the legitimate material for literature. It is revolutionary because it heralds the end of domination by the white Literary Establishment, which is, in essence, colonialist, and the beginning of the establishment of black criteria and black critics for the proper evaluation of that literature born of the black experience.

In this first volume of *NOMMO*, the OBAC writers demonstrate that they are moving onward toward the black aesthetic.

Foreword to *NOMMO*

Hoyt W. Fuller
(1971)

It is five years now since the Committee for the Arts, the precursor of the Organization of Black American Culture (OBAC), called together a group of interested Chicagoans in the main chamber of the South Side Community Art Center to launch a movement to encourage Black expression in the Arts. That general goal, of course, was not new; dozens of organizations concerned with the arts are formed annually in a city the size of Chicago, and most of them fade away after a few months, partly out of apathy, which is an omnipresent condition of Black life, but also partly out of confusion and frustration, which are inherent in the original quest. The Committee for the Arts recognized at the outset that its chances for some success over a more extended period of time resided in its special vision of how expression in the arts could be related to the basic problems of the community. It was the premise of the Committee that the apathy which seems always to be with us is a manifestation of the feeling of powerlessness and outsideness, which generates a sense of worthlessness, of nobodiness in Black people; and the Committee was convinced that, by releasing that natural, pent-up store of creativity within the community, by urging Black people toward an identification with and an acceptance of themselves and their images, their history, their humanity, art itself would achieve a fresh interpretation rooted in the lives, the aspirations—in a word, the experiences—of the community. The idea was revolutionary; it proposed that the usual approach to artistic expression which had been foisted upon Black people over the centuries had, of and in itself, inhibited when it did not destroy the Black creative impulse; and it suggested that the seeds of liberation—political and economic and social, as well as aesthetic—would be planted in the Black psyche through this new approach to artistic expression. The interest then was primarily political; art for the sake of Black empowerment was the principle.

As it turned out, there was more than a little logic in the fact that two esteemed writers (who are primarily poets) appeared as guests on that fateful afternoon. One was Arna Bontemps, a virtual "history of Black literature on the hoof," who then was visiting professor at the Circle Campus of the University of Illinois. The other writer was Margaret Danner, a poet who had been quietly demonstrating for decades in her strong but gentle poems what the Black Aesthetic is all about. Mr. Bon-

temps had begun his literary career in the early Twenties and was a friend
and associate of many of the writers of the Harlem Renaissance. Over the
years, his contribution—as poet, novelist, anthologist, historian and librarian at Fisk University—has been formidable; and on that Sunday afternoon at the Art Center he delivered a casually beautiful account of his
sojourn in the Black world of letters. Miss Danner, much younger than Mr.
Bontemps, but a veteran nevertheless in the task of opening Black people
to their beauty and to their possibilities, introduced the audience to her
work.

That was the beginning. At this point, there were only three
people associated with what was to become OBAC—Gerald McWorter
(now Abdul Hakimu Ibn Alkalimat), Conrad Kent Rivers (now deceased)
and this writer. A council of seven additional members was formed (Jeff R.
Donaldson, E. Duke McNeil, Joseph R. Simpson, Donald H. Smith,
George R. Ricks, Bennett J. Johnson and Ronald C. Dunham) to adminis-
ter the parent organization, and workshops were established in "community arts," art and literature.

In the spring of 1967, the Organization of Black American Culture—aptly named by Jeff Donaldson to incorporate the Yoruba word for
leader, *oba*, in the catch-letters—was introduced in a swift-paced, excite-
ment-generating program in the auditorium of the old Lincoln Center
(now the Center for Inner-City studies, a branch of Northeastern Illinois
State University). The community responded, and OBAC became one of
several new local institutions (Afro-Arts Theater, the AACM, the Black
Women's Committee, the Topographical Center) which promised to raise
the consciousness of Black people in Chicago to unprecedented levels of
responsibility and action.

The first year proved fruitful. Under Joe Simpson's direction, the
OBAC Community Workshop brought in relevant people like Imamu
Amiri Baraka (then still LeRoi Jones) and Ron Karenga to lend their
insight to the solution of problems facing the community, and encouraged
plain people to articulate their grievances and their aspirations. The
OBAC Artists Workshop, under the leadership of William Walker and Jeff
Donaldson, painted the original Wall of Respect at 43rd and Langley, the
landmark wall mural which was to serve as model and inspiration for a
whole new movement in people's art across the country. And the OBAC
Writers' Workshop, fortunately, supported by an extraordinarily talented
group of young people, moved out into taverns, churches and community
centers, preaching the unorthodox religion of the Beauty of Blackness to
scores of ordinary people who proved by their eager response that they
needed to believe. For a while during 1968, the OBAC Drama Workshop
flourished under the guidance of Ann Smith.

The first session of the Organization of Black American Culture
Writers' Workshop was held on the second floor of the South Side Community Art Center. It was the spring of 1967, and the community was
animated by an excitement that seemed, at the time, to portend great and
significant changes. In OBAC's second year, only the Writers' Workshop
remained to carry the burden of the aims of the original organization. The

workshop was beset by all the routine and unavoidable threats which loom over any Black institution trying to pursue positive goals, but it had been fortunately strengthened from the beginning by the presence of several young people of uncommon talent and determination, and the faith of these young people in both their own abilities and in the validity of the workshop's purpose served to anchor and to preserve the workshop. Looking back now, some of the threats seem ludicrous: there were, for example, Blacks who resisted the idea of the uniqueness of the Black experience and who tried to impose upon the workshop the notion that honest literary art could emerge through the screen of appropriated culture, style and aesthetics; there were disruptions by "writers" carrying the banner for Jesus, so militant in their missionary duty that they literally would not be moved; and there were the sick ones—lost, defiant, unteachable—dedicated to the proposition that every neurotic one of us is equal to the task of leading in a million different directions the way to Black salvation. Would-be writers came and went, gaining a measure of their potential in the process. Non-writers came and listened, and sometimes talked, and invariably went away impressed that there was something here, some seed, some richness. The famous writers came, Imamu Amiri Baraka, John A. Williams, Maya Angelou, Louise Meriwether, Nikki Giovanni, sometimes as guests, sometimes as visitors, and some personages became patrons, among them Sammy Davis, Jr., Brock Peters and the inestimable Gwendolyn Brooks.

After two years of rewarding residence at the South Side Community Art Center and then in the main hall of the Du Sable Museum of African American History and Art (courtesy of the always sympathetic Charles and Margaret Burroughs), OBAC found a storefront home on Thirty-fifth Street. With the aid of a small grant from the Illinois Sesquicentennial Commission (through the Illinois Art Council), OBAC published the first issue of what it hoped would be its quarterly journal, *NOMMO*. A brief time later, the OBAC *Newslettah* appeared. There was a second issue of *NOMMO* months later and another issue of the *Newslettah*, and then it became evident that OBAC was suffering from the same afflictions which inevitably bedevil voluntary groups—apathy, exhaustion, other-directedness. Furthermore, the flame of the revolution burned very low everywhere, and it was apparent that new blood and new outlooks would have to be added. Some of the members who had helped to launch OBAC as a contributing community organization dropped out, or moved on, and others moved in, encouraged by the accomplishments of the departed.

Meanwhile, OBAC had gained a reputation across the country, and several of its original members—Don L. Lee, Carolyn Rodgers, Johari Amini—were known internationally. The culturally aware in the city were as familiar with the organization as they were of much older, more economically viable institutions. A Speakers' Bureau had been organized to provide OBAC writers for school and community programs. In the spring semester, 1971, five OBAC members collaborated in designing and teaching a course in Black American Literature at Indiana University at

Bloomington. Sterling Plumpp, a poet steadily growing in power, organized a Young People's Writing Workshop. And Angela Jackson, Randson Boykin and Mwalimu took turns, with OBAC volunteers (Ann Smith, Donna Parks), in conducting a successful reading program for children at the Hall Branch Library. Altogether, OBAC members have published more than 25 volumes.

After more than four years, then, after upheavals and dark periods and even some nasty dissension, OBAC thrives. In late 1971, only two of the original members remain fully active—Don L. Lee and Johari Amini—but it so happens that they have been, from the beginning, two who embodied all the virtues of the organization. Active members now include Sister Zubena (Cynthia Conley), A. J. Wassaiah (Andrew J. Whitfield), Angela Jackson, Randson Boykin, Sigmonde (Kharlos) Wimberli, Sterling Plumpp, Eunice Favors, Johari Amini, Don L. Lee, Ronda Davis and Barbara Mahone McBain. Temporarily inactive members include Maga Jackson, Walter Bradford, and Carolyn Rodgers, the latter two both original members. The members contrive to maintain for the community a place of assembly, where those interested in writing and exchanging ideas may come and, in an atmosphere of cordiality and informality, learn from each other. OBAC asks only what it has always asked: that those who occupy its space and who take advantage of its time understand that the Black experience in all its infinite subtlety, variety, complexity and substance is what is *of the essence* at OBAC.

■■■■■■■■■■■■■■■■■■■■■■■■

OBAC and Black Children

Sterling D. Plumpp
(1972)

The Organization of Black American Culture's Writers' Workshop, better known as OBAC (oh-*bah*-see), was founded to be a community organization. This means that the primary focus of the organization would be to provide a structure for the Black people of the immediate community and the general Black community, at large, to come and contribute/learn/teach/participate in the development of a valid Black Aesthetics growing from the rich soil of Black Life. The initial impact made by OBAC was through the first group of competent, dedicated, and articulate poets, critics, rappers—workers who spread relevant messages to Black People in forms as natural as the melody of "Swing Low, Sweet Chariot." Due to the nature of our struggle at the time when OBAC was arriving, many activities were of the nature such that OBAC members went out and communicated with other groups, shared with others what had been nourished on 35th Street. But the programmatic aspect whereby day-to-day contacts with the developing members of the Black community were made regular and systematic, was somewhat delayed. There are good reasons for this. First, there was an immense amount of burden placed upon the key people in OBAC who had to try to write/teach/lecture/and be a part of an emerging new Black Writing society national in scope.

One of my biggest biases is that if you want people to become something, then you must sacrifice time/energy/and money to provide the kinds of experience that will allow them to become that. I, personally, have grown greater—by growing, I mean that my interactions with the people I have come in contact with in OBAC meetings have been a source of change in me, a source of renewal. In fact, had it not been for OBAC, I probably would not have seriously reassessed what I wanted to do as a writer and teacher of Black Literature. I decided that any folk idiom can be utilized to communicate to Black People; it does not matter whether it be a fast parkerlike riff, a coletrane soliloquy, a fast rap, a slow sad blues, a rich flowing spiritual, a funeral sermon, a lullabye, a happy reminiscence, or the dozens—they all can be made to work for you if the writer sacrifices enough time to explore them. Thus when I got free time I decided that I would spend the time necessary with Black children whose eyes are familiar with the life styles of 35th Street and let them discover ways of relating, housing, systematizing their very relevant messages. I came in contact

21

with the first class of OBAC children through the good graces of Mrs. Virginia Johnson, a teacher at Douglass Upper Grade Center. Mrs. Virginia Johnson had sponsored an assembly where numerous students had written poems (in fact over six hundred participated) and the winners read theirs during an assembly and were given prizes.

I thought that the first writing school for Black children in OBAC should be somewhat experimental in nature; my intentions were really to find out how well Black children would respond to the call to create if there were no assignment given. Again through the efforts of Mrs. Virginia Johnson, who volunteered to be a counselor for the young writers, I sent out invitations to members of the Douglass Upper grade Center to join a workshop for children. The response was great; fifteen students signed up and even got permission slips from their parents. I decided that my role as teacher/facilitator/advisor would be just to provide an atmosphere where they could express themselves as freely as possible. Since the school was founded during the regular school year, I thought that we should meet twice weekly on Mondays and Fridays, one hour on each occasion. I felt that to meet once a week would not be sufficient to establish any kind of working rapport with them. I must admit that I've been very encouraged by the way the young writers have worked and participated. The average attendance is about ten per session and nearly 100% read their work.

The brief experience I've had with Black children in a writers' workshop makes me know that they want to be heard—they are not interested in being told. They listened very intently when I played a Langston Hughes record, of poetry read by Ruby Dee and Ossie Davis. They even remembered the poems a month later. They respond very well to guests who come in and read for them or lecture, but they expect the guests to listen to their creations. Everyday they go away with books from the Hoyt Fuller Library. It is a joy to watch them become what all Black people are becoming—more aware, more conscious. Their poetry is them in its many shades. It is the Black Aesthetic, the Black Life, though in its unmined, unexpurgated, yet real rich form. They speak in clear, loud, and condemning tones. Let us listen to their honesty, their ripe expressions, their truth. [**Editor's note:** Following are two of the 13 children's works published in the Summer 1972 *NOMMO.*]

Not without Laughter

Look There he stands
Where all eyes can see;
a little child, Dark?

Naturally.

His eyes see, how bad
a world can be, to a
child that's Black,

Naturally.

Look There he stands,
Where all eyes can see,
a child; only a child,
A Black Child, but
not without Laughter,

Naturally.

—Darryl Beasley, 14

The Hidden Part

The mothers worries
Houses ragged
Enjoyments are few.

Horrifying sounds
Invisible faces
Danger in the air
Defending only themselves
Endless alleys
Neighborhood quiet.

People afraid
airy halls
Rats scamper
The hidden Part

Rat
Small Gray
Pest
Bites
Dangerous

—Sherry Faulkner, 14

■■■■■■■■■■■■■■■■■■■■■■

Preface To *Cumbaya*

Angela Jackson
(1976)

Heartstrong: brothers and sisters in the word. We are bloods together in nommo. Magic in power. Flesh and blood we find ourselves so like our people: clumsy with feet of clay but bird-dreaming freedom. Learning first our word-walk then our wings.

These are tremendous times.

"8 Years Ancient" was the underlying chant of the OBAC Celebration at the Kuumba Workshop Building, November 9, 1975. Present were writers from our far geographies and long generations: Shirley Graham Du Bois, West Indian Rex Nettleford, Azanians Peter Clarke and Dennis Brutus. Poets Mari Evans, Gwendolyn Brooks, Sarah W. Fabio, Zack Gilbert, Haki Madhubuti, Johari Amini Kunjufu, Laila Mannan [Sonia Sanchez], Henry and Nora Blakely, Walter Bradford.

Other writers: Ted Ward, Al Duckett, Lerone Bennett, Addison Gayle, Darwin Turner, Mike Cook, Sam Greenlee.

Other notables: Jeff Donaldson, Ann E. Smith, Richard Newhouse, Margaret Burroughs, hosts Val and Francis Ward. And The Black Community present in a fine force of 350 to 400.

OBAC members active and otherwise there: Melvin Lewis, Jabari Aziz Ra, Johnnie Lott, David and Denise Sims, Angela Jackson, Omar Shuayb, Warren Foulkes, Eileen Cherry, Pat Washington, Debra Anderson, Alfreda Collins Nady, Andrew J. Wasaiah, Birdie Williams, Uriah Carr, Hoyt Fuller and comedian Billy Wallace.

It was a great day crowded with atmosphere, refreshments for body and soul. A special thank you to Sisters Rosemary Jackson and Gwendolyn Fowkes who hosted thru thick and thin.

In the wake of our celebration the following tragedies:

The untimely death of former member Kharlos Wimberli.

The devastation by fire and water of OBAC Headquarters at 77 East 35th St. Center for Inner City Studies brothers and sisters wonderfully assisted in salvaging books and memorabilia and storing them temporarily at their facility. OBAC is meeting thru the courtesy of the Burroughs [family] at 3806 S. Michigan (basement), one of our original homes. We will announce our new headquarters in the near future.

Congratulations to Safisha and Haki Madhubuti on the birth of a daughter.

Why OBAC Is

Angela Jackson
(1980)

The OBAC Writers Workshop is alive and well. Our health and vitality is a thermometer of the weather for African-American life. How we are is how We are.

OBAC was founded in 1967: This is 1980. Thirteen is not an unlucky number. It has a misunderstood magic—like black cats. (Some sisters at LifeLine Center in Robert Taylor Homes tell me how one day a black cat sauntered through the open door of the Center. He circled the room royally, brushing each wall. After this arrogant promenade he sauntered out the Center door. That day the Center received word of the long awaited funding. Money. Black cats bear blessings. They are much maligned.)

What seems like bad luck may be good.

It is a harsh season. A season of sweltering heat and storms that break trees in the night. We fumble for resources, jobs, grants, loans. The KKK rises like an old dog with new teeth. Fangs. Ronald Reagan's face is the face of war. In his wrinkled countenance is the would-be dream of Blackmen turned to dust. They drum up the draft, and wish to send our remaining sons into the devastating wind.

These brown-faced children who belong to us, who are our mission and commission, and the life-handlers' omission, these brown-faced children who cannot read their names in the news or write their names in this earth which is ours, these children—our business is their being and absolute and full flowering. They are us and we will *read* and write our names in the news, and we will read and write the news. Make it happen.

For inside this heavy and obvious oppression, under the harsh harsh wing we are coming to some ultimate decision to live and be. (Is there any choice?) The process of living and evolving, our own fallibility, could tear us limb from limb, or seem to. But it will not. We will not succumb to the mortal sins of the structured denial and aggression against the spirit and the material reality. We will not succumb to the venial sins we commit against Family, as well as our coercions with murderers. We will not succumb.

The season wants its clarity. It wants its music. It calls for our

25

strong imaginations. (This is the reality: Richard Allen, chief foreign policy advisor for president-elect Ronald Reagan, employee of the Portuguese during the Portuguese-African Wars, denies documented atrocities committed against the people of Mozambique. Always the murderers deny the murder. This is the reality. Need we number the lies? Look at the unemployment line in your neighborhood. Need we number the lies which are as many as the petty crimes we commit against ourselves? Need we number them?) The season demands our clarity. It wants us to see ourselves whole and holy. To dance inside our sanctity and sanity. *To guard our sacred humanity. To build a world in the interest of its people.*

Such a world demands our imaginations. (Imagination because we don't see it everyday. It is hidden under the dross and the manufactured lie of our worthlessness constantly beaten into our heads. It is obscured beneath the status quo: We think the way they say it's supposed to be is the way it's supposed to be.) We must see ourselves in our natural dignity. We need to see with new eyes, clarified vision. We speak the words to conjure forth ourselves. Ourselves as we truly are: intelligent, just, demanding, relentless, self-equipped, aesthetic, and kind. And so certainly sensible. Even ourselves as we are underneath the harsh wing of the great denial is multiples more complex than they tell us we are and tell us we are.

But, finally, it is no matter because it must not matter. We have too much of our own business to watch and handle. If the song will be ours we must sing it. If the plays will be ours we must write them. (Didn't Langston say this?) If the novels, essays, films, and the poems will be ours we must produce and publish them. (Brothers as diverse as Sidney Poitier and Haki R. Madhubuti have said this!) There is so very much work to do. And when you are doing the work you were meant for there is so much personal and specific joy to enjoy. The responsibility is exhilarating and *good*. There is so much work to be done, individually and collectively.

The OBAC (Organization of Black American Culture)—(Oba meaning leader or king, Oba-Culture) Writers' Workshop is a work place and a gathering of workers. Our work is in the Word. No place is more sacred or serious.

We speak the words. And that is why OBAC is. To consistently search for the clarity inside our experience, to seek the untouched magnificence, the rueful but striving imperfection of our moments in time.

We seek to identify and exalt the peculiar movement and music of our experience. To touch the rhythm and turn it to the Word. To affirm in the face of structured denial. (Listen to this.) *To affirm in the midst of structured denial.* This is as meaningful as medicine or religion. As profoundly important as physical war. As life-giving and life-preserving.

We speak now *to notify* each other of the storms, the whirlpools, and the traps. We unveil the lie.

We speak forever to the world that must be ours because it is ours. A humanized sphere. We do not take our duties, our responsibilities lightly because, in the words of [OBAC associate] Ginger Mance, this is "spirit work." We are a Black Writers Workshop. We ask only the blessings of the God who makes things powerful and excellent. We demand the notice and energy—listening and actualized—of our people.

We tell you now, we tell us now, it is time for new vision, a new word and world. Ourselves, African in our Diaspora, made whole again and making wholeness. It is a large and challenging task for a people born for greatness.

Don't it make you wanna shout?

■■■■■■■■■■■■■■■■■■■■■■■

Black Poetry—Where It's At

Carolyn M. Rodgers
(1969)

In the last few years, we have seen a significant increase in the amount of Black Poetry being published. We have also seen a change in style and subject matter. At this point, it is possible to see distinctions in the various types of poetry being written. That is to say, all Black poets don't write the same KIND of poetry, or all Black poems ain't the same kind. They differ. Just as white poems differ and just as white poems come in sonnets, ballads or whatever.

I have attempted to place all Black poetry in several broad categories, all of which have variations on the main form. Very few poems are all one type or another. It is possible and probable that a poem will be three or four different types of poetry at one time. That is, a signifying poem will be a *teachin, spaced, pyramid* poem. Here are the main headings:

1. *signifying*
   a. open
   b. sly
   c. with or about
2. *teachin/rappin*
3. *coversoff*
   a. rundown
   b. hipto
   c. digup
   d. coatpull
4. *spaced* (spiritual)
   a. mindblower (fantasy)
   b. coolout
5. *bein* (self/reflective)
   a. upinself
   b. uptight
   c. dealin/swingin
6. *love*
   a. skin
   b. space (spiritual)
   c. cosmic (ancestral)

7. *shoutin* (angry/cathartic)
   a. badmouth
   b. facetoface (warning/confrontation)
   c. two faced (irony)
8. *jazz*
   a. riffin
   b. cosmic ('Trane)
   c. grounded (Lewis)
9. *du-wah*
   a. dittybop
   b. bebop
10. *pyramid* (getting us together/building/nationhood)

Some of these categories are self-explanatory and familiar. Most poems, as previously stated, fall into more than one category which, to my way of thinking, attests to the flexibility of Black writers. Unconsciously, I think, poets fall into their bag—or bags—and it is no discredit to a writer if he chooses to deal with only one form—or two, or three. . . . However, a Black writer will be classifiable in at least ONE of these categories, although it is conceivable to me that Black writers are creative enough to uncover forms which are yet to be acknowledged. We will know if the writing is Black.

Briefly, I am going to give examples of several of the headings, and then devote a large amount of discussion to signifying poetry since it has reached an exciting unprecedented level of sophistication in the written word.

The *teachin* poem is a poem which seeks to define and give direction to Black people. The two examples chosen and quoted in part here are Ronda Davis's "Towards A Black Aesthetic" and Barbara Mahone's "What Color Is Black."

> if tomorrow's black poetry will
> not EXPLAIN what is
> but BE it
> then pens will be electric with feeling
> igniting
> and the paper shall become the poet
> and the poets shall be earth-clouds . . .
>
> —Ronda Davis

and Mahone:

> Black is the color of
> my little brother's mind,
> the grey streaks
> in my mother's hair.
> Black is the color of
> my yellow cousin's smile,
> the scars upon my neighbor's wrinkled face . . .

The *coversoff, rundown, hipto, digup or coatpull* are basically the same type of poem, so the terms can be used interchangeably. There are many, many examples of this kind of poem today. For example, Cleveland Webber's poem, from his recently released book of poetry, *Africa Africa Africa,* "In America"—

> the people are in all the areas
> we occupy little parts of air,
> telling little lies, taking little trips,
> at least 5 days a week . . .
> . . . ghetto streets get empty while the pig is
> internalized in a suffering too old to be.

or Don L. Lee's poem on "Nigerian Unity"—

> little niggers
> killing
> little niggers
> the weak against the weak
> the ugly against the ugly . . .

These poets hip you to something, pull the covers off of something, or run it down to you, or ask you to just dig it—your coat is being pulled.

The *spaced* poem is very beautiful and many Black poets, after writing a lot of *signifying, coversoff* or *shoutin* poems, find that an inner calm, becomes, and inherent in that, a mystical and positive way of looking at the Black man's relationship to the unvierse. Amiri Baraka (LeRoi Jones) has a poem called "Black People: This Is Our Destiny," and I quote from it here:

> . . . we go to meet the realization of makers knowing who we are
> . . . knowing how to live, and what life is . . .
> . . . we must spin through in our seventh adventures in the end-
> lessness of all existing feeling, all existing forms of life, the
> gasses, the plants, the ghosts minerals the spirits the souls the
> light in the stillness where the storm the glow the nothing in God
> is complete except there is nothing to be incomplete the pulse
> and change of rhythm, blown flight to be anything at all . . .
> vibration holy nuance beating against itself, a rhythm a playing re-
> understood now by one of the 1st race the primitives the first men
> who evolve again to civilize the world . . .

The *spaced* poem returns to the spiritual wisdom of our Egyptian/African forefathers. Returns to the natural laws, the natural state of man before subhuman massacres. Spaced poems say that our ancestors are in the air and will communicate with us. As is the case in Jones' "No Matter, No Matter, The World Is The World"—

A broke dead genius
moved on to dust
will touch you one night . . .
. . . and the stacked dust of a gone brother will
hunch you
some father you needed who left you . . .

We speak of the vibrations, positive and negative, and we believe
again in what we have never truly denied; the power of NOMMO, JU-JU
and the collective force of the positive spirits, moving in time with the
universe. In our poetry, we sing of Sun-Ra and Coltrane, and their life-
motion which is sound. The new Black poets believe that we are the
seventh dimension (as the seventh sun/son). They further believe in the
over-all importance of the astrological signs of people (the writer is Sagit-
tarius—No. 5). The dream is to utilize our beginning to conceptualize and
direct a Black end that is as beautiful as our beginning.

The *mindblower* poem may seem similar to the *spaced* poem, but
the two are not to be confused. There are basic differences. *Mindblower*
poems seek to expand our minds, to break the chains that strangle them,
so that we can begin to imagine alternatives for Black people. They seek
to ridicule and mutilate that which may have formerly been esteemed.
Often these poems predict an awful or glorious future and are gorier than
the *spaced* poem. Sometimes the awful predictions are for Black people,
oftener, for subhumans.

Larry Neal in his book *Black Boogaloo*, in an untitled poem says:

We gathered in the open place
Piled their symbols one on top of the other,
Their flags and their death books; took their holidays rolled
their platitudes into nice burnable heaps,
Gathered and piled this stuff from the stink
pots of the earth which they have made so.
In the distance their cities burn . . .
    We piled their histories skyward with destruction
acknowledgement to our ancestors and gods,
then we light it.
        Singing.

By contrast is Jewel Lattimore's "Folk Fable"—

. . . but the niggas wadn't hip & wadn't hipped
    until they was copped.
    too.
    to work in the mines on the moon
    . . . & the ships had promises had names
    that all the niggas knew names
    like JESUS & HEAVEN & FREEDOM
    to take the niggas to a new world . . .

> . . . & when they was shipped to the moon
>   mainland sold
>   to companies who
>   was bidden
>   while the chasemanhattan bank
>   supervised the auctions . . .

Or Ebon's poem, "The Statute of Liberty Has Her Back to Harlem" (two other alternate titles excluded)—

> I saw them bayonet
> her spine
> and pin her 16th birthday
> to a cross
> where it hung.
> dank and slimey
> it hung,
> like stagnant death
> in shallow pools,
> vomiting blood
> on poets
> and mothers
> and flower children . . .

Surely, he was talking about "them," and he is a master of the gory.

Every poet has written a *bein* poem. In fact, most poets start off writing them. Just writing about the way they be, they friends be, they lovers be, the world be . . . An example presented here is one of my own, from my book *Songs of A Blackbird*—

> it's me
> bathed and ashy
> smellin down with
>   (revlons aquamarine)
> me with my hair black
> and nappy good and rough
> as the ground
> me sitting in my panties
> . . . it's me in the sky
> where pharoah and coltrane playing
> . . . and it's me screammmmmmmming into the box
> and the box is screammmmmmmming back
> . . . in kulu se & karma . . .

And all praise is due ALLAH; we are now getting more, more & more love poems from/about Black men and women. Such is this fragile jewel of Barbara Mahone's. The poem, "With Your Permission," combines *skin & space* (spiritual) aspects, as they should be—

smooth surfaces are easy
. . . i would rather deal with
             what moves you
explore the fire and texture
       of your soul
   with your permission
i would chart a course
       across your skin
   and travel all day
             all night
up and down that rocky road.

And one Black warrior, William Wandick, writes spears of honey:

my eyes took your slender fingers & dreamed on them,
they thinned imagination to a queen called sheba/nefertiti
deeming you royalness/making a fetish of your hand . . .

And there are love poems for all Black people, such as Ronda Davis's poem about the "Wine Dipped Woman." And we need more. And more. More . . .

The *shoutin* poem is perhaps at this time the most familiar to us all. For awhile, it seemed to be the only kind of poem being written. It usually tells the subhuman off. Or offs him with word bullets. An example of the *facetoface poem*, which is an aspect of the *shoutin* type, is one written by Sonia Sanchez in her hard-hitting book of poetry, *Homecoming*—

git the word out
now to the man/boy
taking a holiday
from murder tell him
we hip to his shit and that
the next time he kills one
of our
        blk/princes
             some of his faggots
gonna die
             a stone/cold/death.
                      yeah.

The last category with which I will deal briefly is the *two-faced* poem. As kids, we used to call a person two-faced if they grinned in our faces and talked about us behind our backs. In poetry, this concept takes on similar, but broader, meanings. For example, I will use my poem, "You Name It"—

I will write about things that are universal!
So that hundreds, maybe even thousands of

years from now, White critics and readers
will say of me, Here is a good Black writer,
who wrote about truth and universal topics.
  I will write about people who eat,
      as it was in the beginning
  I will write about people who sleep,
      is now
  I will write about people who fuck,
      and ever shall
  I will write about babies being born,
      world without end
  I will write about Black people
      re-po-sses-sing this earth,
          ah-men.

I would hope that everyone who reads the poem catches the two facededness (irony), implicit in the theme.

Signifying poetry holds a special fascination for me. Probably because I could not/can not signify and have always admired those who can. From a literary point of view, it is a significant, exciting aspect of today's poetry. I know, and you know, that we have always signified. On the corners, in the poolrooms, the playgrounds, anywhere and everywhere we have had the opportunity. "We sig" with somebody, about somebody, and if we can't be open about it, we "sig" on the sly! Langston Hughes' character, Simple, signified: with his landlady, his partners, his girlfriend, everybody . . . And Richard Wright deals it in *Black Boy*. However, to my knowledge, no *group* of Black writers has ever used it as a poetic technique as much as today's writers. It is done with polish. And the audiences love it! Too much *signifying* can be negative, I think; however, most of today's poets are very conscious of how important positive vibrations are, and few have carried signification to an extreme. In the main, it is being used, for constructive destruction.

A quick, or lengthy, look at the poetry of Don L. Lee, Nikki Giovanni or Sonia Sanchez shows that these three poets *signify* with their readers and the objects of their poems. *Signify*—fuh days . . .

  "wallace for president
  his mamma for vice-president"
                  —Don L. Lee

and—

  Memorial. The supremes—cuz they dead
                  —Sonia Sanchez

or Nikki Giovanni—

      ever notice how its only the ugly
      honkies
      who hate . . .

and of course the master of it all, Amiri Baraka (LeRoi Jones), on wigs—

> . . . why don't you take that thing
> off yo haid
> you look like Miss Muffet in a
> runaway ugly machine. I mean,
> like that."

Signifying is a way of saying the truth that hurts with a laugh, a way of capping on (shutting up) someone. Getting even talking bout people's mammas & such. It's a love/hate exercise in exorcising one's hostilities. It's a funny way of saying something negative that is obviously untrue like:
"you look like you been whupped wid uh ugly stick"
or saying something that is negative as:

> . . . nigger: standing on the corner, thought him was
>   cool. him still
> standing there. it's winter time, him cool.

Signifying is very often a bloody knife job, with a vocal touch. It moves in progressions sometimes and it is both general and specific. In *Black Boy*, by Richard Wright, we are taken through a dozens scene or *signifying* scene (to me they are the same), and each phrase is labeled in terms of its significance.

> "You eat yet?" [uneasily trying to make conversation]
> "Yeah, man I done really fed my face." [casually]
> "I had cabbage & potatoes." [confidently]
> "I had buttermilk & blackeye peas." [meekly informational]
> "Hell, I ain't gonna stand near you, nigger!" [pronouncement]
> "How come?" [feigned innocence]
> "Cause you gonna smell up this air in a minute!" [a shouted accusation]
> "Nigger your mind's in a ditch." [amusingly moralistic]
> "Ditch, nothing! Nigger, you going to break wind any minute now!" [triumphant pronouncement creating suspense]
> "Yeah, when them black-eyed peas tell that buttermilk to move over, that buttermilk ain't gonna wanna move and there's gonna be war in your guts and your stomach's gonna swell up and bust!" [climax]

As you see, every line leads up to the cap, the final one. And the last statement is based on a reality that all Blacks know. Peas, buttermilk, cabbage & potatoes will cause you to fart! It is a four-to-four balanced way of making love to—while poking hurt/fun at—one's self and one's life-styles.

A great deal of what today's poets do is hit & run *signifying*—or, another way of saying it: spot-*signifying*. That is, they do not usually sustain the length of a standard *signifying* circle. But they are traveling too fast. They hit—

yo mamma!

and keep on moving to the next point—

your daddy too!
or

if dracula came to town now
he'd look like daley
booing senator ribicoff
no pretty man himself
but at least out of the beast
category
—Nikki Giovanni

The poets *signify* with/about a whole lot of people in one poem, hitting one, then another, and usually, though not always, one theme holds the poem together.

When two people *signify* with each other, one feeds the other for progression, dramatic buildup to impact, but the object of ridicule doesn't have to be around or vocal. Responses can be imagined or drawn from the poet's own experiences—

you followed him niggers
all of you—
        yes you did,
i saw ya. [implied response—no, I didn't]
        —Don L. Lee

Now, because *signifying* often contains such a broad base of truth, it has been known to cause—in fact, it is famous for causing—a fight or a death. It can get too down, too real, so true and personal it uncovers too much. If the signifyer can REALLY get down (and in grammar school the last word was "yo mama is uh man . . .") the second party who cannot move his tongue to balance the scale may use his fists to do so—or his knife, or both. And it is a matter of pride. No Black person wants to be "sigged" about or capped all over . . .

No Black person can listen to some *signifying* without responding in some way. It pulls us in and we identify with the bad "signifyer." Obviously, this style of poetry has the power to involve Black people and to MOVE them. It is a familiar mover, and is probably the most dynamic type of poetry I have mentioned up to now.

I trust that I have initiated here a rather complete incomplete picture of where Black poetry is at. Some may quibble with the actual attempt to label what Black writers are doing. Others may take issue with the labels.

We do not (it cannot be said too often) want subhumans defining what we be doing. There is no human reference point. And objectivity does not REALLY exist in criticism. There is, perhaps, reason, tempered by a good strong sense of what is reasonable, what is fair. Ultimately, one's life-style is his point of view.

Black Poetry is becoming what it has always been but has not quite *beed*. And we have love and the spirit of our ancestors to guide us.

Angela Jackson

David L. Crockett Smith
(1985)

Angela Jackson is generally recognized as the most versatile and richly talented of the writers to emerge from Chicago's Organization of Black American Culture (OBAC) Writers Workshop during the 1970's. She is the author of three volumes of poems, several short stories, a popular romance (coauthored pseudonymously), and a novel in progress. Despite her versatility, however, she is known primarily as a poet and especially admired for her technically deft, densely metaphorical, and constantly inventive language. She is also celebrated as a brilliant reader of her own poetry and fiction. Apart from her purely literary accomplishments, Jackson is known for her role as the coordinator and sustaining presence in the OBAC Workshop after Hoyt Fuller's departure in 1976.

Jackson, the fifth of nine children, was born in Greenville, Mississippi, to George and Angeline Jackson. Her parents moved to Chicago while she was a small child. Consequently, she grew up in Chicago and developed a sense of language which was fundamentally Southern yet tempered by urban and Midwestern influences. While she was an undergraduate at Northwestern University, Jackson began to receive literary recognition. In 1973, she received the Conrad Kent Rivers Memorial Award, a literary prize bestowed annually by *Black World*. In 1974 Northwestern awarded her both the Edwin Schulman Fiction 2nd Prize and an Academy of American Poets Prize.

Despite her education at Northwestern, her most important literary influence was her involvement with the OBAC Workshop, which she joined in 1970. OBAC, a community-based organization, was founded to encourage "the conscious development and articulation of a Black Aesthetic." In keeping with this general goal, the Workshop pursued three explicit objectives: "(1) the encouragement of the highest quality of literary expression reflecting the Black Experience; (2) the establishment and definition of the standards by which that creative writing which reflects the Black Experience is to be judged and evaluated; and (3) the encouragement of the growth and development of Black critics who are fully qualified to judge and to evaluate Black literature on its own terms, while at the same time, cognizant of the 'traditional' values and standards of Western literature and fully competent to articulate the essential differences between the two literatures." Led by Hoyt Fuller, the editor of

Black World, the workshop's founding members had included such distinguished poets as Haki Madhubuti (Don L. Lee), Carolyn Rodgers, and Johari Amini (Jewel Latimore). While the OBAC writers were strong individuals, they shared a set of concerns and a general sense of style which marked them as a distinctive "school" or movement. Angela Jackson's own style developed out of this context.

This influence is readily apparent in her first book, *Voo Doo/Love Magic* (1974). She herself notes: "i am more than grateful for the grooming and growth allowed me in the workshop; for the dedications i have gained as a Blackperson and the commitment to Black/craftsmanship and Black/communication." She dedicates the book to her family, to members of OBAC, and to Hoyt Fuller. *Voo Doo/Love Magic* is a collection of fifteen poems, mostly concerned with a longing for love, family experiences, and the exploration of cultural resources. Yet even more fundamentally, it is an experiment in style. These poems are ebullient in spirit, and deeply rooted in Afro-American vernacular speech. The main technical challenge which they pose is the dilemma of how to capture the authentic rhythms and inflections of vernacular speech, yet at the same time to produce a language which is creative, not merely imitative.

These poems succeed remarkably well at capturing the mannerisms of vernacular speech, but the spacing and virgules which Jackson uses to indicate inflection may mystify the uninitiated reader. Sometimes, indeed, they seem gratuitous, as in these lines from "Woman Walk/n Down a Mississippi Road":

> i wuz the young april after noon
> breathed into this mississippi
> breeze /n fold/ed myself
> into the fresh/ ness of his arms.

Here, one needs the poet's own remarkably subtle ear to reproduce the rhythmic pattern; and even then, these lines rely too much on the inflections for them to stimulate other interest. Even a reader who can distinguish between the inflections of "afternoon" and "after noon" or "fold/ed" and "fresh/ness" may conclude that this passage offers more sound than substance. The best poems, however, skillfully combine authenticity and creative resourcefulness.

An example of a well-balanced poem is "Second Meeting," which suggests African antecedents to an encounter between a young man and woman in a Chicago subway car. It begins:

> memba the time . . .
>   we met at home
>   that slow age ago. one day.
> me.
>   with a water jar balanced
>   on my head/
> to fetch from the river

                    and u
                    and u wuz
        hone/n a spear for the
        hunt   that nite

In the middle section of the poem, the female speaker recollects their previous life in Africa and reminds the young man of it with her smile. He responds, haltingly:

        (don't i know u
                from
                    sum/
                        where??
                            u said. and
        i nod/ed softly: yes.
                        afraid i'd tip/ ova
                    the water jar
            i always think
                    is
                        balanced
            on my head . . .

This poem works because the inflections and pauses, the general sense of style, are not just mannerisms. They are part of the subject of the poem, which is concerned with how personal style is mediated through deeper cultural memory. The subtle and precise language used here typifies Jackson at her best. Another of her special talents, one which appears only occasionally in these poems, is her ability to create what Stephen Henderson has called "mascon" images: that is, images which evoke a dense cross-section of Afro-American experience. For example, the speaker of "lovin u rite" promises to

        make home as home as buttermilk an
        cornbread outta mayonnaise jar.

The "home" here is "downhome"—the Deep South—where people do, indeed, relish the delicacy which she describes. Her love, by implication, will strike a resonance equally deep.

        In her concern with Afro-American vernacular speech, Afro-American music ("Make/n My Music"), the continuity of African culture and the endeavor to make serious art accessible to a popular black audience, Angela Jackson's work reflects directly the influence of OBAC and Hoyt Fuller. Yet her poems are never polemical, as Madhubuti's often are, and like Carolyn Rodgers, she often grounds her politics in a call for strong community ties and a general love for black people (for example, "because we failed"). Also, like Rodgers, she sharply criticizes the hypocrisy of people whose militancy is merely talk ("Revolution"). Nevertheless, even in this first book, she exhibits a distinctive, highly personal voice. No one has developed a more complex and subtly modulated vernacular-based poetic diction than she. In *Voo Doo/Love Magic* her command of rhythmical language is most apparent. In her next book, *The Greenville Club* (1977), her gift for creating complex metaphors blossoms.

During the mid-1970's she became active with the Poets-in-the-Schools Program in Illinois and she began to be frequently demanded as a reader. As her inclusion in *15 Chicago Poets* (1976) demonstrates, her reputation had grown beyond the context of OBAC. *The Greenville Club* was published in *Four Black Poets*, a collection of chapbooks bound into a single volume. Most of these poems express reminiscences of growing up in an urban, black community, and they cover a broader range of perspectives than the previous collection. They exhibit a more restrained style and, generally, a greater maturity.

The opening poem, "The Cost of Living," exemplifies this volume's strengths. It begins:

> The cost of living
>   is far
>   too high
> life will split you along your back
> like the fisherman's wife who tears
> the blackspine from the
>   shrimp
>   for her gumbo

This poem, addressed to a black man, is about the need for love and the consequence of not having it. Love, in the poem, spares one from the cost of living alone: to risk being split open like a shrimp. Given an alternative, the poem concludes, "the heart cannot afford/such expensive feasts." Even more striking than the poem's message, however, is the poet's creation of metaphor. In comparing the black man to a shrimp, the poet stresses the destructive power of the world around us, which not only humbles but emasculates black men. The brilliant coinage "blackspine" is both physical strength (backbone) and blackness (cultural heritage and identity). Finally, gumbo requires lots of shrimp, and black men, this image implies, are as vulnerable and expendable as shrimp. (Gumbo, incidentally, is both a Bantu word for okra and a classic dish in soul food cuisine. "Gumbo," therefore, links African and Afro-American cultures.) In sum, the poet evokes castration without mentioning the knife and expresses a political consciousness without a word about politics. Such richness and subtlety of meaning are typical of Jackson's mature work.

In contrast to *Voo Doo/Love Magic*'s celebratory exuberance, several poems in *The Greenville Club* evince a preoccupation with the elusiveness and destructive power of love. "Brokenhearted, Alabama" presents an especially memorable portrait of a woman driven mad by love. Its densely evocative opening lines describe her:

> bananapeelings her bruisedskin
> brushing against her hair a bitten sun
> running its noon
> she shades her face
> worrybunched and blotched
> and waits
> it's too much. they heard her say.

This acute awareness of pain also extends into Jackson's treatment of political topics. One of her most memorable poems is "from a speech delivered in freedom hall on Afrikan liberation day: words from a welfare mother." A masterpiece of understated outrage, this poem expresses the response of poor women to those who impugn their integrity:

> the
> president
> is a welfare-chiseler
>
> he
> chip away my sons life
> scale
> his years
> like flakes from fish
>
> cluttering the kitchen floor
> with tears

These shocking images make the president a symbol for the most exploitative aspects of an oppressive system, which wreaks "nonchalant" destruction in the lives of poor people. Protesting forced abortions, the speaker quips:

> he flush my daughters
> futures
> down the clinic toilet

Finally, adding another sardonic twist to the "chiseler" image, the poem reaches its crescendo of contempt with the factual observation: "he pay no income tax." Jackson concludes this blistering poem by simply repeating the opening lines. This incisive and mordant poem, like most of *The Greenville Club*, reveals a sensitive, clear-headed, and fiery poet at the height of her powers.

In her most recent book, *Solo in the Boxcar Third Floor E* (1985), Jackson continues her earlier thematic concerns. These new poems are spoken in the voices of various tenants in an apartment building, not in the poet's own voice. In this respect, *Solo* seems very closely related to the fiction writing which has been Jackson's dominant concern during the 1980's.

Jackson's fiction, like her poetry, is especially notable for its sharp images and metaphorically rich language. Indeed, her novel-in-progress, "Treemont Stone," grew out of an unpublished series of narrative poems called, "A House of Extended Families." (*The Greenville Club* is actually a part of this larger collection.) Some of her ideas, originally conceived as poems, apparently demanded fictional treatment. In her fiction, Jackson's primary concern has been to capture the quality of her characters' lives through a precise and evocative rendering of their own use of language. Though she writes beautiful, descriptive prose, her most memorable trait as a fiction writer is her ability to create voice and to let the characters speak for themseves. Her most notable early stories include "Dreamer," which appeared in the premier issue of *First World* (1977) and "Witchdoctor," which appeared in *Chicago Review* and won an Illinois State Arts Council Award in 1978.

The following passage from "Witchdoctor" illustrates the most memorable qualities of Jackson's prose. It describes the protagonist's thoughts after a final tryst with her adulterous, but deeply cherished, lover:

> I rose, laughed, left and rinsed my body. Foamed between my legs with a face towel. Water fell from my faucet. I sang that man from under the last cover. I bathing. He sleeping bones and lost semen. I hummed across the water cupping under my breasts. I scattered scents and singing. His name was steam. I tempted him to wash my back; to touch mahogany into ashy fire. I beckoned him from bed through the closed bathroom door. He did not come. I slapped at his silence with a dry towel: frisked my free body. Calling to him.
>
> I stood in the doorway searching for him. The stripped bed was an empty white page. The rest of his poems were written in this silence I am constantly reading inside my head.

Like her poems of this period, her stories evince a poignant awareness of the pain associated with unrequited love. The power of these stories derives not from the movement of plot, but from the vividly present consciousness of her characters and their sense of themselves, of each other, and of the world.

The performances of Jackson's dramatic work have been enthusiastically received. *Witness!*, an "anthology" of her poetry and prose, was performed in Chicago and Milwaukee by the Ebony Talent Readers Theatre in 1978 and 1979. Her full-length poetic drama, *Shango Diaspora: An African-American Myth of Womanhood and Love* (produced in 1980) has been produced in several cities, including Chicago (1980, 1981, 1984), Cleveland (1982), and New York (1982). The New York production was produced by Woodie King, Jr., at the New Federal Theatre. King described the play's one-week run as "stupendous." Based on a long sequence of poems, *Shango Diaspora* chronicles a young woman's initiation into the mysteries of sexuality and love. It utilizes a freely interpreted version of African mythology as well as the blues and various other elements of Afro-American culture. While *Shango Diaspora* might be compared to Ntozake Shange's *for colored girls who have considered suicide/when the rainbow isn't enuf,* its general style more closely resembles such plays of Federico Garcia Lorca as *Blood Wedding* and *Don Perlimplín.*

Angela Jackson received international recognition when she was selected to represent the United States at the Second World Festival of Black and African Arts and Culture (FESTAC) in Lagos, Nigeria (1977). Her work has been included in Dial-a-Poem and Poetry-on-the-Buses, and in 1979 she received one of two premier Illinois State Arts Council Creative Writing Fellowships. The following year she received a creative writing fellowship from the National Endowment for the Arts. She was listed in *Outstanding Young Women of America* in 1979, and *Ebony* magazine, in its August 1982 issue, included her among "Women to Watch in the 1980's." In 1983 she received the second Hoyt W. Fuller Award for Literary Excellence. Beginning in September 1983, she became Writer-in-Residence at Stephens College in Columbia, Missouri. She was elected Chairperson of the Board of Directors for the Coordinating Council of Literary Magazines (CCLM) during 1984. *Solo in the Boxcar Third Floor E* received an American Book Award from the Before Columbus Foundation in 1985.

Among her recent publications, an excerpt from "Treemont Stone" has appeared in *Tri-Quarterly* (Spring 1984), and a selection of poems from her forthcoming book, "The House of Spider," appeared in *Open Places* (Spring 1984). A new play, *When the Wind Blows,* was produced in Chicago in October 1984. A full-length volume of poems, "The Midnight Market of Memory and Dream," has been accepted for publication by Third World Press, but at the time of this writing, no publication date has been set. At present, Jackson is completing another book of poems, "Dark Legs and Silk Kisses."

References:

Edith Herman, "Verse Things Could Happen When a Poet Visits the School," *Chicago Tribune,* 30 May 1977, II: 5,7;
"Women to Watch," *Ebony,* 37 (August 1982): 56.

■■■■■■■■■■■■■■■■■■■■■■■■

Bag People

S. Brandi Barnes
(1986)

When hearing the words "Bag People," one visualizes the common meaning and usage in the vernacular of America. The words bring images of society drop-outs, male and female, who have no home. They sleep in streets, on park benches, and at charity missions. Their life possessions and belongings are contained in remnants and other forms of shopping bags. They dress in rags, and most smell as if they have not bathed in months, though it's really been a few weeks.

But a new type of bag person is emerging in Black America. They too are a distinct group. They come in all ages. I have personally seen Black toddlers transformed into bag people. Their cute little faces, framed in plastic. What happened to safety precautions concerning plastic?

A few years ago, Carefree Curl made its debut in Black Society. Then imitators immediately followed. Blacks are now wearing Carefree Curls, California Curls, Freedom Curls, and any type of curl. Each curl carries a mandatory requirement; *"You must wear a plastic bag over the curl."* After all, how else will it stay soft, moist and drippy?

Imagine fully, out of all the usages of plastic, it is now used for curl protection.

Initially, the bags were colorless and transparent, made of cheap plastic sewn on an equally cheap band of rubber. Most beauty supply houses sell them at the rate of five for $1.00. Manufacturers have expanded on creativity and now produce them in green, pink, and blue tints, still transparent.

The bags have become a fad among curl wearers. Bag People are instantly recognizable because they wear their bags *everywhere;* on public transportation, at laundromats, grocery stores, courtrooms, afternoon excursions, and places as simple as college classrooms or a quiet picnic for two.

I'm all for fad and fashion—but I do have limitations. I began to dislike the bag look (not to be mistaken for baggy clothes). I'd dream of all types of bags—shopping bags, laundry bags, lunch bags, *etc.* All of my dream bags were fashioned as shower caps. Sometime I dream in color and all my bags are multicolored like those on Black heads—male, female, toddlers, adolescents—you name it, I dreamed it.

I fantasized about snatching a bag off of someone's head, then

45

asked myself, "Is a plastic bag worth dying over?" Bag people appear very serious about their bags.

Early college psychology lessons abandon me and I strain for self-control when I see a bag person of the hair kind. I was told by none other than a bag wearer, why he wears a plastic bag. Said he, "I don't want my curl to dry." I shuddered inwardly.

One morning, waiting for an elevated train on public transportation, I was surrounded by bag wearers. But next to me stood a very elegant woman. This was no classless person. Her facial features were striking and magnetic. It was freezing winter, and her full length fox coat was more than adequate, along with the expensive boots and purse. She was a refreshing sight among the swell of bag people. Her hat was soft, black mohair. I sat next to her when the "L" arrived. I was hoping some of her elegance would rub off on me. As she turned to gaze out of the window, something hung out from under the hat. Then I noticed it peeking from the sides as well. I felt my anger swelling inside, mixed with utter compulsion and disappointment. She was a bag person of the hair kind!! I froze. She turned and rose. I would not move. I wanted her exit to be difficult. I didn't have the nerve to go for her bag.

At home that evening, I rationalized on everyone having freedom of choice, but I didn't feel any better toward bag people of the hair kind.

Well, winter is gone. Summer and hot days and nights are at hand. So are the bag people. They have come out of their winter hats as fast as pop corn pops.

Beaches will soon be polka dotted with plastic bag wearers, bobbing up and down in the water.

I don't know what other people feel when they see the unsightly plastic bag wearers. Nor do I know what I'm going to do. Since there are more curl wearers this year, naturally there will be more bag wearers.

I have decided to pray. If the summer sun would melt just one, just one plastic bag on someone's head, I would forever hold my peace. I figure word will spread about melting and *presto*, there'd be no more heads covered with plastic bags.

If praying doesn't work, I have been considering a little scientific experiment. For example, what would happen to the bag if sprayed with a can of Mace, or other explosive? Will I get arrested for assault? Are the bags protected by law?

Well, that's my problem. *It ought to be a law!!* There should be a law about processed hair, doo rags, and curl wearers with plastic bags. Get my drip? . . . Ooops . . . drift?

Why Foreign Policy Is Foreign To Most African-Americans

Haki R. Madhubuti
(1986)

International affairs has to do with relationships, the reasons these relationships exist, and in whose interest. It also has to do with power. Raw, unadulterated force and fear, the kind of fear that makes men piss in their pants and blow their brains out. Such power has forced nations to spend sixty percent of their national budget on weapons systems, as their people seek nourishment from the garbage of tourists. In the last quarter of the twentieth century, on the heels of modern computer technology and satellite communication, the conducting of foreign policy is still the game of running the world.

Simply stated, the relationship that one country has with another country or countries is defined as its foreign policy. A nation's foreign affairs can range anywhere from trade to "constructive engagement," from scientific, cultural and educational exchange to war. Generally speaking, the foreign policy of a nation is set by its ruling body, in the United States the executive branch. In effect, the President is charged with the formation of a foreign policy that must be, at some point, confirmed by the Congress. To really understand a nation's foreign policy requires serious study. Most people in the United States, whites as well as Blacks, do not have any idea about what this country is doing around the world, with the possible exception of its "War on terrorism" that is explained in thirty-second slots each night on the evening news. This country's foreign policy is calculated in body counts as the sophisticated theft of nations goes unnoticed. The role the CIA and KGB play in the world's destabilization is seldom explored in the popular press.

The citizen-consumer in the United States plays checkers and video games while the world-runners (politicians, businessmen, military and academics) continuously restructure the world's chessboard. Unlike in the game of chess learned as a youth, the opponents on the world stage do not start with an equal chance to checkmate. The game of world-running is fixed, according to Holly Sklar's book, *Trilateralism*. The stakes are too enormous to be left to the skill or luck of a single player. These are gigantic gang wars in which the combatants fight outside the ring in the form of surrogate wars without referees or rules. The major gangs are the United States and the North Atlantic Treaty Organization versus the Soviet Union and the Warsaw Pact. Each gang, with some consultation

47

with its membership, has carved up the world into "Spheres of Influence."

What is clear but not talked or written about in great detail is that white people, who are less than nine percent of the world's population *run it all* and that all others fall into one of the two camps or into the ineffective non-aligned nations. White world supremacy, operating in the areas of business, law, education, language, religion, sports, entertainment, military and foreign affairs, is the most serious problem facing African-Americans and other people of color, argues Neely Fuller in *The United Independent Compensatory Code/System/Concept.*

If the function of a gang, which is to acquire, develop and protect one's turf—in effect, its economic market—is understood, the analogy of a nation to a gang's operation is not too farfetched. The old Anglo-Saxon proverb, "The only successful war is the one that is won," operates daily in the Pentagon and on the streets, which is why the United States can, with a confident arrogance, ignore the World Court's decision condemning its activities in the not so "secret" war against Nicaragua. This is also why the USSR and the USA can, with little difficulty, tie up the votes in the United Nations that they feel go against their best interests. The United States and the Soviet Union are modern gangs that, in the final analysis, listen only to each other. And even though each country speaks a different language and operates out of dissimilar cultural imperatives, each one's message is the same: *we run it.*

To fully understand the foreign policy of the United States, one has to have a lot of time and an appreciation for serious money. The major stimulants for the foreign affairs of the United States are its "national security" and profits. Imperialism may be a little understood word on the block, but for most of the world it is a dangerously non-negotiable reality. The unequal relationship between rich and poor countries, the involvement of politics and international economics and the effective use of economic and military power to create dependency, exploitation and dominance speaks to the type of imperialism at which the United States is the reigning master. The foreign policy of the United States is predicated on three principles: (1) expanding markets, (2) national security and anti-communism, (3) global economic and political hegemony. At one level, this is deep stuff which will require the average person to give up evenings, weekends, holidays, and even dating to grasp its meaning. But, on the other hand, there are some close-to-home and recent observations that may help clarify the crippling influence of U.S. foreign policy.

Ferdinand Marcos, formerly the dictator of the Philippines, ruled that country by using force and crony capitalism for over twenty years. Marcos, on a salary less than that of the lowest paid state governor in the United States, amassed a fortune that is estimated to be somewhere between three billion and nineteen billion dollars. Only his wife, mistress, accountants, and lawyers know the exact amount, and they are only talking to each other. Today, seventy-two percent of the Philippine population lives in poverty, compared with twenty-seven percent in 1965. In twenty years of dictatorial rule, Marcos killed, imprisoned and politically crushed his opponents with the aid and blessing of the United States government. What did the United States get out of this deal? The use of land in the Philippines for U.S. military bases. From Lyndon Johnson to Ronald Reagan, the U.S. foreign policy in the Philippines has been structured around the needs of the U.S., at the cruel expense of the Filipino people.

The poorest country in the western hemisphere is Haiti. Jean Claude "Baby-Doc" Duvalier, and his father before him, have ruled that small nation like a family business for over a quarter of a century. The poverty is so great in Haiti, that fresh water in the interior is viewed as a luxury. The military and economic oppression was so great that any people involved in progressive political movement could expect instant imprisonment, torture or death, if caught. If a young person cried for food, work and education, she or he was in danger of being branded a communist. The United States provided millions and millions of dollars of aid to Haiti; little if any went directly to the people. Trickled-down economics has not arrived in that part of the world.

Baby Doc's show of concern for his people was for him and his wife to drive through town throwing coins to the populace. However, in February of 1986, the "Baby" and his family fled in the night with the United States providing the taxi service. Before he left, he had robbed the country white. According to *The New York Times*, he left less than one million dollars in the central bank. Corruption in Haiti was a prerequisite for success. The former dictator's wealth is estimated to be between three hundred to nine hundred million dollars, all stolen from the Haitian people. He and his wife are believed to have real estate and monies stashed throughout the West, mainly in the United States, France, and Mexico. Marcos and Duvalier are both looking for a home, and they're doing it in style.

The final example is South Africa. The history of South Africa, in broad terms, closely resembles that of the United States. George M. Frederickson, in his book *White Supremacy: A Comparative Study in American and South African History*, draws many cogent parallels. The most obvious is that Europeans settled both lands and, on each continent, slowly but effectively instituted a reign of terror that would seek to reduce and subjugate the indigenous population. In the U.S., the term genocide would be a polite description of the "success" Europeans have had in reducing the indigenous population and securing the North American continent. The white South Africans, with much help from their brothers, are still working at it—still working at stealing Africa.

What is obvious, however, is that the annihilation of the African has not worked and will not work. What has worked is the effective neutralization of many African people and their reduction to a dependent people in their own land. Also, the whites, through the use of rewards and punishment, have been able to split some of the Blacks into battling factions that fight each other rather than the true enemy. This is the classic victim's reaction to oppression. The Afrikaaners, with their ideology of white supremacy, have developed a system of calculated terror that functions like a well-oiled machine twenty-four hours a day, three hundred sixty-five days a year. At this writing, there are over seven thousand Black Africans who are being detained in South African prisons without charges or legal representation.

The white minority, about four million of the population, has structured a completely separate and unequal system that is designed to totally contain the movement and development of the country's majority Black population of twenty-five million plus. The national government has classified and segregated everything from education to housing, politics to food production, employment to sports, entertainment to health care. This system of hatred and social disease flourishes in part because of the United States and other western nations' support, and in particular, through the use of multi-national corporations such as IBM, Ford, General Motors and others. The bottom line is that the U.S. chose to fight communism by instituting a boycott against Poland and initiating a private war against the people of Nicaragua, but all it can do for African Blacks, in the wake of ten Black deaths a day, and indescribable oppression, is talk. The major excuse from the administration is that "constructive engagement" is working, but few actually give the real reasons why this country continues to back such a racist regime.

First, white South Africans and white Americans are blood brothers. Secondly, the U.S. imports over one billion dollars a year in chromium, manganese and platinum for its industrial, economic and military uses. The human rights of people of color are secondary to the racial policies, national defense and profits of the United States. Bantustans of South Africa are similar to the Black ghettos of the United States. The racial and economic deprivation our brothers and sisters suffer in South Africa actually exists in the U.S., but at a much more subtle yet effective level. In fact, many, many African-Americans do not believe that they are oppressed. To fully explain this will require another essay. However, it is clear that America's Black "permanent underclass," with its high unemployment, frightening illiteracy, enormous prison population, homelessness, and huge addiction to drugs and alcohol, is in itself a dependent and enslaved people. To truly comprehend the state of Black America is a social science course in itself—see Pinkney's *The Myth of Black Progress.* Blacks here are just a boatride away from the type of enslavement that exists in South Africa. Think about this: people in the U.S. seldom if ever talk about a permanent white underclass.

The racist duplicity and contradictions of U.S. foreign policy can be easily illustrated by looking at its actions in Grenada, Libya, the Middle East, Chile, Ghana and other nations. The U.S. actions in the Philippines, Haiti and South Africa represent state terrorism at its highest stages. The people of the Philippines and Haiti are actively initiating change that has little to do with the corrective actions of the United States. This country jumped on the train of the Haitian and Filipino people when it saw change in the wind. South Africa remains a serious, serious problem that has Third World War possibilities if substantive changes do not come soon.

There are several observations here for African-Americans: (1) all people do what they've been taught to do, and most of them act in the way that they perceive is in their best interest, with the basis of these actions both cultural and biological; (2) Black people in the United States have, most certainly since 1865, been mainly concerned with surviving and developing in the western hemisphere. Even though the majority of Black people have forgotten their holocaust—the middle passage—many have not completely forgotten the genocide committed against the indigenous people of this land, those persons renamed Indians or Native Americans. Most Blacks by now understand that treaties and contracts with the western world are like sports records, made to be broken.

The African-American's view of the world is colored by his or her view of him or herself. That is, acculturation has prepared Blacks to see what they are taught to see and to believe what they have been taught to believe. The saying that "It is easier to believe than think" is quite apropos for the Black situation in the United States. Foreign policy is foreign because most African-Americans have been too busy trying to master, translate and understand domestic policy.

Whereas serious struggle is multi-faceted, most Blacks are still one dimensional and strait-jacketed to a European-centered worldview. Many Blacks are like smokers who feel that the warning label on the package is for someone else. Death and taxes are indeed certain, but for the chained mind, slavery is too. It is difficult to win a war when people have to buy weapons from the enemy. Most buyers will never be sold or given weapons from the top of the line. Nations are not taken seriously when they can't do fundamental things like feed themselves. Imperialism has reached its highest stages when the sons and daughters of a given nation, mainly from the First World (Africa) who study abroad, choose to stay and participate in the building of that nation, rather than return home. The brain drain from the First World is unbelievable and crippling to that people.

The war, whether on the battlefield or in the classrooms, is with ideas. Actually, ideas run the world. Foreign policy is being fashioned in the popular, as well as the national culture. We can see this from the foreign policy of the Catholic Church, where every few months the Pope goes on diplomatic trips around the world, and most certainly we can see it in the popular culture with such movies as *Red Dawn*, *Rambo*, *Rocky IV*, and the latest, *Top Gun*. Ideas are important. Two bad ideas are that Black people think that they are a minority people in the world, and that African countries continue to tie their currency and development to Europe, in effect, the West. My point is that Black people represent over one billion people in the world, and if Blacks cannot recognize their own strength world-wide in terms of numbers, landmass, resources, and cannot at some point organize such vast wealth, they are lost. Cheikh Anta Diop, in his book *Black Africa*, calls for the formation of a United Black Africa into a single economic and cultural federated state. It is quite clear that white people are organized at a world level for the perpetuation and continuation of their rule. African people can do no less.

Very seldom will an African trained at Harvard Business School or the London School of Economics create ideas that are self-reliant out of that academic experience, unless he or she is a Kwama Nkrumah, W.E.B. DuBois, Indira Gandhi, Winnie Mandela or Patrice Lumumba. The only time a great many Black people get involved in the U.S.A. foreign policy is in its implementation as foot soldiers in foreign wars. Black people are the people who fight the wars for this country against other people of color around the world. Recent examples are Viet Nam and Grenada.

If African-Americans are ever to have a serious impact on the U.S. foreign policy, accurate information is needed. At the end of this essay, there is a list of books, newspapers, magazines and quarterlies that the interested reader can start with. The major rules to follow in gathering data about the world are 1) do not depend on one source of information; 2) mix the reading, be flexible by studying right and left leaning materials; 3) take policital science courses at local universities; 4) travel whenever possible to other nations; 5) make friends with foreign students, visitors and citizens; 6) start a personal library; 7) work with progressive Black organizations; 8) attend foreign policy lectures that are open to the public; 9) form foreign policy study groups; 10) don't become overwhelmed with what you will discover; and 11) watch and consult with legislators on foreign policy issues.

The attitude one brings to this subject is crucial. Don't be afraid to admit ignorance. The world we live in is very political and extremely complicated. Most things in this world are political, from the food one eats to the clothes one buys. The western world is racist, sexist, class-conscious, and youth oriented. If a person is Black and conscious and living in America, there is one thing that is absolutely certain—he or she is *fighting daily* or has been defeated.

The United States uses over sixty percent of the world's natural resources with less than seven percent of the world's people. Much of those resources comes from Africa. If one cannot see the inequality in this arrangement, it only confirms the effectiveness of western acculturation and the dominance of the Eurocentered world-view. The most important foreign policy question facing African-Americans is Africa. Blacks in the U.S. must pressure the State Department and Congress to pursue a just and balanced policy. We can learn from the Polish and Jewish people in their capable lobbying for Poland and Israel. African-Americans will remain powerless and pawns in the international chess game unless Africa and its future become central in Black thought and action. The 21st century is upon us, memory is calling, and this generation will truly be judged by its children—if they are alive and productive. Using the knowledge and technology of the present, we must pull from the wisdom and vision of our foreparents to issue on this earth a better world.

Bibliography/Reading List

Any bibliography of this inexhaustible subject can only be very selective.

Aliber, Robert Z., *The International Money Game* (New York, 1976)
Agee, Philip, *Inside The Company: CIA Diary* (New York, 1975)
Barraclough, Geoffrey, *Turning Points in World History* (London, 1979)
Biko, Steve, *I Write What I Like* (San Francisco, 1986)
Brown, Lester R., *State of the World 1986* (New York, 1986)
Cline, Ray S., *Secrets, Spies and Scholars* (Washington, D.C., 1976)
Cohen, Benjamin J., *The Question of Imperialism* (New York, 1973)
Diop, Cheikh Anta, *Black Africa* (Westport, 1978)
    The Cultural Unity of Black Africa (Chicago, 1978)
Dower, John W., *War Without Mercy* (New York, 1986)
Dunnigan, James F. and Bay, Austin, *A Quick And Dirty Guide to War* (New York, 1986)
Fallows, James, *National Defense* (New York, 1981)
Franck, Thomas M. and Weisband, Eward, eds., *Secrecy and Foreign Policy* (London, 1974)
Fredrickson, George M., *White Supremacy* (New York, 1981)
Fuller, Jr., Neely, *The United Independent Compensatory Code/System/Concept: A Textbook/Workbook For Thought, Speech and/Or Action For Victims of Racism* (Washington, D.C., 1984)
Garwood, Darrell, *Undercover: 35 Years of CIA Deception* (New York, 1985)
Herman, Edward S., *The Real Terror Network* (Boston, 1982)
Kolko, Joyce, *America and the Crisis of World Capitalism* (Boston, 1974)
Kwitny, Jonathan, *Endless Enemies* (New York, 1984)
Nalty, Bernard C., *Strength For The Fight* (New York, 1986)
Nkrumah, Kwame, *Neo-Colonialism* (New York, 1965)
Omond, Roger, *The Apartheid Handbook* (New York, 1985)
Pinkney, Alphonso, *The Myths of Black Progress* (Cambridge, 1985)
Sampson, Anthony, *The Money Lenders* (New York, 1982)
Sklar, Holly, ed., *Trilateralism* (Boston, 1980)
Smith, Anthony, *The Geopolitics of Information: How Western Culture Dominates the World* (New York, 1980)
Stockwell, John, *In Search of Enemies* (New York, 1978)
Williams, Chancellor, *The Destruction of Black Civilization* (Chicago, 1974)
Wright, Bobby E., *Psychopathic Racial Personality and Other Essays* (Chicago, 1986)

Newspapers

New York Times
Washington Post
Wall Street Journal
Los Angeles Times

Philadelphia Inquirer
Chicago Tribune
Miami Herald
In These Times

Quarterlies and Magazines

Foreign Affairs
Foreign Policy
New York Review of Books
New African
The Nation
The Progressive
West Africa
African Concord

The New Republic
The National Review
Commentary
Black Scholar
Mother Jones
The New International
African Guardian

The African Reunion: A Surpassing Urgency

Hoyt W. Fuller
(1980)

"Until Africa is free, the descendants of Africa the world over cannot escape chains!"

—W.E.B. DuBois, *Dusk of Dawn*

Last summer, to my great surprise, I found myself participating in one of those family reunions which have become so popular in the wake of *Roots*. Surprising because, while I grew up in a very closely-knit family and have always had a strong attachment to my immediate maternal relatives, my interest in long-lost cousins was not highly developed. My participation was encouraged, shall we say, by my 83-year-old aunt who is the true daughter of her mother; that is, this aunt reflects, whether willfully or not, the outstanding characteristics of her mother, my grandmother, who was, I now understand, one of the most extraordinary individuals it has been my privilege to know.

To my claims that I was bogged down in so many projects and obligations that I did not have time to spend with a lot of people I did not know and had never heard of, my aunt's response was simple and unarguable: "Nothing you've got to do is more important than knowing where you came from," she said. And so, I found myself engaged in the logistics of reserving hotel rooms and sending out maps and drawing up itineraries. At the family dinner, I ended up emceeing the program. . . .

And so, the family reunion that I initially had considered only a nuisance and a burden ended with my determination to return to east-central Georgia to delve into the county records and whatever other documents are available which will enable me to piece together the missing parts of the saga of George and Eliza Brady. That determination had very little to do with the rather routine effort to construct a family tree: rather, I now know, it has to do with a search I have been engaged in all the days of my life, a search for nothing so mundane and banal as roots, but a search for a spiritual essence that will enable me, at last, to find a kind of peace.

I am not at home in America.

This, despite the fact that I am fully aware that Black people have as much—or more—right to this land as do the white people who control it. No, I am not home here for quite another reason: it is because there lies at the very core of the civilization which dominates the land—and everybody in it—a poison so dreadful and pervasive that it drains from all of us the strength of spirit that would make us whole. Without that strength, without that spirituality, it is my opinion that we will forever languish here, impotent and afraid.

My mother was a lovely woman, small and delicate, but wracked all her life by pain and illness. She was the opposite of my grandmother, who was buxom and strong (at least when I was a child), and who was too busy and forceful until the end of her life to surrender to disability. And though I remember my mother with as much love and tenderness as I am capable of, it was my grandmother who had the greater influence over what I became.

One of my earliest and dearest memories is of her nestling me close to her ample bosom, laughing and teasing and singing to me in the swing on the front porch of her house. That swing, by the way, is still there; and my aunt, who now lives alone in her mother's house, likes to tell my friends who visit of how I used to "talk back" to my grandmother as she sang to me, although I was too young to know a language. Then, and in later years, my grandmother talked to me, and while I always paid attention, it was not until many years later, when it was too late, that I understood *something* of what she tried to tell me.

Eugenia Brady Thomas was a leading citizen of her community. When I first knew her, she was a pillar of her church, the central figure of the Eastern Star. A serious advocate of education, she did all she could to persuade her brood of 11 children to attend college, preferably Morris Brown, the AME institution in downtown Atlanta that her husband accused her of supporting singlehandedly. Like many AME church people of her era, she had an abiding interest in Africa. She worked hard as a church missionary, collecting pennies to send to the college and to the bishop to aid the Africans on the Continent, as well as those studying in the AME schools. When one of my cousins, a golden-haired fellow with green eyes, told me that I was not really a member of the family but that my mother had found me in a cabbage patch, my grandmother soothed my wounded feelings by suggesting that I was the descendant of African kings. It was an idea that never quite shook itself free from my psyche.

But Africa interested me for what seemed to me the simplest of reasons, long before I had ever met Alex Haley or heard of *Roots*. Black people came from *somewhere;* and Black people had a history, despite what our historians told—or did not tell—us. Since I could not bring myself to accept, now or ever, the idea of Black inferiority—having no reasons whatever, at anytime, to envision myself as inferior—I instinctively *knew* that all these descendants of Africans in this place had been separated from *something* of the most special importance which had defined our worldview and our humanity. I *knew* that *something* was there, that it *existed*, for it had shaped the peculiar genius of my grandmother, had given her the strength and the vision to go against the awesome grain of the American ethic. In the face of formidable pressure to conform, she refused to surrender—or even to compromise—the construct of spirit and humanity in which she functioned. That construct was full and omni-dimensional for her, for it enabled her to be whole. When it was decided that I should go to live and be educated in Detroit, my grandmother's acquiescence was reluctant. She recognized the advantage of greater opportunity in the northern environment at that time, but the selling point for her had to do with the element of safety. She had taught me not to be afraid, to never, ever, compromise my sense of dignity, and she knew that in the Deep South of my early childhood, that could be a prescription for disaster. And so, she let me go. But not before extracting from me two promises that I would not keep: one, that I would return to Atlanta and attend Morris Brown College, and two, that I would one day live in her house and take care of the little land she and her husband had won through the kind of travail that, because of them, I would never experience. "It's going to be much better here one day," she told me. "You will see."

I did not believe her. I thought her optimism was an article of her faith in God. There was nothing I saw around me that indicated that the rigid, hateful rule of white people in Georgia would ever be moderated. But she knew that things would change, as she knew many other things that baffled me: she had known the enemy intimately, as I had not, and she knew he was as vulnerable and as subject to the fear of man as any other mortal. And she knew, because she knew herself, that men will be free, that freedom was the goal of that long, unbroken line of struggle that predated The Middle Passage.

My grandmother did not live to see me go off to Africa. When I left Chicago in 1957 because I could no longer live in America, she had been dead a year. At that time, the "independent" countries in Africa were Liberia, Ethiopia and recently Ghana, where I wanted to go. But I stopped off, en route, on the Spanish island of Mallorca, where I spent—off and on—the next three years. It was, after a fashion, a therapeutic experience. I relaxed there, was free. I gave myself over to being young and, as it happened, to being the happiest I had ever been since puberty.

I lived for the first year in an idyllic little salmon-colored villa in the middle of a black-square garden overlooking the Bay of Palma. There was one hitch to my enjoyment of that lovely place: every morning I religiously took my breakfast coffee in Plaza Gomila, where I read the Paris edition of *The New York Herald Tribune* to keep track of what was going on back home. That done, I could release myself to the day, to swimming, motorcycling over the mountains, to writing, or whatever I felt like doing. I was free.

Or thought I was: Africa possessed me. One day, after Sekou Toure stood up to the French and declared Guinea independent, I got on board a French boat and sailed around the western bulge of Africa to Conakry. That was 1958, my first time on the Continent. After that, I went back many times, once on a John Hay Whitney Fellowship, spending almost nine months in Senegal. The first visit had been inspirational primarily, but also sobering. It robbed me of all my romantic notions about Africa. And I learned, unhappily, that the same deadly virus which had afflicted Africans in America had, even more tragically, diseased the minds of Africans on this Continent, all of us to one degree or another suffering the weight of recent history, wanting to be Europeans in Black skin.

I made an absolutely devastating discovery: **I also was not at home in Africa.**

The Black Consciousness Movement of the Sixties saved my life. Africans in America, a significant number of them, for the first *effective* time in our history—rejected the American, the Western, ethic. **We do not want to be white people in Black skins,** the Movement leaders said. **We are an African people, and we want to rid ourselves of our inbred allegiances to the European ethic and reclaim those spiritual values which have sustained and guided our people for centuries.** On the surface level, this rejectionist movement took the form of "natural" hair-do's, dashikis, adoption of African and Swahili names and, in certain communities, a turn toward Islam.

While we now know that much of this movement never delved beneath the surface, it nevertheless had a deep and far-reaching effect: Blackness lost its identification with degradation. After centuries of being persuaded by the Europeans who had conquered our ancestral lands and enslaved our ancestors that, by the will of God, we had been eternally condemned to squalor, gracelessness and servitude, Black people proclaimed ourselves "beautiful"—and, the miracle is, most of us believed it.

But, I also believe, most of us failed to move beyond the surface, failed to follow the unblazed direction in which our new sense of ourselves would lead us. Because we made it clear, in the Sixties, that we no longer would tolerate in silence and submission the society's affront to our dignity as human beings and as citizens, those who control this society backed down, made concessions and, again, on the surface, at any rate, indicated that the old order no longer prevailed. In fact, some old and hated barriers did fall: we could eat in restaurants, sleep in hotels, work in department stores, and even be elected—once more, as during the *first* Reconstruction—as aldermen and representatives, even as mayors. The industrial boom of the Sixties made it relatively easy for those who control the society to allow us into the corporate world for the first time; we became computer programmers and middle managers and highly paid functionaries at Xerox and IBM and General Motors.

Some of us decided that we had arrived, that the "American Dream," at last, also included us. Sure enough, in the new communities that exploded in the wake of the industrial expansion, a substantial number of Blacks bought split-level homes, an extra family car, sent our children to schools far away from the old ghettos. We proved, for the doubters, that we were just like "other" people, really, that all we wanted was a chance: God's in His Heaven; all's right with the world.

And now, in the Eighties, when the former colonial peoples of the world are saying to America and the Western world, "Our resources are our own, and you, the industrialized powers, will no longer have access at your will, exploiting our wealth for your stockholders in the suburbs of New York and Jackson and San Francisco," those who control America are designing a brand-new script for "the land of freedom and opportunity." *There are no new frontiers,* they are saying; *retrenchment is now in order;* from now and onward, those who "have not" will no longer find it profitable to make demands on those who "have."

Because the barriers have been lowered at IBM and the state house, those Blacks who are not "making it" can no longer cry "racism": the new analysis points to *class* as the problem, not *race*. (Even a learned "brother" at the University of Chicago has validated this: his book, *The Declining Significance of Race,* is the Bible to be sworn by. In essence, he argues that capable and qualified Blacks now have access to whatever their white peers have access to, and that those Blacks who are left out must blame their frustrations on the operations of the class system rather than on racism.)

To such analysts, the rising tide of bitterness and hatred on the Right stem from "reverse discrimination" in the work place, from affirmative-action programs taking jobs from white people, and giving them to minorities. That explains, in other words, the Ku Klux Klan preparing for guerilla warfare; murderers waylaying Black taxi drivers in Buffalo, cutting out their hearts, and judges from California to Texas to Florida routinely freeing the killers of Black men and women. Some of us with a sense of history wonder: Is the Second Reconstruction now underway?

That Black men and women, like white and brown ones, wish to be "at home" and unthreatened in the country of their birth and allegiance is not strange. It is the most natural of aspirations. But what kind of country do we want to be "at home" in?

In a course I am teaching in the History of Afro-American Literature, my students are considering the parallels between the language and message of David Walker's *Appeal,* written in 1829, and the tape of a speech delivered at Cornell University in 1980 by Louis Farrakhan. The similarities are astonishing—and dismaying: What they show us is that, in more than 150 years, the relative situations and concerns of sensitive and activist Black Americans have changed very little. Despite the Civil War, despite Reconstruction I, despite World Wars I and II, the Korean War, the Vietnam War, and despite the Black Revolution of the Sixties.

Less there is an inclination to "pooh pooh" this comparison, it should be remembered that there were Blacks who owned slaves. There is, in short, nothing new about Black millionaires and Black prosperity in the midst of general deprivation and growing despair. That prosperity, however, is ultimately meaningless unless it is used to make a difference in the kind of world we live in.

A century and a half ago, while most of our ancestors were still in slavery, leaders like John Russwurm and Sam Cornish and Martin Delany made it clear that their allegiance was to God and to the idea of man as the child of God, that those who condoned or allowed the domination of man by man violated the central laws of humanity and were the outlaws of civilization. To degrade the human spirit, they understood, was to defy the will of God. They were superior men, those gallant forebears of ours, for they championed the human spirit and held it sacrosanct in the face of the most brutal onslaught against it. It was that legacy, that moral superiority, which possessed Martin Luther King Jr. and made him immortal. But something has happened. We have lost our way. Speaking of our dilemma and of our leaders' failure to lead us, Joseph Lowery of the SCLC said in Pennsylvania recently: "We had the moral leadership, and we vacated it." Yes. We forgot the lessons our history would teach. We betray our destiny when we seek merely to enter the kingdom of America. **It is our task to transform America so that we can be at home in it.**

We have not been paying attention. Since the profoundly revolutionary days of the Sixties, the forces of reaction in America have been gathering strength. For more than a decade, the Neo-Conservative Movement has been recruiting intellectuals and government officials in crucial places. A central emphasis of that movement is the reassertion of European values and priorities, of High Culture, if you like, in the face of mounting threats to that High Culture's domination. Europeanism is on the rise. In Georgia, Congressman Larry McDonald, a member of the John Birch Society, has established the Western Goals foundation, with the innocuous sounding purpose which states that it is "dedicated to the rebuilding and strengthening of the political, economic and social structures of the U. S. and Western Civilization so as to make any merger with totalitarianism impossible." One of this foundation's urgent projects is the defense of racist South Africa, where some 18 million Blacks are held in economic serfdom by six million whites.

Last year, a book called *Empire As A Way of Life* was published in this country and the author, William Appleton Williams, president of the Organization of American Historians, warns that the country in which we live is an imperialist power bent on controlling other people and their resources for the profit of Americans. He says this:

> To think and act in terms of world power is to deal with straight-line projections of getting hold of history and making it conform to American preferences and conveniences. There is no end to that, no inherent limit, and hence it generates an escalating arms race and an attitude of mind that defines the national interest in terms of trying to control or influence everything that happens around the world. . . .

He asks, "Is our welfare, is our democracy, dependent upon empire?"

And I ask: Do we want to be party to a conspiracy to control the world for the comfort of stockholders in the suburbs—or even for Black men and women with token jobs at powerful corporations? Will we, finally, be at home in such a place? It was Western Civilization that gave us The Middle Passage, 250 years of slavery, and another 100 years of segregation and degradation. And it was Western Civilization that gave us the Holocaust and six million murdered Jews.

Listen to a few more observations by this courageous man who fully recognizes the danger and folly of his country's drive toward controlling the world:

> From the beginning, the Western Europeans went for global empire. We Americans were conceived and born and bred of that imperial conception and way of life. We can explain that, even defend it, but we cannot deny it. A way of life is the pattern of assumptions and perceptions, and values, methods and objectives, that characterize and guide the actions of a culture.

Professor Williams speaks of the religion that is common to most of us, but he speaks of it with rare candor. Christianity was once a vital part of Western European expansionism. It provoked and justified all kinds of imperial activity: accumulating capital by conquest, striking terror into the hearts and minds of the heathens who wanted to keep their wealth for themselves and forcibly changing other peoples' ways of life the better to convert them to the true religion.

"Make no mistake about," he writes, "the imperial way of life produced the promised rewards. It generated great economic wealth and effectively limited the scope and intensity of social discontent." But there were costs, and Professor Williams points out that, "the greatest price was paid in the coin of our sensitivity about what we were doing and how that was understood by other people. We began to define security as the national right to empire." And there were other costs: "Americans became so habituated to empire . . . that they demanded ever more freedom and ever more empire."

What is our relationship to America? Are we now—will we ever be—just Americans like all other Americans? One of our most beloved poets once posed that question in a well known poem. "America," he said, "never *was* America to me." And the great W. E. B. DuBois, after a lifetime—a very long lifetime—of struggle here, finally surrendered to the proposition that America would never be America to him, and so, a few years before his death at 95 in 1963, he became a citizen of Ghana. Back to Africa. Back to the source. Not simply to the place from which his ultimately identifying ancestor had come but, infinitely more important, back to the source of hope—hope both for the children of Africa wherever they languish, and because he believed in a moral link for all humankind, hope for the world.

What is our relationship to America? Is there evidence anywhere that we shall ever be "inside" America? Have we, without admitting it, accepted and adjusted to the proposition that it is our fate here to struggle forever, to be the perennial "other," doomed to hacking away at the massive granite wall of racism until kingdom come? Are we afraid to recognize our "outsideness" at last, to understand our experiential and political kinship with all the colonized and former colonized peoples of the world? Our faith and our loyalty remain steady beyond all comprehension. What is it we have faith in? What are we loyal to?

In discussing the nation's routine betrayal of Black trust and hope, Professor Williams reminds his readers of Franklin Delano Roosevelt's ruse in defusing A. Philip Randolph's planned massive march on Washington to force the New Deal to honor its rhetoric and promises to the poor and the Blacks and other minorities. (President) Roosevelt wanted nothing of that nature to confuse the issues and so, after six months of shilly-shallying, he finessed the crisis by issuing an executive order ostensibly ending discrimination in war-related industries, the military and the civilian Federal bureaucracy. There were no penalties for failure to comply, but it was enough to abort the demonstration.

The niggers were contained. Once again. A bone had been thrown, and there was silence. But in its imperial thrust, America sought to treat all its adversaries as niggers.

The Roosevelts, the Trumans·and the Achesons, and most of their successors, fundamentally misconceived the deeply patriotic—even loving—commitment of American Blacks to what Martin Luther King Jr. called The Dream of America. And because they could not acknowledge the existence of an American empire, they could not comprehend—let alone understand—that other so-called inferiors felt the same love for their cultures; and that, viewing America as an empire that threatened the integrity and existence of their cultures, they would ultimately fight rather than accept indirect destruction. . . .

And so there was Vietnam, and Panama, and Iran. And as the poor and demeaned peoples of the world serve notice that their resources no longer will be at the command of multi-national corporations, the poor and demeaned in America are being programmed to passively accept their poverty. If the pie will be smaller, then those who receive the least must be prepared to accept even less than that.

What is our relationship to America? It is time we knew that. It is not strange these days to hear Black men who have risen to positions of prominence—and I use prominence quite deliberately, rather than power—it is not strange to hear such men speak as though they have conferred with the oracles, have concluded that the way of General Motors, indeed, is the way of the world. But these men should be wary; they should listen to the voices of their own history. Greed and injustice can build no lasting edifices, so long as men and women remain wedded to the idea of freedom and self-respect, so long as that elusive but all-pervasive thing called spirit links human beings to that force we know as God.

Those who came here in chains brought with them a view of the world and a deep connection with all living things that centuries of brutality and degradation have not erased. Perhaps, after all, that was a positive benefit of our legacy of oppression in this place. In our striving to become "American," it is true that we have abandoned much of that legacy, and that was inevitable. But it is my purpose here to suggest that in reclaiming that legacy, we will do ourselves a great honor and possibly contribute to the salvation of America.

My grandmother was no English-woman, though she spoke English, and spoke it moderately well. It is true that she adapted to the English forms which were the models for life in this country, particularly in the Deep South; but the substance of her life and longing was something else again. Africa lived in her: *that* was the secret of her strength that held no hint of hardness; *that* was the source of wisdom that enabled her to see clearly and even compassionately the people whose every act seemed dedicated to her degradation; *that* was the inarticulate lesson she tried to teach me when her lips were silent and her eyes as eloquent as song. She knew the utter danger to the human soul of compromise with evil, even if the purpose was to combat and destroy it.

A generation ago, in response to Frenchmen's taunts that Africans had never invented or built anything of consequence, a group of French-speaking men of African descent defended themselves and their culture with the philosophy of *Negritude*. Like all such defenses of the quality of humanity, *Negritude* was unnecessary. However, its proponents did focus in on the "softness" of the African approach to life, in contrast to the "hardness" of the European approach. What they meant, essentially, was that Africans traditionally sought to live in harmony with their surroundings, to respect all living things, for God in His infinite wisdom had created all things for purpose and interdependency, while Europeans found great virtue in destruction and domination. One way leads to wholeness, the other to eternal fragmentation.

There is a brilliant young African writer who has been trying all his adult life to urge African people to return to their source to rediscover the healing powers of the Spirit. Ayi Kwei Armah is the modern version of the endless wanderer. Born in Ghana, he finds he cannot live there, so infected are the Ghanaians with the fever of alien values; but he also finds the same infestation wherever he goes—in Tanzania, in Lesotho, in Algieria, in Senegal, and especially in America.

Everywhere, Black people have surrendered the healing gift of Spirit. In Brother Armah's most recent novel, *The Healers*, the chief character, Damfo, makes this observation:

> . . . The events that have shattered our people were not simply painful events. They were disasters. They were strange, unnatural catastrophes. Those who survived them could only survive in part because they found ways to forget the catastrophes. When you're still close to past dangers that threatened to wipe you out, even remembrance pains you. Our people forgot a lot of things in order to survive. We even went beyond forgetfulness. To forget thoroughly the shattering and the dispersal of a people that was once whole, we have gone so far as to pretend we have always been these silly little fragments each calling itself a nation.

There is horror in the world. And there is hope. But the hopeful can find no wholeness by accepting the horror. It is our duty to reject America's inclination toward the horrible. **It is our task to transform America so that we can be at home here, at last.**

POEMS
1967-1976

Ronda M. Davis

Towards A Black Aesthetic

if tomorrow's black poetry will
not EXPLAIN what is
but BE it
then pens will be electric with feeling
igniting
and the paper shall become the poet
and poets shall be earth-clouds
transcending life
while living it
they shall be insane with liquid inspiration
daring us to blend with their rising vapors
and they will die soon
but never really leave us . . .

suhmtymz

suhmtymz
whehn ah gaht suhmthihn
ohn mah myn
ahm naht shoour
whehthuh ah bee seyihn iht
ohur juhs bee thihnkihn iht

an whihn peepoh uhrown mee
stahrt tawkihn uhbowt
whuht ahm thihnkihn unbowt
ahm naht shoour
ihf they hurd iht
ohr fehlt iht

suhmtymz
ah bee thihnkihn soh hahrd
ah thihnk
peepoh muhs heeyuh mah myn moov
juhs lyk
suhmtymz
they see mah lihps
doo thuh seym thihng

66

wine-dipped woman

a weaving woman with wine-wilted eyes
who reeks of unaged pluck
is a juicy communion

a dripping candle,
she is a light
a means to an end

unfuckedup,
she is a righteous reason.

how else
could she melt u
with a soft stare
when she asks u for a dime?

Haki R. Madhubuti

communication in whi-te

dee dee dee dee dee wee weeeeeeeeee wee we
    deweeeeeeee ee ee ee nig
nig nig nig niggggggggggggggggggg cleek cleek cleek
    cleeeeee cleekcleek
rip rip rip rip rip/rip/rip/rip/rip/ripripripripripripripri
    pi pi pi pi pip
bom bom bom bom bom/bom/bom/bombombombom
    bombbombbombbombbombbomb
deathtocleekdeathtocleekdeathtocleekdeathtocleek
    deathtocleekdeathtodeathto
allllllllllallllllllll allllllllll deathtoallllllll allllllllll
    allllllleeeeeeee
te te te te te te   te/te/te/te/te/te/tetetetetetetetetete
    tetetetetetete:
the paris peace talks, 1968.

But He Was Cool
or: he even stopped for green lights

super-cool
ultrablack
a tan/purple
had a beautiful shade.

he had a double-natural
that wd put the sisters to shame.
his dashikis were tailor made
& his beads were imported sea shells
    (from some blk/country i never heard of)
he was triple-hip.

his tikis were hand carved
out of ivory
& came express from the motherland.

68

he would greet u in swahili
& say good-by in yoruba.
wooooooooooo-jim he bes so cool & ill tel li gent
     cool-cool is so cool he was un-cooled by
      other niggers' cool
     cool-cool ultracool was bop-cool/ice box
      cool so cool cold cool
     his wine didn't have to be cooled, him was
      air conditioned cool
     cool-cool/real cool made me cool—now
      ain't that cool
     cool-cool so cool him nick-named refrigerator.

cool-cool so cool
he didn't know,
after detroit, newark, chicago &c.,
we had to hip
    cool-cool/ super-cool/ real cool
  that
to be black
is
to be
very-hot.

Gwendolyn Brooks

she doesn't wear
costume jewelry
& she knew that walt disney
was/is making a fortune off
false-eyelashes and that time magazine is the
authority on the knee/grow.
her makeup is total-real.

a negro english instructor called her:
  "a fine negro poet."
a whi-te critic said:
  "she's a credit to the negro race."
somebody else called her:
  "a pure negro writer."
johnnie mae, who's a senior in high school said:
  "she & langston are the only negro poets we've
  read in school and i understand her."
pee wee used to carry one of her poems around in his
 back pocket;
  the one about being cool. that was befo pee wee
  was cooled by a cop's warning shot.

into the sixties
a word was born . . . . BLACK
& with black came poets
& from the poet's ball points came:
black doubleblack purpleblack blueblack beenblack was
black daybeforeyesterday blackerthan ultrablack super
black blackblack yellowblack niggerblack blackwhi-te-
      man
blackerthanyoueverbes ¼ black unblack coldblack clear
black my momma's blackerthanyourmomma pimpleblack
      fall
black so black we can't even see you black on black in
black by black technically black mantanblack winter
black coolblack 360degreesblack coalblack midnight
black black when it's convenient rustyblack moonblack
black starblack summerblack, electronblack spaceman
black shoeshineblack jimshoeblack underwearblack ugly
black auntjimammablack, uncleben'srice black
      williebest
black blackisbeautifulblack i justdiscoveredblack negro
black unsubstanceblack.

and everywhere the
lady "negro poet"
appeared the poets were there.
they listened & questioned
& went home feeling uncomfortable/unsound & so-
      untogether
they read/re-read/wrote & re-wrote
& came back the next time to tell the
lady "negro poet"
how beautiful she was/is & how she had helped them
& she came back with:
      how necessary they were and how they've helped her.
the poets walked & as space filled the vacuum between
      them & the
lady "negro poet"
u could hear one of the blackpoets say:
      "bro, they been callin that sister by the wrong name."

Sandra Jackson-Opoku

Untitled

Here is my voice
on the bloom
    female spirits
    swelling like spirituals
    inside

    Here
    is Queen Nzinga's freedom chant
  grandmama's Mississippi wisdom
my own urban blues and

        Here
        Mari sings and Gwendolyn
        teaches
        Ella swings &
        Angela reaches & I
        poet
        because I have to

In this institution
there is my full voice
    there are many
female, delicious, and whole

    The tart Black berry
      the sweeter the juice
        to roll on your tongue
        and burst
      like sun
    in your mouth

        Here is the song
        ripe and ready
        sweetswollen on the vine

Taste it.

Ancestors: In Praise of the Imperishable

Much more than just one woman,
there are endless spirits
roaming inside me
River Mothers
moving, and
memory much
older
I
And
who but we
fall heir to such
memory, such dream?

River Mothers moving,
History wrapped around my tongue

There are spirits, stirring inside me

Black birds

our soul knows
what it is to go flying
in nightly dreamtrips soaring
over L-track cities/whispers
on the nightwind laughing
shadows flapping
free
Owl eyes that see
and know the quiet
lives below shiver
to the caresses of cold moon
fingers/wild spirits
escaping days cages
princes of the night

Yet twilight shows
our nakedness/hungry
sunbeasts climbing
over skyscraped horizons
chasing souls
back to daybeds

With the night our spirit is hungry
and yearns to be fed

Carolyn M. Rodgers

how i got ovah

i can tell you
about them
i have shaken rivers
out of my eyes
i have waded eyelash deep
have crossed rivers
have shaken the water weed out
of my lungs
have swam for strength
pulled by strength
through waterfalls with electric beats
i have bore the shocks
of water deep deep
waterlogs are my bones
i have shaken the water free of my hair
have kneeled on the banks
and kissed my ancestors of the dirt
whose rich dark root fingers rose up reached out
grabbed and pulled me rocked me cupped me
gentle strong and firm
carried me
made me swim for strength
cross rivers
though i shivered
was wet was cold
and wanted to sink down
and float as water, yea—
i can tell you.
i have shaken rivers
out of my eyes.

mo luv
to Gwen

if i were a painter
        it would be easier
i suppose
        though paint i know
has its limitations.
                        how do you paint
    the pulse
                or mix the essence of
                    the tender heart
    what color is love, throbbing
        through the black veins.

if i were a musician,
                perhaps
i
    could write a score
            with notes
        and special combinations
    advanced sounds, beyond directions
        or, you could hear
    a voice ringing around the air
            heavy, vibrato with encouragement
jazz timing at the throat
                            or i could beat drums
        and you would hear
                        but
    what is the beat of care,
    how rolls the rhythm of tender

For H. W. Fuller

a man, standing in the shadows of a
white marble building
chipping at the stones earnestly, tirelessly,
moving with the changes of the hours,
the days,
the seasons and years,
using the shadows to shield him
such a man,
can go un noticed. . . .

a Black Man standing in the shadows
is not like the one who straggles
through open spaces, hurls bricks at
windows, shatters glass,
yanks or kicks the doors down and
beats his chest scream/proclaiming his glory—
these ones are removed, swiftly.

but the man who grows inside the shadows,
chipping at the foundation, long after
windows and door have been replaced,
the man, who becomes the dark shadow of a
white marble building, will
pick the foundation to pieces,
chip by chip, and
      the
      building
      will
      fall.

Kharlos Wimberli

The Shadows of Your Frown

For Hoyt Fuller (who probably will not like this poem at all)

From far away
the furrows in your brow
seem deeper.
In between
the skinfolds of concern
I see the hurting.
Your dismay
leaps loudly
from the pores
that cry the sweat
of anxious
to be on with
what we must be on with.
The revolution is not near...
and you know why
but cannot let
the understanding patience
intersect the knowing why
    I see you better
from this distance now
and cannot longer bear
the pain
of such sharp seeing
    I come closer
knowing little else
to really do
but blur the stinging
vision
with "a closer walk with thee"
and let you
fan the spark
until it flames again.

Yakie Yakubu

Your Deal

like i used to wonder
who the dealer was
in this game
     and where
         in hell he got
the marked cards
cause i never got as much as a
pair of deuces and my mind
was the only thang that ran wild

but then i got high hip
        found out
a *man* deals his own hand
and says what the games gon be

Jagged Balagoon

. . . out of struggle between him
and all else, all is and was

Whatever was, was cause man
faut wit it; grabbed it round
the neck and wrestled it into
Being—Something

Whatever is, is because we done
hasseled and kicked and bit—
and still is

And whatever will be—will because
we gon always humbug, and struggle

Yeah, man was, is, and will always be
whatever he was, is, and will be
cause of constant, never ending
unpredictable struggle

cause that's the way thangs is

Sterling D. Plumpp

Stand Up Stepping To
Sounds of Coming Men

Stand up stepping to sounds of coming men
or die waiting in colonized promises . . .
Rise on tomorrow's skylines
with bullet kisses/brawns to brew
airborne drafts of Malcolm-mug days
Stepping on sounds of coming men
stand to taste Lumumba rains moving
like prayers through the ears of time
stand to up Dessaline's cup of historical vision
drink to dramas of Chaka drums
giving rhythms to unhip winds
afraid to try Nyerere's new steps down by
Toure shuffles and uhuru bopping Frelimos
Stepping on promises sound as Osagyefo
cowardice withers like a brief joy of love-making
or like the shrinking candle of loud rhetoric
or like the frivolous touch that
was youth yawning on green lawns of idle days
step onto the stand of people buds
blowing with life saxophonic prosperity
Way down yonder under the whip of capitalism
black men stand up to sounds of coming new men
rising from the rinsed vowels of Padmore
doright men a-humming through DuBois's dreams
brave men reclining in the whirlwind of Garvey's love

Stand up stepping to sounds of coming men
or die waiting in colonized promises. . . .

78

Omar A. Shuayb

John Henry Revisited

i saw ol' bad
john henry today
all dressed
in black britches
britches
pulled high
that bragged
on his bigness
whoomp
he smiled
up a breeze
shinin' his boast
all over my
face/muscles
in his arms
talked shit
as he gripped
da hammer
whoomp
i ain't laid
no damn hammer

down
been hammin'
on railroads
highways
skyways
and blues-ways
i chews steel
for tabacco
whoomp
got de man's
tech tired...
niggers
betta fetch
da time
quit frettin'
'bout a piece
of pie
and bust
da whole
cherry
thang.

Ebon Dooley

The Mighty John Hancock Building or
The bigger they are the harder they fall

it was a normal day
in the Loop. . . .

the sun was morning warm
and bounced spring sparkles
from the neon billboards
above Michigan Avenue.
yellow cabhorns honked
and warned mini-skirted mannequins
away from curbs
and changing amber lights.

it was a tuesday scene
and rather quiet
for near/noon traffic sounds.
(the sharp fast sound of
high heels; and dull/worn
rubber soles
dragging on ruffled concrete)

lunch hour crowds
crowded the street.
(window shopping on the
Northern Slope) crowding
around Big John.
crawling
like millions of pink/plumb
ants
beneath Big John
when it happened. . . .

when the Mighty Hancock
roared in pain
and sprawled
down the "magnificent mile"

when smoldering powder/smells
mingled in the air
with dust and bricks
    and steel and glass and
concrete balls of fire

when burning bricks
crushed crowded corners;
and silver spears of glass
shattered spines
and pinned pink bellies
to the pavement

When Big Bad John Hancock
fell
and crumbled concrete
floated in pools of blood
it was a quiet day. . . .

it was a quiet day
when it happened. . . .

Johnnie Lott

Facing the Storm

When we face the storm
Our minds sink
Beneath the horizon
As a tornado
Ravages across the sun
Water spills from
A wounded man
And blood comes in
Torrents from the sky
Forming lakes and rivers
And starts its slow
Progress toward the sea
Everything is blue
And green and red
Except the flowers
In the flower bed
Black has captured them
And in the center is
A white man's head
The lips are opened
As if to speak
And the eyes are
Wide as if to seek
But nothing is said
And nothing is seen
Because there's nothing
In the land of the dead
Especially if it's nothing
But a white man's head.

Eunice Favors

Nature and Naturalness

i ain't never been scared
of lightning
or thunder
or night;
like to me,
night ain't nothin'
but a festival of Blackness,
thunder's like the rumbling of drums,
and lightning's like
a spark of lovin' when it hits right.

Barbara D. Mahone

what color is black?

black is the color of
my little brother's mind
the grey streaks
in my mother's hair
black is the color of
my yellow cousin's smile
the scars upon my
neighbor's wrinkled face.
the color of
the blood we lose
the color of our eyes
is black.
our love of self
of others
brothers sisters
people of a thousand
shades of black
all one.
black is the color of
the feeling that we share
the love we must express
the color of our strength
is black.

A Sea of Brown Boys

a sea of brown boys
streetwise and tough
remembering their fathers
never ached after anything
saw their name in lights
their manhood swapped for
dollars and fixes.

their old men had been
fighting drunk
prisoners of the world wars
dead or missing in some action.

a bridge over trouble
never was needed more—
new heroes ripped off constantly
snatching the sexes
fathers from sons.

they came in studs and spades
in all manner of purses and high heels.

shaft   superfly   sweetback

where did our love go?

Debra Anderson

(Untitled)

I feel sorry
    for blk cats
in wte patten leather
    shoes
And white nylon
    socks
with their initials
    sewn on the side
For cats
    in
wte double knit no-iron
two pleated 3 button
    pants
With wte
    silk shirts
that have been
    Taylor made
For cats in
wte sombreros
that carry brims

wide as Baptist
    Church ladies'
I feel sorry
    for these cats
'Cause they go 'home'
to Yazoo, and Tupelo
    to Augusta and
        Newport
To show it off
And spend Sat nite
standing
    against the wall
        of the Eldorado Inn
With one hand in one
    pocket
Trying to look cool
But only looking cripple

Warren Foulks

#5 The Courts

I was raised on the courts with nothing but my
attitude for protection taking funerals to the
hoop cause I didn't want to end up
                                        shoppin storefront images.
I've been a cigarette smoke dance blown through
a storm of cities. Like I say I was raised on the courts
with a clash by night following a death of
                                        dust storms.
You couldn't call us weak for chanting fate
at our mothers on the way to the night lite
downtown rhythms of whispering
                                        cause hell everybodys coming home.
You couldn't call us weak if we cried or
eased ourselves in the sexrites of dance
cause I was raised on the courts starving
on environmental chilli and watching my family
                                        become falling voices.
That's why I can understand romantic violence
in your eyes. That's why I can accept a gift of
sounds and wrapped touches, knowing we may have blues for dinner
and still offer you a gift for tides.

I was raised on the courts and since my
        dialogue was singing and the sister raps
            we often shared caste kisses,
                but why couldn't we launch a rescue of suffering?

Cause after all the trading of gifts and everybody
coming home, the courts are a cologne image, the
climax has swept by and I'm still taking funerals to
the hoop, prayin that somebody don't pin my shit.

Maga Jackson

Change-Up

who would have thought that at
        my age i'd still be going thru changes...not goin
thru them in the same way...but changin just the same.
        Looked in the mirror
          this morning
           saw a different/face
               from yesterday
yea-yesterdays done come
        and gone and left me only
          tomorrows
      and them tomorrows kinda creep up
          on you and
           slide right by...
Funny how today is
     that day i dreamed about
          minute-mile-years age
      'cept i'm not the tomorrow-woman i'd be...
i'm going thru changes and the changes   this morning   ain't
     changed
        just going thru um
           different.

II
Time?
   who got the time?
      i guess i do
       got to get my self straight
        back on the productive-narrow
    been wastin too much
      time...who got it?
      i guess i do.

88

III

Called Life yesterday

      got one of them funny tones

   operator said

         Life's number was

            un-listed

            couldn't be reached by phone

            on a cause a

        the wires

            were subject to get

                    crossed

     Had mine got

         crossed?

i said yes...

        ...told me she'd give me the address

        didn't think Life'ud mind if

           i dropped by...

i said

   thank you

     and put on my coat.

Helen King

To Be Black, Here

To be black, here
A long, low eternal blues.
A fire-red fire
A loud, electric
Laughing
Joying
Loving—
That is crying, really.
Disfigured young
Ancient teens
Unsmiling women
Wretching, hollow-laughing young men
Holding their own
Thang on the corner
Old men
Dry-rotting in
The cold sun, here
A dismantled people
Seeking warmth.
Giving,
Sharing pain.
Cooking;

Diggin' meat
And wine
And smoke
And God
Stifling in a world full of room
Away from home
And running scared
Still—
One day the blood will chill
The eyes will
See/into/through
The agony
Set the minds—
The whole world, afire.
An unyielding young
Will rise
All/all/all
The energy here
Will turn and forge
A new image/man/world
Till black is right—
Or not at all!

Tony Williams

(Untitled)

Women, black
U a token
    Dropped
        in
    CTA bag,
(Colored Tokens of
        America.)
    Or u joined
And they bus u
        u busted
                along
    bus/lined (lying) systems,
And slotted
into programmed station.
    A put on.
    Putting u on . . . .
        News shows,
Amos & Andy shows, ...
And yeah   it shows.
        but don't show me it
                show it to them,
                    it - self
        bussing/systematic/program
                    put owner
                    show it to it
            but show me us,
Cause   I'm tired of seeing
                        old news,
        on new (nude) faces

91

Denise Love

The Zoo

Look at the people perform
Step right up my good man
and feast your eyes
on the spec tac u lar feats.

Each and everyone
Escaping life and himself
in some unique but common
                              way.

Look at them over there
makin all that noise
playin a silly game of cards.

Look at the sister
she's so hung up on
her looks and new clothes
that she knows
               she is what's happening.
She leaves nothing
to the imagination
          and if she smiled
         her face would
                    CRACK.
She can hardly open
her eyes for the weights
she has glued on them.
Now here is Mr. Hard Times.
He roams all the cracks and corners
of
    Bad Times.
He'll sing you a song
            in Blue
                Green
                     Red
                        and Purple
          for a hand out.

A hand out that shortens
his life by one day.
They flash bright colors
        demons
         sexy women
          dreams of flight
   and reality is just a figment of
            someone's
               nightmares.

Now we come to Mr. Jive Time.
He's so together that he's
falling apart.
He's got the whole world
in his hip pocket...
        Jackson, Hamilton . . .
If it wears a skirt
He'll flash a smile
and his eyes will do a dance
that will make some
sweet unsuspecting soul
left standing
      naked.
His words are
so sweet they
   melt like
      butter
and leave a feeling of
        emptiness.
He has polluted ice water
   in his veins
and nothing
     and no one
can cramp his style.

Just look at all the
fools in the zoo.
They're like baboons in a
      cage.

Call them Brothers and Sisters
and they snap
    "Don't rap that Blackness
    shit to me. Don't you see
    my 'fro is together."
yeh
    Their 'fro is together
        But
   their
       brains
          is
              fried.

Andrew Jazzmar Wasaiah

cold ft

we talk a whole
lodda shit sometimes,
   "my main bru/sista
   why u know we tight as
   the twist in a knot.
   aint no way the shoe
   gone cum off."
& when come time
to shit,
we b so constipated.
"right on" frontin
tryin to smell sweet.
& all the time
just full of shit,
as someone is left...
bare feet.

Alfreda Collins

Common Ground

intellects   rejects
teachers   preachers
had been men
bearded down
beady eyes
red veins   broken
slim thin
winos dopies
sleepin on the streets
leanin against the wall
rappin
bout
those days that was.

mostly women
had
drained strained
made
swollen blueblack
minds blisterbust
when seein
backdays
replays
flashbacks
of
those days that was.

looked at me
Stranger
thinkin
umgon rob them
when
all the time
we was
on
common ground.

Johari M. Amini-Hudson

A Hip Tale in the Death Style

You were a god once before the filth began
when the earth was still warm
and all things lived according to their music
because no strangeness moved
across the face of real blood

you were a god
when the momentum of mountains
above green hollowed bottoms
was new drums pumping chants of lifeblood
under and through the leaves of ancient trees
tall wide shading the moist air
and the richness of living things

you were a god once

but then the trip came
and your blood is full of it
and you blasphemed yourself
because the drums don't pump lifeblood chants
on 43rd street over
the sound of waving fingertips
which point to the feeling of the needles
over the sound of the death style

the drums in the galleries on 43rd street
don't pump lifeblood chants
because the strangeness is here
and the face of the blood
is shot into a thin shell that holds no life

(the strangeness has chants of its own
and the chants pump through shooting galleries
where the carriers of death
have brought you their gift
of powered crystals in time
to the chants of strangeness
drumming thinness in the blood
and drumming your godhead away
where the death carriers destroy it

97

and the genocide of our days is crystalled
into suicide

o yes
suicide is warm and o d is the End
and the strange chants pumped it
from your tied veins
to the tear in your throat
to the rip in your face
that screamed your talk into the phone
AGGGGHHHHHHHH   IMA EVERYTHING   GET HERE

and when i got there you pulled my hand
to a half time tune
slicing my heart
on the half beat of your blood

(o how blood is thin now
your shit filled blood fallen thin
in one inch pools on the floor
marking off where the wood drinks
the circle of your ritual

and you rolled in the dream of galleries
that reached from 43rd to 59th

you really were a god once

but when they gave you the crystalled filth
you took it and loved it
and died from your blasphemy

You really were a god once. . . .

Signals

(1)
is yo eye so empty
in the moonlight of yo smoke
u cant see me waitin
for u to sway my way
sway   fine & black & o so cool
a swift swayin tree
swayin bendin down
& catchin me up into yo movement
pleasin u?
is yo eye so empty
in the moonlight of yo smoke
u cant see me waitin

(2)
o my man
our beginning will be
as beginnings be
total through all the sweet secretions
from your prime cause

and i will be a womanfire
orbiting your night

and you will protect my burning softness
because you wont be
out.
of
it
when i need you

UNTITLED
(in commemoration of the blk/family)

we will be no generashuns to cum for blks r killing
r.selves did u hear bros.did u hear the killings did u hear
the sounds of the killing the raping of the urgency of r
soil consuming r own babies burned n the acid dri con-
figurashuns of the cycles balancing did u hear.did u
hear. hear the sounds of the balancing & checking off
checking off erasing r existence from the count of the
cosmos while r mother moans for the loss of r funkshun
& who we will never be did u hear bros.hear .hear.hear
the sounds of r mother of her moaning as she moans
while we allow her to lie stretch ing herself from Dakar
to Dar es Salaam & she moans & tears her flesh &
gushes did u hear the gushing bros.did u hear.hear. did
u hear the sounds of the gushing oil from her members
spraying the auto mated powers of a foreign god who
ruts in.to her did u hear the sounds.sounds. bros.
sounds of the rutting did u hear. hear did u hear the
rutting of the animal with the golden hair rutting in.to
her urgency eating the sacrificed & futile fetuses erupt-
ed n the fascinated juices of the cycles of pills which
will control the number of her mouths did u hear. did u
hear the cycles turning bros. did u hear them we   will
be no mor. . .

Jamila-Ra

ODE TO MAGUS: THOU ART THAT
(In 8 Parts)

Dedicated to Science the Everlasting Universal Mind
(Part I Sound)

Magus (magi pl.) A member of the Ancient Persian priestly caste, one
skilled in Oriental Magic and Astrology, an ancient magician or sorcerer.

CB noise   10-4   10-4, CB noise 10-4
a quad nadgate
caused communication from without to within
the universe to become blocked,
a Triadic, Triadic, melodic, harmony
composed to ignite 360 degrees × 10, 10 times
enough ohms of power propelling me into infinity
and beyond
thru the Black Holes in Space.
Vast gas astro archways into the ineffable
a dynamic encounter encompassing
10-24 sq. cm enough volts to jolt
the robots trained and programmed
in nescience nonsense,
ultrasonic, super-sonic, electronic
electric mmuuuuuussic
wanting to bedeviled than bedazzled
by the spontaneous spectacle of creating
a diablastula spectacular
busting, breaking, multiplying, growing
unfolding rhapsody's
CB noise10-30, repeat 10-30, repeat 10-30.

Astronautical wizards since Thoth, Hermes, Trismegistus
Rumi, Magus through Bird's "Master Takes"
and "Further Explorations" of Silver
from the "Helio-Centric Worlds of Sun-Ra"
passing on higher degrees in
Neology, Barology, Nephology, Sciagraphy and Cosmology.

Using amazing powers she
travels along the axon of his body
he syncopates the rhythm
their songs produce "Such Sweet Thunder"
that satellites are launched from Earth
on Oct 4, 1957 latitude 50 degrees, longitude the same
brought to you by Duke Ellington.
The visionary quantum equals Einstein, Elvis
Max Planck, Atari, Pythagoras, tissue, acrylic
cyclotrons, optacons, thalidomide, polyester
infections, penicillin, amounts in dollars, cents, stocks
shares, options turning mah jong into backgammon then chess
communication passing from piece to piece
pawn to king
a pedagogy invented out of need for a recorded history
discography "The Complete Genius" rcognizes
all music is not DISCO ROCK
and can be transmitted
on all frequencies
to show pictures with words and writing
shake your T.V. shake your T.V.   TV. T.V.
the continuing tragedy of plastic
manipulating minds altering circumstances
denying light waves to eclipse
the body the beat goes on
Shake, Shake, Shake, Shake
Late, Late, Late, Late
"Some Girls" sing I LOVE LOVE LOVE LOVE
"All My Children" because they are
so "Young and Restless"
even more anti-phonal when she
turns out to be he
and they turn out to be you
the connection is broken.
"Rumours" have it that "Pills"
are rotating the earth toward "Helter Skelter"
change the record to another channel
ERDA, HEW, USDA, WWII
CB noise 10-9 10-9
this is WXYZ
we bring you *much more* mmuuuuuussic
but no transfusion.

The magnificent exigent captivation
of the infinite kaleidoscope
of spirit and space . . . the UNIVERSE
commands/demands us back
and we will travel on an Aeolian Mode
played on an African Kora
a Sura's sweet sound
projected astrally through
the atmosphere into Eros
everlastingly ours, and
beyond.

Randson C. Boykin (Reshain)

Peace of Mind

Ritual
To be Spoken ALOUD
in celebration of All African Peoples
holiday
BLACK WORLD DAY. January 1, of every year.

> All that we need
>   And its so hard to find
> Is some peace peace
>   Peace of Mind
> When the mother and the father
>   Fuss and fight all the time
> When the sister and the brother
>   Have no time to rhyme
> All that we need
>   And its so hard to find
> Is some peace peace
> Peace of mind.
>   Wood (As sung by Nina Simone)

Old ladies in little black hats
     sitting on the missionaries bench,
sitting in the sanctified seat; looking
for a little peace peace
Peace of mind.

Om!   Peace.
Mani!   Peace of
Padme!   Mind
            chant: just some peace of mind
                    just some peace of mind
                    just some peace of mind . . .

Allahu!   Peace.
Akbar!   Peace of
Miiiind!
            just some peace of mind
            just some peace of mind
            just some peace of mind . . .

104

Osiris roaming through the deserts of
time   Osiris roaming through the deserts of
time,   "Pleez Ra RaRaRaRa cum
O,   Pleez cum   cum to a place of pleez cum
to a place of peace of peace of: Arabia."*
A-ray-be-a melting my suns into soils of themselves
their turmoil washing in the valley of their souls; they need
sum peace   sum peace of mind   just sum peace of mind . . .
                              chant: just some peace of mind
                                    just some peace of mind
                                    just some peace of mind . . .

        Ra, your daughters children: the Afro-Asian
                              the Afro-Caribbean   the
                              Afro-American the Afro-African
are captive in leprous clutches   they have no peace of mind
        In our mothers head Egypt sits
festering in its own insolence;
While Africkas breasts flow
creating an Ivory coast,
diamond studded nipples
protrude into the ageless sea;
Black sumptuous womb
echoing Voodoo incantations/   rising
from its fertile crescents . . . she has no peace of mind
            the Congo flows
as she pisses down her legs; her
shackled ankles bound by the Boers
with their apartheid
wresting the riches of her children . . .
        And she moans and groans in agony
As she wheezes curdling vomits
From her Mind!
                When
All that we need
        And its so hard to find
Is some peace peace
Peace of mind
                just some peace of mind
                just some peace peace
                Peace of mind.

*Reference is to all of the Middle East.

Jim Cunningham (Olumo)

music to accompany
jack johnson to a fast
funeral/for miles

1.
take that, take this
person strolling
with sounds in the head
evening calls
from a low skyscraper
where visible wind
blows a blue man
scrambling evening in his hands
take that, take this
person strolling over strings
with sounds in his hands
just right for night steps
or dreaming
hot pursuit across red clay

2.
night steps
no heaviness in sight
day far away
and people too forget
to move
before the swift collage of silences

3.
night steps
into openness
arrows moving
like spirit shadows
of floating bears
move
twilight breaks
our backs
are floating
like drum rims eclipsing
the sky giants
who play impulsive music
while strolling
into openness

Birdie Williams

Roses, Love

Perhaps to wait awhile
but only a little time
for the roots have washed away
and only the roses remain

A deceitful beauty hobbling about
a servant of time, have changed with time,
just a matter of time.

Here,
but already gone
a whisp of roseness free of its bounds
to suppose the promise of reincarnation.

May return again, as love again,
but who is to say?
Am I to wait
and pretend that the roses
are not wilting?

Melvin E. Lewis

Seasons of Love and Juju

For Sandra and Kofi

We are joyous teardrops and wide laughter
caught in the fussy hair and mist of morning jades
we evaporate on the scented leaves and pellets of our
father mums and *azucenas*

We are the children
of the moment
where the stars and sun kissed

We are the *Oriente* wind and whooping cranes
that carve and weather
songs and rocks along the southern coasts
and plantation fields of the world

We are the horns and sea gulls
that blow steam from the Black Star Line
and carry the juju of freedom, uhuru
and *la brigada venceremos* throughout the diaspora

Our assimilated and *casa* tarred home
is not a place where the toes
and seasonal temperaments of our ancestors
find cool water, burning incense and fruit for their
journeys and wisdom
the libations do not reach the rivers of silent movement
the towns we have stepped-in
known the morning traditions of the market women,
slept in the ginger root and shrimp, *pelau* gumbos
have flowered our dictionaries and morning breath.
the songs of our grandfathers prayers
float over our eyes before the signs of lakes
and cities that have changed their names
they would say in gravel and soft voices:
(voice 1)   you do not belong here
(voice 2)   see where the waves start, the Nile is still
                         and the moon yellow
(voice 1)   and come back for my seat on this porch
(voice 2)   sit near my stool under this willow tree

(voice 1 & 2)   for the smoke of iron birds, red bricks
and copper ovens have clogged our pores
for we had names, winter winds and death-marches
before the rivers tops were crusted by oil
and the bottoms belonged to industrial silt
and the caprice of generals.

It is rare for the sun and moon to meet and join
it is woven in autumn stems, monsoon bamboo
Indian leaves and maroon cane in the tablets of the
coastal rivers, when they have walked together

Sandra H. Royster

First Blues

on Saturday nights
they'd take their
grown folks laughter
and leave me just the echoes
and the smoke of fresh-fried hair
to keep me company
nose pressed against cold pane
making misty clouds
i'd watch
them disappear
my eyes on stems
to catch the last of rhinestone twinkles
as they clickety-clicked away
into the evening world
of thick blue music
and the sweet/sour smell
of highball breath
i'd wander through the sudden quiet
of discarded rooms
rubbing lipstick smears
implanted on my cheek
in perfumed flurries of cool silk
and finger treasure troves of woolworth gems
that *i* would wear
someday
on Saturday nights...

Carl Chamberlain

Say It Ain't So

Burnt umber bluish soft dark afro napped hair
crowning your face like the moon reflecting the sun
and gleam glowing love beats.
Eyes, deep liquid pools
hiding a secret smile sayin I know somethin you don't know.

Yeah, got me doin a number
like lookin at your picture
dream slidin, sun slappin, and sky grabbin
for hours at a time...
even got me talkin to the picture...answerin too.

SHO NUFF DIG YO STUFF.

You got me on a blazer
high on dreams of you cause my heart is singin again
and the song is sweet as candied yams and spring kisses.
The last time I felt like this
i had my feelings hurt...
                    please woman
                              say
                                  it
                                    ain't
                                       so.

David Sims (Kiilu)

Midnight Blues Note

...once we made music
like
    'Trane blew his baadd horn's lovesupreme----
      a mellowsmooth soprano inflection
      raving alto SCREAMS
            into each other's
            space;
    and sad,
      misty notes of tender reflection.
like
    Yusef & Rhassan's flute-songs
    trillchimed against windwhispers
    not unlike laughter,
        laughter of tussling, tangled
        playful floor-embrace touch.
Mahogany body
    beating conga-rich tones
    sprayed
    in
    browneyed
    lustre.
Ebony passage of rhythm-chant love
    accented by bongo stac cat os
    pulse-merging w/thumb piano echoooeeesss
    on coconut-oiled oak frame.
We used to compose the funky lifebeats
of shared cosmic sensuality
    ...on linen sheets lined w/the staff
    of my manhood &
    the inner space it
      merged with
    creating the harmony
      of woman-touch
      & man-smell
      of heaving
      happiness
      & "uh good-god"
      tempo...

No one else's diamond needle or 4 channel speakers will
    replay
    that furious fugue of blended lovetones . . .
  ...but the song must fade
    & i know that it hasn't ended tho
    i guess the pitch has wavered...
          maybe
            i should've practiced alone
                first
              -because
              the
              best
              notes
              came
                too soon.

Adalisha Safi

(Untitled)

remember one early morning a little while ago
Oh i'm sure you do
                    you/me/we have had so few of them lately
we rapped till day broke and rapped some more
                                        can you dig it
i told you of the cold winter here and that i could tell i was gittin sick
we rapped about the open door
you not only had a key but i kept the door propped open so that in case
of emergency you wouldn't have to look for your key
                                        and you said i can dig it
there i stood in the door like a dummy/as you left me
NAKED VULNERABLE PREGNANT with empty promises the grape and
the dull green in chocolit papers brought from you to me
                                        you can dig it
there was a knock on the already open door
                                can you dig it
and the sun of the east poured its light on the entryway
a smile and hey Mama, the hawk is dealing out there
you ain't Home where its warm
                        come inside
                        you will freeze and die
                                standin in the cold
i told him i had to keep the door open
that you were out there some where
but with a shove of his foot
                        shut the door
                                can you still dig it
you may have some trouble if you try to use the/that KEY
the door is still there
                        oak with a little willow in it
beautiful as ever
it continues to be the entryway for only the living
and
                        i can dig it.

Nora Brooks Blakely

Negavitism

I am tired of men
I have stepped out of line
        given up my space
Four-footed minds on two legs
Cesspool/swamp mud that was mistakenly allowed to breathe.
Here it comes—a lion pit surrounded by mintgreen forests
        luring me in.

A firefly light//lights out when you need it.
Let me stop . . . I shouldn't say all this,
      I said I wouldn't look no the *good* side. . . . . . .
It's just that I'm so tired of fireplaces----------with arctic ashes.

Reconsideration

Well, it ain't all bad
There are warm cuddle nights
      lampeyes that softglow when we laugh
      cheer/chimes in his voice
      firecracker brains with sparkler ideas
        that cracklebright my mind into new life.
A sun that honeys my existence
hmmm. Reverse mental bubblegum—
      the longer my mind chews these thoughts the sweeter men get

HEY!   can I have my place back?

Philip M. Royster

Intimacy

Our hands touch
but do not hold
even when we grasp
they do not enfold.

Honesty . . . Truth

Honesty
    is darker than
    your woman's nipples
    and more thrilling.

Truth
    is deeper than her navel
    and more vital.

CONDEMNED

Each sight unsought cracks
my consciousness with a flash
of disappointment:
The car lights the motel curtain
until I can see she is merely a child
who does not smile when I ask her
to get dressed without touching her,
and though I tell her to hurry home
the crowd catches me at the field
of weeds against the tracks.
It is my wife who breaks from the edge
to condemn me, her pointing finger
bursts my rising plea, her anger
pounds my face to skull,
her whisper, the ghost of mercy,
Jail him before her father comes.
The crowd marches me past my brother
slouched against our abandoned shack
and I regret that this may be the last
time that he will fix me with his eyes.

Smalley M. (Mike) Cook, Jr.

Mikado Quartet
To H.J.

SWEET SPIRIT, BLACK PASSION
THROWN HIGH BY
SWIRLING CREST OF PIRATE CYCLONE

DANGER DANCE DOWN UNCOMPASSED PATH
GENEROUS FLIGHT OVER BITTER ROCK

NO DIAMONDS HARD, RUBIES RED
NO GOLD PURE ENOUGH
FOR YOUR LOYALTY

PAST THE DRAMA OF CHANGING SEASONS
I HEAR YOU THROUGH THE PLAYERS MASQUE

Pauline Cole-Onyango

I Drink to the Glory of
My God

the first man i ever had is my man
in him i dig for diamond coal
pulling out chips and chunks
of stone-turned soil
with my bare hands
and the honey sweat sap
of his strength
is my nourishment

abandoned in a hell's pit
he makes a clearing around us
freeing me to grow into him
like siamese sunflower seeds
planted in childhood of blackness
and blooming
on a cool spring morning
before the sun
breaks the earth
in half

E. Van Higgs

Bushwoman

bushwoman bends over washboard
wipin browsweat on hand
blublkblush brown flesh
rubbed rough on ridges

she cups coffee coloured child
tender tips of touch
holds face

an sits a throne
strong
strength sweeps softly
coconutmilk sweetens
her honeythick moist lips
nostrils quiver
at presence of her man

bushwoman moves
a washin wave
baobab/calabash bottom
mu-sic movements
liquid free form
w/rhythmic changes.

Janice Dawson

Stop and Shop

Pssssst. You there.
Look in my eyes.
Look in my eyes and see
and see me.

Pssssst. You there.
See me looking at you.
See me checking you out.
Can you feel the vibrationnnnns too!

Pssssst. You there.
Look at me again.
Can you tell I want you.
No! Not now! Not later!
Soon - Thursday - Forever.

Pssssst. You there.
Better stop me.
Better grab me.
Better hold on forever.
'cause I'm channnnnging without you.

Pssssst. You there
Like me this way?
Then take me home,
take me home,
take me home,
with you.

Angela Jackson

Second Meeting

memba the time . . .
            we met at home
        that slow age ago.   one day.
me.
    with a water jar balanced
    on my head /
    to fetch from the river
                and u
                and u wuz
    hone / n a spear for the
    hunt   that nite
    do u think about / —when
                we'd met befo
        in a   / once life.   one nite.
we shared the bitter ripe / ness
                            of a
            mango /   togetha
    moved a   fertility dance
        beneath the warm east sky . . .

    but i guess / u forgot . . . til
                    we met   again.
            in this cold /   place
    chicago.   the subway.
        like:
            hey sista   wuts happen / n
        . . . and
        i reminded
        u   in a smile
(don't i know u
        from
            sum /
                where??
                        u said. and
    i nod / ed softly: yes.
                    afraid i'd tip / ova
                the water jar
            i always think
                    is
                        balanced
            on my head. . . .

in my fathers garden
(anyway and how)

my mother does work in my fathers garden.

this afternoon without wind
        of september in heat

the monkeycigartree once struck by lightning
grows anyway and how

its roots have begun again to be
                at a awkwardheight
and this afternoon of lazysun   bloomed in heat

the tree bends and touches the greens
and squash in my fathers garden begun from brick and rocks

we thought
        the only thing that would grow in this city
        would be brokenglass
on vacantlot and faithshovelled
my father planted anyway and how.

he set his task. and grew his greens too close
like people in tenementrooms.
           and my cousin fixed the seeds
                that opened crampedyellow
        transplanted them in sun and soil and air.
        her hands are whiskey and kindness. like
        herself.

my fathers garden grew.
he never knew my cousins sharing. her healingcare.

now. ready for evening my mother does work in
my fathers garden.

the monkeycigartree my brothers smoked stalkthings that grew
from it pumped magic in their heads   once
grows again and bends and touches the greens the squash the beans

and my mother bends and touches like treeshadow her orangedress
signals sun to set.
my fathers planting sprawls thicklimbed and sound.

tomorrow. some stranger will pass and ask
           how did he break this unfriendlyground?

Walter Bradford

Sermon for the sake of my children;
a message to my youth

You may think it all belongs to you
the weight of working on the world
to make it right
the way people say it should be
but ain't
and you may think this world insane, at least,
since father left no hand to feel and
history lies lonely on a page
water talk talk full men swallow
all, they can hold up to
and you may think it a shame
to find your soul
still a victum
in this age of muscle monkeys
chinning on the moon.
It is
not so
it is, simply
your turn.
That evil is as evil do is evil just the same
that evil is the hope you saved is true and laced with pain
not new pain but the same pain the
over and over again pain the
same pain passed on.
But you, pebble from a glowing stone, have work in this world
you, despite it all, must not fall the way
of some before you, so,
watch each motion you make and
becareful on the way to your soul
for all begins there
know what it contains and
what it sings after and
what it leaves behind
your fathers did
as theirs did
and did
and did
and did
until it came to you, you

lords of tomorrow
make the wind a magic spear in your hand and
show it where to go, you
front streets heroes
be the songs your fathers could not sing and
the rain turned round and handsoaked back to god and
be the men of cast and color under
temples of corroded gold that sit
grinning like neon angels
peaceful in the city night and
be the dust from mountains where
kuroo calls you home, you
little stone, little cold black stone
and you troy
and you gangster
and you shug and
bay-bay 'nem too
be the men
be the men
to put sorrow to sleep in this world.

Hoyt W. Fuller

Twice Widowed

She sits grave-faced by the window
watching new birds in the pecan trees
and the old dog's stumbling lope to his shambled shed
The children who sneak over the high rear fence
to gather the fallen nuts
are strangers
and the limp-muscled dog ignores their trespass

(Travail and loss came early and huddled about her
Their implacable presence bent her shoulders
and even the child of her loins escaped her embrace)

Beyond the window's view the city looms
The street is filled with unfamiliar faces
She does not raise her still-bright eyes
to the steady stream of aircraft above the trees
and only when she knows her son will visit
is she conscious of the motors' rending roar

There is a precious peace there in the trees
They are a screen against particular storms
She laughs sometimes
remembering pleasures older than her child
and wanders among them, alive again in ancient dreams
In those moments she becomes the child:
her brown eyes glitter and her strong voice purrs
And I am moved toward impotent, desperate prayer:
'God of my mother, let her be happy there'
I am the parent now. Our world has turned.

Eileen Cherry

in the/groves

may be. it is just.
i am silenced. stilled. frozen in gold.
this time.
it is my season to give ear. to listen.

       i have tried speakin to the trees
       but have fallen raw&green
       in my word. they whisper, she wallows in youth.
       too young to yield. too firm
       to be broken by wise teeth.

  i am the freshling seed. locked in lobe/velvet
of un/ready fruit. & i can/only promise
the earth tomorrow may be
a great gittin/up o/future trees tangled
lacin her head like african/crown.
        & i can/only promise
her baskets weaved green w/leaves
drinkin butter/gold of everyday/sun.

may be. it is just.
i am silenced. in the/groves.
frozen in the whispers of wish. row upon row.
the trees know my promises
are yet youthful. know
i have yet to be broken by wise teeth.

127

fat legs

thinking bout
a little ol fat baby
thinkin bout
a drop of fat black
baby child

thinking bout
the miles them little
fat legs would run
drummin they foots high in
the air
        /chub chub
turnin/burnin
        boogedyboogedy
when they could finally
run up a stair

then the bones grow and roll
up under
    tables/hidin
seek under beds
from the strap and laughin

they jump/dance conjurin mischief.

fat legs
growin bones and knees
learnin to
catch cuts and
press ground to
whisper prayer.
fat legs grow bone
to meet in battle
and run the swift and surest.
fat legs
grow to wear the
hip kinda shoe/
                grow
to show
who pimp/strut the purest.
fat legs ripen to firm
thighs and knees/mama taught
to sit right   pressed together
in prayer.

fat legs grow bone.
thinkin bout
what they own
                a man/woman
yam/seeds of knowledge/fat
greasey lotionleened legs do grow
bone
        hustlin to keep from rustin
        til the firm thighs cramp up hard
        as rock or fall to flab/thighs
        wither like figs or bloat

fat legs do too grow bone.

stand/in the need of a new
knee
as they criss/cross stiff
strut to gamble
on ice and forever steeping
stair
press together in prayer

David L. Crockett-Smith

Footnote to a GNP
(After the Film *Last Grave in Dimbaza*)

The graves have been dug in Dimbaza.
They await the malnourished children
with the smugness of open graves.

Prosperity has its price.

The regime has decreed:
"workers ought not be burdened
by superfluous appendages
like women and children."

The Bantustans
exist for the common good.

The graves are smiling in Dimbaza.

Can you hear the sound of gunshots?
The European women
and children
train with police on the pistol range.

Can you hear the children scream?

The graves are empty in Dimbaza,
and small-boned corpses toddle through the streets.

The Bantustans are empty.
The workers' camps are empty.

With the tears of tiny eyes
still burning on their cheeks,
with the pains of the unconceived
already gnawing in their loins,
the people come with thighbones in their hands.

Where are the children of Dimbaza?
The hand that holds the gun
withheld the bread.

And the starved hope of bloodless change
sprawls in an open grave.

For the emptiness that fills the children's eyes
for the women's hearts and a toast of broken skulls
may the factories die in a blood of liquid flame.

There can be no peace nor sleep nor thought of love
in a land of open graves.
The graves have been dug in Dimbaza.
Let the graves now be filled.

SPRING SONG

I want you to know
the azaleas are blazing
in Montgomery
and the Alabama River
is cleared at last of snags.
I have heard it said
the setting moon found
robins in her nest
and all the floods of spring
will fail to wash the swallowtails away.

Spring has carried her heat
to Alabama, and the grass
blades spring up in excitement.
Wild roses race with honeysuckle
to stake out the turf,
and O, the women prowl
with foxfire in their eyes.

I want you to know
I was born in the corpse of winter
where Creeks once ran naked,
I was born in Tuskegee,
raised among cotton fields in Mt. Meigs.
The mantis taught me my poise.
The mockingbird speaks my tongue.

I was planted in a soil of books
and sprinkled with blood
from the T.V. mouths of newsmen.
I grew gray in my greenest days.

I grew gray, and I am here
where the air is heavy,
where raindrops taste more bitter than tears.

It is spring.
Gunbursts bloom like roses
in South Africa. The new day in California
breaks on a procession
of men in sheets. A voice
is grasping at teenage girls:
"I want you, baby. I want you!"

I want you to understand
the wildfire spring ignites my blood,
the world is hoarfrost on my heart.

But I know
the child who waits to be born
calls out to me from the womb
in a silent tongue.
He does not know
I am two eyes
which see too much,
I am a heart
which never holds enough.
All he knows is the need of a child,
as all the flowers know
is to bloom in spring.

There is dirt beneath my feet.
A river sings in my veins.
Though the dogs are mad with pain,
and Nazis goosestep march
in the face of a bloodied moon,
though twisted men
are singing in the street,
though brambles strangle the flowers
and curl about my door,
I want you to know
I will go forth
with a sickle in my hand.

I want you to know
I have no fear of death.
The unborn child
is walking at my side.
He is speaking with my voice.
I go out to meet the spring.

CREATIVE PROSE

The Doe

Cecil M. Brown
(1969)

The two of them, boy and Uncle. Standing at the edge of a field where tobacco stalks had only two weeks ago been chopped in, not far from where five years ago, the time around which he went off to school, there was a hog pen, and where now stood a fine green bunch of mongrel plants. The only patch of fertility in fact, for miles, if one didn't consider the pines that had been there all during his life fertility—which he didn't. More like sterility. Their greenness a facade, a put-on, because the fact of the matter was the land had long been raped of its energy, suffered humiliation at the hands of Riegal Paper Company; in their hands the animals frightened away by ugly white paddies from up North some-where. Once some hillbilly even set the woods on fire. Immoral beast.

A calm afternoon, Paul and his uncle Jed standing in the field, his uncle Jed holding his 12 gauge shotgun ready, both of them holding their breath, listening to the pattern in which Red Rooster was running, know-ing if he ran in a straight line it was a buck, and, if in a circle, a doe; so calm, that only that sound, plus the sound of his Uncle Jed's sudden dry swallow, could be heard, the swallow like the liquid movement of fluids in the stomach, drawing his attention to uncle Jed's Adam's apple. Uncle Jed didn't have the Black man's nose, nor the skin, nor the hair. He had the white man's features, but the Red man's skin, the skin dark red, black-ened in certain crevices by the intense late August sun, blackened, too, by age and toil. Fifty-six and teeth falling out. There was, too, a hump in his back that became more pronounced as the year passed, a boulder in the sea that became more exposed as the sea level fades.

Raised him, took pride in telling people that he was his son, probably because he never had children of his own.

Ten minutes gone, still standing, trying to figure out what Red Rooster was up to. "Well," Uncle Jed said, slightly grinning, "reckon it's a doe, huh?" Paul looked at him, only for a moment. He knew; knew that the Uncle knew. Once when Paul was 12, Uncle Jed burst into the yellow kerosene-lit kitchen, announced proudly that he had "got one" and they went out into the back field with a flashlight, pushed back the shadowy brush and found a mangled doe. An emptiness filled his stomach to the point of sickness; it was like cheating, and for many years he disliked his uncle, thought him a coward.

"Yeah," Paul said, vacantly, "I think so." And then, glancing over to his uncle, "guess we have to let hit go." He watched his uncle fidget, reluctantly easing the hammer of the shotgun forward, breaking the barrel and taking out the shell, a surge of triumph growing in the boy's chest.

His uncle chuckled to himself, as if to say that if Paul was not around he would have a deer, which was the kind of thing his uncle was capable of saying. The chuckle and silence forcing Paul to advance his moral objection into the open. "Part of the pleasure in doing anything," he said, almost to himself, and certainly to the calm blue afternoon, "is doing it by the rules."

"'Cept not everybody don't have the same rules." Chuckle. "Now you take them paddy boys, now ifn' a deer run by their gun, they don't care what it is, it's just a dead deer." The boy wheeling quickly, "Yeah, but don't you see, Uncle Jed, that's the way white people are, they're immoral, but we don't have to be that way." His uncle coughed, "Yep, that may be true but they the ones get all the meat. Ha."

Then there was a speck of dust coming about a mile off down the dirt road.

"You think that's mommy and them?"

"Looks like them Martin boys' truck," Uncle Jed said.

"Uncle Jed, you mean to tell me Daddy still lets them crackers hunt on our land?"

"Ha, ha, well, ain't nothing wrong with it. That the Bible says do unto—"

"But Uncle Jed, don't you understand if *they* owned this land and if there were deer on it, do you think *they'd* let *us* hunt on it, do you really think they would?"

"Ha, ha, no, them devils shore wouldn't. They wouldn't even let a Negro even set foot on it."

"Then why do y'all still let them hunt on our land?"

"You better talk to your daddy 'bout that, I tell ya."

"I don't understand it," Paul said, shaking his Afro-fixed head. "Why don't y'all—" he wanted to indict his uncle personally because he knew his uncle and father were of the same belief—"charge these crackers a fee. That's what they would do for you. They'd have you—"

"Well, you know what your daddy'll say to that; he'd say we's all the same and you got to live with your neighbor. Now, see here, you can say all this and talk about Black Power, but you don't have to live with rednecks, you get back on the plane and go back up North, but we have to live here with them—"

"But, Uncle Jed, I would feel the same way if I lived here. I mean, you mustn't forget that I lived here all my life, too. But I tell you we have to treat them the way they treat us. Because as long as we pretend to be more moral than they, we'll never get anywhere politically. In fact, our moral superiority is what these crackers thrive on, because for one thing these bastards"—a year ago he wouldn't have used such strong language in his uncle's presence—"don't believe they live in the same moral community with us and, second, they interpret your generosity for Uncle Tomism."

"We still have to live wit' him," was his uncle's evasive grumble.

"I am going to tell the crackers myself," Paul said, watching Uncle Jed begin to throw his eyes around uncomfortably.

"Them poor pecks ain't gonna listen to Negroes. Jokers rather die and go to hell"—this was said with feigned militancy, designed unconsciously to assuage Paul's anger—"before they listen to a Negro."

The truck was approaching quickly now, keeping only inches ahead of a trail of grey dust. Paul watched it intensely, with a silent hate, watched the truck as it slid up to his feet. Both doors flew open, and one of the Martin boys, the oldest one, got out with an expensive-looking gun; the other cracker Paul did not know.

The two men ran a few feet from the vehicle and froze. Their ears cocked to Red Rooster's wailing. "Well, Jed, what you reckon it is?," the driver said, knowing it was a doe. The uncle grinned and dug the toe of his shoe in the black soil. "Looks like it's meat to me."

Paul looked at the uncle. *Uncle Tom* bastard.

In his jacket pocket he flipped over in his fingers a double -O-buckshot. Uncle Jed wouldn't or would understand. Really, it didn't matter.

"Hey, Jed," the tall white boy was saying, as his Adam's apple, sharp as a knife, sliced up and down in the calm afternoon balminess. "Jed, you don't care about no doe, do you, meat is meat, ain't that right, Jed? Ha. Ha. Huh, Jed!"

But meat was not meat. God's Covenant law had established this. White man's law was not God's, nor nature's, nor the Black man's. The soil, now a wasteland, because of dumb crackers, and Uncle Jed's cowing before the symbol of destruction which he mistakes (?) for. . .what?. . .I really don't know . . . maybe he thinks the white boys will shoot him with their fancy guns. The single buckshot, however, twirling over in hiding in the jacket pocket. White crackers die, too, Uncle Jed. Paul knew, visualized that there were two more buck shots in the glove pocket of the truck. Then remembering his Uncle Jack's death. Death by buck shot. The terrible hole it made. His wife believing that he loved other women more did it for him. A waste, really. The terrible hole it made in sleep right beneath the left shoulder. And the single buck shot twirling indecisively between his fingers like the ghost of Hamlet, action's enemy, the liberal's sanctuary.

"Hey, look Joey," the tall white boy said, a twig jumping between his gnashing teeth, "let's get that doe, huh? Jed's right, meat is meat." The white boy looked as though he would have slapped Jed on his back, or hugged him even, had he been in reach. "What you say, Joey."

The other, shy, reticent, more conscious of the enemy, had not ceased pretending to be listening to the dog. Paul looked directly in his watery blue eyes, saw his eyes run away frightened and dwell on some material aspect of the head lamp. Then, suddenly, his eyes leaped up, unexpectedly, determined, wild. "Hell, what's so sacred about killing a doe? God made 'em, I ain't gonna grade em." And then, almost as if to confirm or to gain complicity, he turned to Paul, "Ain't that what you say, boy?"

"My name is not 'boy'" was the first blow. The cracker was more audacious than one expected, but then, this could have been bright fear, wearing the mask of self-righteous arrogance.

Uncle Jed kicked a clod of dirt with the ferocity of a mule. The kick succeeded in serving as a refutation, as an absorber, really, a convention by which one could begin talking about something else, or by which they could hide behind and pretend what Paul had said had not been said; was so successful that, indeed, it was as if not only had Paul not said what he had said, but Paul did not even exist.

The three had agreed tacitly, the way lovers agree, upon a course of action or a texture of criticism in the midst of others, agreed, despite the pit of shared hate among them, despite their slave-master differences. They had agreed most assuredly on one thing: This person who said his name was not "boy" did not exist. Nothing more was to be said to him, for one cannot speak to a Black man who doesn't answer to "boy," in the same way one cannot speak to a ghost.

And then the second blow—a young fighter swinging in the air, yet swinging. Fighting windmills is still essentially fighting, although, and here Uncle Jed fell extremely short, ass-kissing was still Emily Post:

"Get off my father's land, off my land, you white mother-fuckers! Get your immoral asses off my land. You beasts! Shoot a deer here and I'll have you locked up, crackers."

A scream was really what it was, and they didn't hear. Swinging in the wind. Shadow-boxing. Because the tall one turned to the shy, watery-eyed one and said, "Joey, c'mon let's go!"

The engine revived like an animal surprised in its morning bed. Shot onward, watched by Uncle Jed's tired and frightened eyes. And by the ghost's. And Uncle Jed had not heard (?). Because: "ha-ha—them paddy boys gonna get that po' doe."

And then: Uncle Jed, don't you see how you cowed before these white boys, just because they are immorally superior to you, because they are better at being beast than you, and you licking their shitty cracks that resemble nothing so much as an old woman's spittled-covered mouth, you acting immoral because it is only through such an act that they can see you as existing. Is such an existence so very valuable? No, rather, Uncle Jed, be a ghost like me and keep your manhood, for, after all, there is virtue in being a spirit: you can see through empty souls and walk through opaque walls, for example.

And then Paul had the shotgun with which he had killed his first buck nine years ago in The Bottom, out of Uncle Jed's hands and running down towards The Bottom where he knew the doe would stop and the men waiting for the soft vunerable head to peak from the brown-yellowish greenery, running as he fumbled the buck shot into the nose of the gun held together partly by a black piece of adhesive tape, running with the wind bringing the telegraphic "Paul," "Paul" from his Uncle Jed's tooth-less mouth, "Paul," "Paul," the sound of a desparate man who is not quite sure what desperation is or, if this is it now, the controlled sense of desperation that remembers not to be embarrassing. And so he ran, was running, ahead of his body, already aiming the crooked barrel that always had to be aimed just about a quarter of an inch off to hit anything, already seeing half of the tall cracker's face lit up with blood as the other half watched that half fall to the ground between his shoes, already ensconced in the green woods which he loved and which loved him, green woods that protected fugitive slaves since the beginning of America, already escaped into the woods living in moral liberation, already sure that he had finally succeeded in embarrassing Uncle Jed, succeeded in becoming an exis-tence, in having a voice in a silent world. Already there before his body. An unfortunate Hamlet-like position.

Blues for Little Prez

Sam Greenlee
(1973)

The garbage collectors found Little Prez in the alley near Six-trey, OD'd away, layin' there cool and stiff, the tools of his burglar trade beside him and the shit for his fix there, too. He'd run across some of that almost pure smack only the rich white folks can get nowadays stuck behind a real Picasso drawing in a Bradburg Village townhouse on the North Side. Didn' pull no capers usually on the North Side 'cause rippin' off white folks was a one-way ticket to the slam, but he turned on all the afternoon before with some junkies he knew lived in Old Town, turnin' on, noddin' an' diggin' teevee an' the nex' mornin' everybody was gone an' no smack aroun' when he woke up an' he needed a fix quick so he walked over to the Village an' dug a back-door with a lock jus' beggin' to be picked. So he slid in through the Sci-fi electronic computerized plastic kitchen that could do everything except fuck an' cook food you could taste, past the big color console TV sittin' squat an' fat like some bloated Buddha gon' wrong diggin' him with its big charcoal-grey cyclops eye, an' on past the little brother Sony TV in the bedroom 'cause any Pig seein' a nigger walkin' down North State Street with a idiot box was gon' jack you up for sure. Dug a cassette recorder good enough for a fix, but the real score after he emptied all the dresser drawers on the floor looking for a stash of cash was a fancy wrist watch good enough for the first fix of the day an' he could stick it in his pocket, an' then he dug the picture wasn' hangin' right in the way junkies have of focusin' in on jus' one thing an' foun' the package taped behind it and stuck it in his pocket when he heard a noise before he could check it out. He slid on back out the kitchen door of the white man's pad like his momma been doin' for more years than Little Prez been livin'. On out into the eye-blinkin' hard hot sun cuttin' through his shades like razor blades an' lettin' him know once more that daylight and junkies ain' no match. On down into the dank damp tube of the subway feelin' more like home where no daylight an' no eyeball burnin' sun could come. Bought two Hershey bars in the vending machine on the platform, his junkie juices flowing in his mouth askin' for some sugar, an' he tried to cool his junkie nerves jumpin' up and down his spine like grasshoppers up a long stalk of ragweed in a Woodlawn vacant lot where he used to play an' catch grasshoppers and make 'em spit tobacco an' tell ladybirds to fly away home 'cause they pad was on fire an' he didn' ever step on ants 'cause that would make it rain an' when it rained he'd have to stay in his funky crib in the middle of the rats and roaches an' the sound of the soap opera down the hall dealin' with silly-ass so-called hangups of jive-ass white folks whose ghost-white voices walked into the room an' took over. Tol' his grasshopper nerves to cool it an' his monkey to take a vacation 'cause he was gon' turn on soon as he hustled that fancy-ass watch layin' in his pocket nex' to his long unused dick cause smack been for a longtime his only ol' lady. Was sniffin' an' scratchin' but bein' cool with it 'cause they might be a undercover pig sittin' in the subway car waitin' to jack up some junkie 'cause he didn' have nothin' else to do an' it was easier than messin' with some beret-wearin' gangbanger who didn' give a shit an' might kick some pig's ass or worse an', shit, he sure wished the pigs would get off his back but he been cool since the last time he got out of the slam in Joliet an' he was stoolin' for the pigs now and so they let him alone an' even laid a lid on him now an' then when he said somethin' they wanted to hear, but right now he was out of his 'hood an' some motherfuckin' rookie lookin' for a promotion an' didn' know Little Prez might bust him or even rip him off 'cause the quickest way for a honky pig cop to get a promotion in Chicago was to off a nigger. So he wished the damn train would get him the hell on back to the South Side where he belonged an' he could get him a fix an' all his hangups take a vacation along with his monkey, an' all the time he had the best smack he ever had in his pocket but he forgot about it like everything else when he needed a fix, jus' thinkin' how much he needed to turn on an' how good he be feelin' after he shoot up an' all the down things be movin' in his head while he noddin'. The El came on up out of the tube and the sunlight hit him across his eyes right through his shades as hard as a pig from the Southwes' Side hatin' niggers an' hungup an' evil 'cause one of his neighbors sold his crib to a nigger jus' three blocks away an' even though the pig pumped a full magazine of buckshot in through the nigger's picture window they jus' boarded it over an' now they was "for sale" signs all over the block an' nex' thing you know they be takin' over his neighborhood an' he moved twice already gettin' away from niggers. Little Prez knew how to read all that shit in a honky pig's face, an' how much shit the pig gon' make him take an' how much smilin' some- times didn' do no good 'cause a lot of them pigs got they kicks stompin' niggers.

Little Prez got off at Fifty-fifth, glad he was back in his own 'hood, an' he hustled the watch to a barber for 35 bills, bought his shit, hurried to his crib an' knew he could make a thing out of his make 'cause his monkey not buggin' him too much. Let himself into his funky-junky pad with jus' a mattress on the floor an' a table an' a refrigerator (didn' usually have nothin' in it, the only thing in the crib worth anything the stereo an' color teevee). He dug sittin' an' noddin' diggin' TV with the sound off an' his earphones on, diggin' the sounds an' watchin' TV with- out havin' to listen to them screechy tacky voices sounding like somebody scratchin' his fingernails across a blackboard when he high. He had a small white enamel sterilizer he ripped off from an abortionist one time an' that was a good score 'cause he foun' two shoeboxes full of cash an' he didn' have to steal nothin' for months after that caper. Little Prez dug he was a different kind of junkie shootin' up with sterile needles and the only tracks in his arms was when he turned on someplace else with some junkie friends or when he was too strung-out to wait for the red light to go on on the sterilizer. But he was scared of dirty needles; his momma aways tol' him 'bout germs an' shit, an' he knew a lota junkies got wasted from hepatitis an' shit from turnin' on with dirty needles. He turned on the TV without no sound to that soap opera always had somebody Black on it talkin' to white folks all the time, an' Little Prez used to make up what they talkin' about between nods diggin' the sounds on his headphones. Then he took his time puttin' on a stack o' sounds: Prez, Stitt, Jug, Trane an' a old Wardell outa print nowadays an' he tol' everybody it was one of his "collector's items." He had some of the new sounds an' dug 'em, but when he was turned on he mainly listened to the sounds that was the sounds in the streets when he first got out there in 'em. He put the records on the box then started gettin' his make together diggin' Prez during his first administration winnin' the election for all-time in front of that bad-ass Basie band. He put the needle in the sterilizer. "Rock-a-Bye Basie," diggin' Earl Warren doin' a few Johnny Hodges type bars, then Prez fatter-toned than usual, the band riffin' so bad behind him, an' then Sweets blowin' like he invented the Harmon mute. Little Prez hummin' along with 'em everyone of 'em and the band too, an' not missin' a note, gettin' the make ready, careful like he was gettin' his horn together in some funky backstage like Prez gettin' ready to blow. The red light went on an' tol' him the needle was ready, an' he got the rest of the make together while Prez was doin' trippin'-type things on "Taxi War Dance." Took out the needle and the tablespoon with the handle bent over double, made up over an alcohol lamp, Prez wailin' now, bootin' the band an' they talkin' to each other, Prez an' the brass section, an' Prez, four bars each an' them cats could say more in four bars than some of these young dudes in four sides. Herschel Evans blowin' now, deeper-toned than Prez, earthy sound like he had to keep his feet planted on the ground 'cause Prez always wantin' to fly, big fat sound no reed squeek, sound soundin' like it an' Herschel the same thing with the rhythm section rock-steady an' swingin' behind him. Whole band riffin' now an' Little Prez puttin' the rubber hose roun' his pipestem arm, flexin' his fist an' lookin' for a collapsed vein to show, gettin' uptight now 'cause it so close an', shit, where was the motherfucker, the needle ready an' Prez sayin' things an' the earphones right there, shit, where was it, wantin' to put it in his arm an' beggin' for pussy he knew he wasn' go get, never as bad as waitin' for that vein to show an' give him a target for the clean dickhead of his needle, an' one showed an' he hit it an' slow slow makin' it last shot up an' pulled the needle out, still proud an' hard even when empty an' his own dick never been like that even when he was a stud an' hustlin' a stable of four of the finest whores on the South Side. He put the dick/needle in the sterilizer, put on the earphones an' waited for the flash, better than any orgasm he ever had an' didn' miss anymore 'cause he had all the sex he needed every day in Miss Skag an' it hit him an' he moaned an' Prez blowin' "D. B.

Blues" an' Little Prez layin' there an' noddin' an' diggin' Lester, his man, President of all the tenor men.

II

We called him Little Prez 'cause he dug Lester so much. Could scat all Prez's solos note for note in the right key standin' there near the basketball backboard in McCosh playground, his hands shoulder high, holdin' an imaginary tenor like Prez downstage at the Regal Theater blowin' with that bootin' Basie band behind him, Jo Jones kickin' on drums, Freddie Green rockin' steady an' Walter Page walkin' strong, the brass bright an' bitin' punctuatin' the saxophone riffs, an' Prez would start out with his tenor hangin' low an' like it gettin' good to him comin' up slow 'til it shoulder-high an' him steppin' in place in time like it so good he can't stan' still an' the band kickin' twelve-bar ass behind him, an' we could see an' hear all that on a sunny day when bored with basketball, an' Little Prez doin' his thing. Was a little nigger, Little Prez, with a head too big for his scrawny body, lookin' skinny even under all those clothes his momma made him wear to keep him from catchin' cold but didn' work too well he was always sniffin', even in the summertime. Little Prez couldn' do nothin' but rap, was the Rap Master of the 'hood. Couldn' fight like Tampy, play basketball like Raby, football like Fuzz, run like C. B., hit a softball like Junior. Couldn' sing, dance, drink, fuck, steal, play games, hunt rats. Wasn' dumb or smart in school, didn' have a fine momma with a sharp boyfrien' with a big Cadillac or Lincoln. Couldn' do shit but rap, lie an' signify. Could play the dozens for days, talk about your momma bad enough to make you cry, run off 42 verses without repeatin' hisself. Sing-say the "Signifyin' Monkey" like nobody else. Couldn' do nothin' else 'cep rap an' he could rap like the real Prez blew, an' when Little Prez got big everybody knew he was gonna blow tenor too an' he would walk down to the pawnshop near Cottage Grove an' dig the horns in the barred window, mostly old beatup Martins and Selmers, but sometimes one or two lookin' bran' new, lef' by some strungout junky musician. Cheated on his lunch money, delivered the Tribune in the mornin's, sold the Defender an' the Courier on Fridays, hauled groceries from Kroger's in his wagon, an' finally he had the bread an' got his Selmer, walked out with it in the case on down Sixty-third in a crablike shuffle jus' like Prez, an' everybody said if Little Prez could blow like he talked he'd be a bitch. He dug every tenor goin', dug Jug offin' everybody every Saturday afternoon at Al Benson's Battle of the Bands at the Pershing. Dug E. Parker McDougal an' Johnny Griffin still blowin' with the DuSable High School band before Hamp came through. Dug Dexter an' heard the cats in the playgroun' tryin' to put down Prez to the tune o' "Dexter's Deck": "My name's Dexter, outblow Lester anyday . . ." and he laughed. Dug Jug an' Stitt, Wardell, Lockjaw an' Gator Tail, Quinichette, the vice pres, Ike Quebec, Ben Webster. Dug 'em at the Parkway, Savoy, Pershing, White City an' the Regal. In the Propeller Lounge, Blue Note, Bee Hive an' the Sutherland. Saw 'em come and disappear, saw 'em early an' saw 'em late, saw 'em try to imitate the President, an' Little Prez tried to deal with somethin' we didn't know: that Little Prez couldn' blow. All them sounds and notes and things runnin' roun' in his head and he couldn' bring 'em out through his horn. Wore a black porkpie like Prez, sometimes tossed his head in that faggot put-on like Prez, drank good Gordon's gin, wore eight-sided dark green tea glasses, big bold-look ties, pin-stripe double-breasted box-back suits like Prez. Lived, ate, slept Prez but couldn' blow like Prez. Practiced six, eight, 10 hours a day, treated his horn better than his momma, shaved his reeds, soaked his reeds, changed his mouthpiece, oiled his keys, polished the brass, an' Prez blew his nose better than Little Prez blew his horn. Couldn' deal with it, wouldn' deal with it, didn' want to deal with it 'cause he knew it was a lie 'cause his momma tol' him, his preacher tol' him, teacher tol' him, everybody tol' him hard work and sacrifice would suffice. Didn' know, couldn' know the only people really believed in the Protestant Ethic was Black folks, didn' know even though he'd grown up in a Black Baptist church what a Protestant Ethic was, jus' believed if you wanted somethin' bad enough and worked long enough and hard enough you had to get it, couldn' quit it, had to get it. If you worked hard enough you had to get it and didn', couldn' dig that the people worked hardest had the least. . . . An' all the time Little Prez blowin' an' not knowin' he doin' the right thing for the wrong reasons. Blowin' with visions of Cadillacs dancin' in his head, long an' lavender an' full o' chicks with hydramatic hips, a closet full of clothes an' enough shoes to change everyday for a month an' not wear the same pair twice. Didn' know, wouldn' know, couldn' know music ain' got nothin' to do with them kinda things. Didn' even stop to think Prez didn' have them kinda things, sittin' in a cheap hotel on Broadway lookin' at Birdland through gin-glazed eyes, diggin' all his imitators and emulators draggin' down all the bread for blowin' the shit he'd discarded 20 years before, an' all of 'em white boys.

So Little Prez blew ugly 'cause his head was ugly and he never knew the reason why. Tried everything twice and then once more 'til one day he discovered Smack. Started out sniffin' and found everything turned soft and warm, the hard edges roundin' off an' the sounds, smells and taste becomin' somethin' else, an' when he blew he sounded jus' like Prez—to hisself. Started out sniffin', then skinpoppin' an' had to put away his horn to go out in the streets to support his habit. Started snatchin' pocketbooks 'til a welfare mother with her check jus' cashed and five hungry kids to feed kicked his ass an' almos' held him 'til the pigs got there. Ran some whores on Sixty-third and Cottage 'til the shit turned him too greedy and impotent and one day he had to make a choice between a fix an' a payoff and the pig he tried to stall busted him and he spent his first time in the slam and dug he could get all the shit he needed long as he had some bread, and between his momma and hustlin' his ass inside to guards and/or cons he was cool and wasn' even in a hurry to get out, but by the time he got out he'd had a full course in Breaking and Entering, an' now he was a full-time junkie and part-time thief. But the dream never deferred 'cause nex' week he was gon' renew his union card, get a band together, cut a record and blow everybody's mind. Spent time twice in the slam an' went to Lexington three times, not to kick his habit but reduce it when it got too expensive to support. An' you could see him on a corner on Six-trey noddin' his junkie nod and blowin' tenor sounds inside his head loud enough to drown out the racket of the El on its way between Cottage Grove and King Drive, which usta be South Park in his before-junkie days.

III

Little Prez sat up straight out of his nod like he was havin' a bad dream he couldn't remember. The box was still playin' the last record over and over. It was almos' dark outside, the sun comin' pale an' weak down the airshaft and crawlin' into his funky room on weak wino knees. He got up quick an' turned on the lights; big, bright, naked bulb 'cause he was afraid of the dark. A drag for a rip-off junkie, afraid of the dark 'cause the dark is when he had to work, slippin' down alleys in the dark into dark houses an' workin' with not much light, checkin' out whatever would bring the most bread with the least work: portable TV sets, watches an' jewelry and men's suits, if they wasn' too big or too small, but money the bes' 'cause you didn' get ripped off five-to-one by a fence or worse than that if you had to hustle somethin' quick on the streets. Move through the dark pad hopin' you was right they was no dog in it an' no silent burglar alarm, but even so knew no pigs would be in no hurry to answer an alarm from a nigger's home. Check out the bedroom first an' dump all the stuff from the drawers on the floor an' mos' times they was cash in there somewhere 'cause even credit-card niggers didn' really trust banks and usually had a stash somewhere in the pad. It was a drag havin' to work in the dark with the shadows long an' always lookin' like they movin' an' furniture sittin' there lookin' like people, so he always had to turn on before he went inside to keep from climbin' the walls. He got his shit together, his burglar tools in a attaché case—he thought that was cool puttin' rip-off tools in a attaché case of good pigskin he'd ripped off from a pad in Pill Hill but he usually worked Woodlawn where he grew up 'cause the pigs didn' give a damn and the folks lived there couldn' afford to buy and train them big man-eatin' dogs them saditty niggers had roun' the house an' he laughed like hell everytime he read 'bout one of them big motherfuckers turnin' on his owner. He was waitin' for the sterilizer to turn on the red light an' reached in his pocket and pulled out the envelope he forgot he had and opened it up and they was ten packets looked like Horse an' he opened one, wet his finger, dipped it in and tasted an' it was smack, tasted like good shit an' he almos' sat down and cried. Thought 'bout stayin' home an' turnin' on but he'd cased the job for a month an' he decided to do it and took one lid of the new stuff to turn on with before he went inside the pad he had staked out.

IV

He stood listening, in the dark alley not far from Six-trey. Good place for a rip-off an' he'd pulled four capers there in a year, only one dog, old and half-blind down at the other end o' the block and barked at everything including the El, so nobody paid him any mind. Had lived a whole history in Woodlawn alleys: ripped-off his first sweet potato from a store on Six-trey and cooked it over a fire in the alley; shot his first basketball and missed; smoked his first cigarette, his first joint, felt his first tit, drank his first wine, had his first fight, an' lost, had his first fuck leanin' against a garage, sniffed his first Horse and pulled his first B & E caper in alleys near Six-trey. Couldn' keep away, an' his momma still lived on Eberhart an' kep' a $20 bill in a sugar bowl so he wouldn' rip off her TV when he was uptight for a fix. Little Prez moved deeper into the shadows, made-up an' hit himself. Took loose the rubber tubing an' waited for the flash an' the white folks' almos' pure Horse galloped through his thin junkie veins an' smacked his ass for the las' time, the Horse too pure, too white for the Black junkie's heart an' they foun' him the nex' day, OD'd away. No more Prez for Little Prez, his horn in its case in the closet. No more dreams of standing in the spotlight in eight-sided dark green tea glasses, his horn held high nex' to his right shoulder. No more rip-offs an' no more monkeys to feed an' somewhere on the South Side a little Black kid saved his pennies to buy a horn so he could blow just like Trane. . . .

A Plundered World

Hoyt Fuller
(1975)

Carl packed the toilet kit in the two-suiter and looked about the room to see if he had forgotten anything. Except for an ashtray with several cigarette butts in it on the top of the dresser, the room was as he had found it when he arrived two days before. It was his old room, the one he had occupied as a child, and the one he always used on visits to his grandmother. His aunt had put fresh white oblong doilies on the dresser and table, a clean blue spread on the huge old mahogany bed, and crisp, filigreed curtains at the window. The throw-rug on the varnished floor, made by his grandmother from old stockings years ago, had been put through the washing machine. The two straw-bottomed chairs looked faded and forlorn, but he knew they also had been washed. He closed the expensive cowhide valise and locked it, put it on the floor, and sat on the bed beside his hat and topcoat.

The door opened and an elderly woman stuck her head inside. She wore a bandana that was wound about her head like a turban. "You 'bout ready?" she said. "Time aint long as it has been."

"Yes, I'm all set, Mrs. Henderson," he said.

Mrs. Henderson was housekeeper and practical nurse for his grandmother. Although old and toothless, she was still agile and strong, and the work was not difficult for her. She had only to make her ward as comfortable as was possible now, and keep the house tidy. Aunt Lou did the more thorough cleaning on the weekend.

"Mister Carl, let me tell you, you the spitting image of your uncle Barnes," she said, closing her filmy eyes and smacking her lips. "Prettiest colored man I ever did see. You just like him, too."

He chuckled, unembarrassed. He knew he did not look like his uncle who, in any case, was not "pretty." His uncle had the light skin and the sharp, near-Nordic features of Carl's grandfather. Carl, on the other hand, had inherited his own father's bold features. And while he liked to think he was not unattractive, he knew very well that his face had the loose, slightly swollen and battered look of the prizefighter. "She's buttering me up," he thought. And, to discourage her, he said nothing. He got out his cigarettes, put one between his lips and lighted it.

"I hope you'll have just a minute to chat with me 'fore you go," she said more soberly, correctly interpreting his silence.

"Sure, Mrs. Henderson, I'll have time."

"Well, alright then, I'll leave you be." She withdrew her head and closed the door.

He let his eyes roam over the room again, wondering vaguely what Mrs. Henderson wanted to say to him. Then he forgot her, concentrating instead on the age-browned oval portrait of a young couple on the opposite wall. The man was stiffly handsome, his quadroon face chiseled. The woman was comely, dark and shy, and wore an improbably grotesque, high-crowned hat. It was a portrait of his grandparents taken after their wedding in the eighteen-eighties. "I never knew those people," he smiled wryly to himself.

Carl tried to remember how his grandparents had looked when his mother first brought him to live with them when he was five years old. He found that he remembered his grandmother with ease but that little else of that time was very clear in his mind. It had been a time of upheaval, confusion and sadness. He remembered his father's funeral only mistily, the gray casket in which he had lain so still, his black face ashened as though powdered, and the huge, box-like black hearse that took him away. His mother wept continuously, it had seemed, even when they moved out of the tall dark building where they had lived and took a train (it had been his first train ride), ending up in the unfamiliar place with the strange people who he learned were his grandparents.

He did remember vividly, however, his mother, still weeping, hurrying to the taxi waiting in front of the house, the driver carrying her bags and loading them on the back seat. She had squeezed and kissed him and told him to be good, and he understood she was going away without him. He became hysterical. His grandfather held him while he kicked and fought and screamed, until the car was out of sight and his mother was gone. In all the years afterwards he had not been fond of his grandfather, and now he wondered if that was perhaps the reason.

His image of his grandfather was of a wizened droopily mustached little man the color of sea-washed sand, with long, tangled gray-black hair that always needed cutting. But that was how his grandfather had looked when he died thirteen years earlier, and he may not have looked that way thirteen years before that.

It was different with his grandmother. He would never forget anything about her. At the time of his first crisis, when he was uprooted and, he thought then, abandoned, she had been there to lessen his loneliness and desperation. She had replenished his plundered world with love. In those days she was a stately woman, sturdy and ample, with a round, sorghum-brown face. Her arms were large and strong and her bosom like a soft warm mountain. She was the most impressive person he had ever known, and there had been nothing in her rotund face and great bulk to link her with the svelte young woman in the photograph.

Time, inexorable and impersonal, had worked still another transformation, and the jolly woman of his childhood bore no resemblance to the gray, arthritic and age-wasted creature now lying asleep under the benevolence of drugs in the next room. The thought drew his face to the drab blue wall. He frowned unconsciously, expelling smoke from his lungs. In a little while he would hold her fleshless hand and speak with her (what could he say?) for the last time on this earth. He felt helpless and useless and, for the first time in his thirty-one years, knew the terrible simplicity of the inevitable.

Carl dislodged the somber reflection with a twist of his head. There would be plenty of time for philosophical musing on the plan. Now he felt he should be talking with Aunt Lou, deciding what was to be done. Surely, however delicate, such talk was appropriate. He got up, squashed the cigarette in the ashtray, and went out in the hallway. The floorboards grumbled under his weight. The corridor was narrow and dingy and smelled of closeness and the odor of freshly brewed coffee. "I guess Mrs. Henderson is having her umpteenth cup," he thought.

At the front of the house he peered into the living room, looking for Aunt Lou. She was not there. He lingered a moment in the doorway. This had once been his favorite of all rooms. He had no memory of the living room in his father's house, but he had many memories of this one. Had it changed much? The piano was still there, black and shiny, with the large tinted family portraits on top, though possibly not in the same place. Even then Aunt Lou was always changing the furniture around, lifting and shoving the divan and two armchairs while he rolled the carpet. Only the big upright Philco, with its stuck panel doors, had remained in the same spot because of all the wires behind it that ran through the window and down the side of the house. The Philco was gone now, and a television set and console record player were added, and probably the divan and chairs and the carpet were new. There was an artificial gas log fire installed in the fireplace where once real wood and coal had burned. He had sprawled in front of it evenings, listening to Little Orphan Annie and Dick Tracy on the radio or playing sultan to his grandmother's Scheherazade as she whisked him away to an exotic pastoral past where coiled rattlers lurked on the smokehouse floor and wily weasels terrorized the barnyard.

Smiling absently, he pushed open the screen door and walked onto the front porch. It was a sunny Georgia autumn afternoon, drowsily warm and crystal despite the gossamer shroud of dust over everything. The narrow, ell-shaped house across the unpaved street, originally white, was rouged with powdered earth. His grandmother's house, also white, was less stained as it stood yards from the street and was shielded from the pervading dust by the two giant oaks in the front lawn.

The dust never failed to depress him. An old bitterness revived and flowed through him everytime he turned off the main street of the town onto the street where his grandmother lived. (He thought: "We have to spend so much of our energy in helpless anger.") For the first two blocks the street was wide and clean, lined with trees and big frame and brick houses. The pavement continued in the next block, but minus the cleanliness and order. The eroded sidewalks grew tangled weeds and bushes, and shabby shanties occupied by outcast whites sat back from the street, half-hidden behind wild chinaberry bushes and poplar trees. This was the buffer zone between the white people who mattered and the Blacks.

Abruptly the pavement ended and the street was red clay, hard and dusty or soft and slushy, depending on the weather. The street improved slightly in his grandmother's block, where the handsomest homes of Blacks were located. Periodically, to pacify these taxpayers, the city spread over the street a layer of gravel. It promptly vanished in the mire when it rained. Only the next street was paved. It was the through-way to the all-white municipal golf course.

A blue sedan rolled slowly up the street and stopped in front of the house, dust billowing behind it. It was Aunt Lou's car. She climbed out and slammed the door and came toward him over the walkway from the cindered sidewalk. She was short and plump, as his grandmother had been at that age, with the same round face and skin the color of the browning leaves. "Hello," she greeted him in her low, tired voice. The voice now saddened him, for he recalled when it had been light and lilting. "Is Mama awake yet?" she asked, forcing a smile as tired and strained as her voice.

"No." He shook his head. He wished she would be gay. "Where'd you sneak off to?"

"To buy food. It's Saturday, you know." The words were a rebuff. "I was coming to ask you to bring the groceries in the house. It's not everyday there's a man around to do that. I might as well take advantage of it."

"Glad to oblige," he said.

He went out to the car and got the huge bags of groceries from the rear seat. When he came back up the walkway she had mounted the three steps to the terraced rock garden and was stooping over the oval-shaped fishpond, raking leaves to one corner with a stick. He put the groceries in one of the straw-bottomed rocking chairs on the porch and leaped over the cement balustrade and joined her in the garden. She twisted her thick neck to look up at him. "The water should be changed," she said, "but I'll wait until the leaves stop falling."

Carl watched her lifting the wet leaves from the pond with her pudgy fingers, her movements slow and awkward. His eyes strayed to her head. The thick hair was oiled and straightened, with feathers of gray in the black mass. He did not know what to say to her. Words had never flowed easily between them. Now, when it seemed really important, it was no easier than it had ever been. When he was a child she had been too busy to bother much with him. She was dedicated to her music, studying, planning and saving. One day she would throw up teaching school and sail to Italy to learn from the great vocal masters. She was too busy even for the men who had courted her—the young minister at the church, the male teachers at her school. When they came calling, she spent much of the time at the piano singing exuberantly, but more for her own pleasure than for theirs. They had not come to hear her sing.

Aunt Lou had once given him piano lessons. But she soon tired of it and sent him instead to another teacher in the next block. He had not liked the woman, and his musical education had ended quickly. He did not care. Music had seemed exciting only when he saw Aunt Lou at the piano, flashing her fingers over the keys and rousing the neighborhood with her arias.

Later, when he was again with his mother and his new stepfather in Detroit, a recital was arranged for Aunt Lou at the Art Institute. She arrived in a plethora of excitement, and her radiance astonished him. She seemed for the first time to be beautiful. Her picture was in the papers and on posters announcing, "Louise Brady, lyric soprano." He was proud. His own Aunt Lou. But all went wrong. The audience was less than entranced and the critics in the newspapers were cruel. She had planned to stay in the city a week but instead went home the next day. And she never again appeared in a public recital.

He knew that disenchantment weighed heavy in her. Not merely because of the shadow now haunting her life. Death, the ultimate surrender, did not rank with the graver failures of spinsterhood and talent. It was rather that the intervals between great disillusions had been so rarely filled with joy. He wanted to say something cheerful. Or comforting, at least, but he could think of nothing that would not sound of pity. And pity would alarm and offend her, and the chasm between them would spread wider still.

"Do you remember how we used to empty the pond?", he asked.

She looked up at him again, cocking her head. "We? Who?"

"You and I."

She laughed softly, with surprise, not mirth, and dropped her head, shaking it. "No, I don't remember at all."

"Well, you showed me how," he said, kneeling beside her. "There was a piece of hose about six or seven feet long. I'd put one end in the bottom of the pond and suck through the other end. The water would start flowing up and out on the ground. I got a mouthful of dirty water every time."

She shook her head again. "No, I don't remember that. It was awfully unsanitary. It might have made you sick."

"It takes more than a little dirty water to make little boys sick."

"I suppose so."

"I often think of some of the things I used to do back in those days. Things that would just about kill me now, I guess."

She stopped raking the leaves and stood up. She regarded him with an odd coldness, straightening the folds of her navy blue skirt. Despite her apparent lack of interest, he went on talking, standing up beside her, looking down into her solemn face.

"I used to sneak off in the woods and go swimming with Sandy in the creek," he said. "You remember Sandy, my dog, I'm sure. Well, there were water moccasins around there, and minnows and tadpoles, the dog, and God alone knows what else. I guess I would swallow a gallon of that dirty water a day. The only bad after-effects, though, was the spanking I got when I got home. You probably don't remember. Mama could tell I'd been in the water. She always knew. I didn't understand until years later that she could tell because of the sand in my hair and the sandy ash on my face."

"Yes, it's easy to tell that way," she said and moved along the cobblestone path toward the house.

He remained still, watching her go, imagining her old and withered, a shawl about her shoulders, shambling among the jonquils and the dahlias and the tall sunflowers. He decided not to pursue her. Perhaps it was better to leave things as they were. She would make the necessary arrangements. Perhaps his efforts at intimacy only discomforted her.

Mrs. Henderson emerged onto the porch and crossed to the balustrade, motioning to him. "Is she awake?" he called out, a knot of anxiety leaping up in his throat.

"Naw, she still sleeping, Mister Carl," Mrs. Henderson said. "But I think you better come in here and have a bite to eat. You ought to have something in your stomach before you go away from here."

"I'm not hungry, Mrs. Henderson," he protested. "And I'll get a meal on the plane."

"Makes no diff'erence," she persisted. "You come on in here and I'll make you some ham and eggs. You'll need it."

He knew it was useless to argue. She was determined to "chat" with him. At the steps to the porch he passed Aunt Lou and took the bag of groceries that Mrs. Henderson was trying to lift. "You're a little young for such a big load," he teased her. Mrs. Henderson held the door open. "I aint young as I used to be, and that's for sure," she said. He entered the house behind Aunt Lou.

In the kitchen, Carl sat at the table while Aunt Lou put the groceries away and Mrs. Henderson fussed at the gas range. "You feel like eating a mouthful, too?" she asked Aunt Lou for the sake of courtesy.

"No, thank you," Aunt Lou replied remotely, moving ponderously about the room. When she had finished storing the groceries, she left without a word.

The kitchen was high-ceilinged, like the rest of the house, pine-paneled, and painted white. In recent years Aunt Lou had installed such modern conveniences as a deep freeze, walls of cabinets, and all manner of electrical mixers, squeezers and toasters. Mrs. Henderson did not know how to use many of the appliances and would not try to. "The old-fashioned way will do me till I die," she would say.

Now, frying the eggs, she repeated what she had already said to Carl at least a half dozen times in the past two days. "Your grandma's so happy to see you, Mister Carl. It's done her old heart really good."

"Well, I'm glad," he said warily. He wished she wouldn't call him "mister," but she had ignored his suggestion that she call him Carl as she had always done. He supposed that she preferred to defer to his status as a "Northern professional man," which was her loose definition of his accountant job. "It's good to see her again too," he added.

"She always talks 'bout you," Mrs. Henderson declared. "A few weeks 'fore you come, she was telling me 'bout the time she made you go to the woods in the dark and bring that old dog back. Weak as she was, she bust out laughing. She said you was the scaredest little boy in Georgia that night. You remember that, Mister Carl?"

"Yes," he nodded, smiling. Yes, he remembered. It was one of his grandmother's favorite stories about him. It had been one of the few times she had severely punished him. He turned back through the clutter of his memory to that time. It stood out clearly among the years like a snapshot still black and white in an album of prints already faint and yellowed with age.

He had been seven or eight years old, for he could read the posted notices that all dogs not innoculated and tagged by a certain date would be taken by the dogcatcher. To punish him for some disobedience he could now no longer recall, his grandmother told him she would refuse to have Sandy innoculated, and none of his frantic entreaties could sway her. To his tearful vows to never disobey again, she remained obdurate. "You're not a good boy and you don't deserve a dog," was all she would say. On the eve of the deadline he conceived a desperate plan. In the woods where he and the dog went exploring was a tarpaper and pasteboard shack occupied by an eccentric but kindly man. The dog catcher would never go there. He took the big, cinnamon-colored German Shepherd to the shack and asked the old man if he could leave the dog there, promising to bring food everyday. The old man agreed. He tied the dog to a tree beside the shack and went home. His joy in saving the dog's life far outweighed his grief in having to leave him in so lonely a place.

After supper, when it was time to feed Sandy, Carl's grandmother became concerned at the animal's failure to appear. As dusk settled she went into the street, calling the dog's name. When he didn't come she decided he had been captured and prepared to go to the city pound to fetch him. At that point, with his conscience twisting him into an emotional rope, Carl confessed.

His grandmother was furious, more for being outwitted than anything else. After threatening to give him "the thrashing of your life," which is what he would have preferred, she hit upon a cleverer punishment. She sent him alone into the darkening woods to bring the dog home.

Carl started out bravely, for the walk to the edge of the woods held no terrors. But suddenly, confronted with the black and forbidding wall of trees and brush, his courage faltered. But he plunged in, futilely trying to shut out of his ears the eerie chirping of cicadas and crickets and the weird trumpeting of tree frogs. His ripe imagination littered the dark path with vicious, crawling reptiles and posted fierce, snarling leopards behind every bush. The woods that in the daytime beckoned with countless intriguing surprises now loomed and crackled like a leafy purgatory. He had not dreamed his grandmother capable of such cruelty.

The shack stretched an eternity away. When finally he approached it, he was running breathlessly along the path. He called out, tears burning his eyes, "Sandy, Sandy." The dog barked in the echoing night, straining at the rope. They collided with such force that he fell to the ground. The dog was all over him, crazy with eagerness. The paws scratched his arms; the hot tongue blinded him, lapping in his face. But he was far happier to see Sandy there in that forsaken place than the dog could possibly have been in seeing him.

"I guess that learned you alright," Mrs. Henderson said, grinning, nodding her bandanaed head. "I guess you behaved yourself after that."

His reminiscent smile widened. "That was the only time in my life I ever hated her," he said. "Especially when I found out she had already had the dog innoculated. I really hated her. If I hadn't just had a terrible time in the woods, I think I would've run away."

Mrs. Henderson cackled. "No, I dare say you never could hate your grandma, Mister Carl, Not you. Not for nothing. She always pinned her hopes on you. After Mister Wesley died, and there was no man around this house, she used to say you was coming back here when you finished your education. 'Carl will come and look after his old grandma's place,' she used to say. 'My little Carl is coming back.' That's what she used to say all the time."

He stared at the old woman with something close to revulsion, as though really seeing for the first time how unlovely she was. She was ocher-colored, with the sharp features and long face of her Anglo-Saxon forebears, and her skin was ash-dry and withered. She was tall, thin, and bent, and her long blue frock touched the tips of her shoes. She wore a faded oxford-gray sweater and a clean white apron that looped over her neck and waist. "She's like some old voodoo witch," Carl thought.

She brought a plate of fried ham and eggs and put it in front of him. Then, moving about with unexpected sprightliness, she provided him with silverware and two slices of toast. "Go ahead and eat," she commanded. "The coffee'll be ready in a minute."

He hadn't told her he wanted coffee, and would've preferred milk, but he said nothing. When she placed a cup and saucer beside his place and put another cup and saucer opposite him, he understood why he was going to have coffee. "This looks good," he said appreciatively, and started to eat.

When the coffee was ready. Mrs. Henderson filled the two cups and sat across from him. She put three heaping teaspoons of sugar in her cup and stirred it slowly. "A big, strapping, fine-looking man like you ought to eat," she said. "You can't depend on that little sandwich they give you in the airplane."

"They don't give you a sandwich," he said. "You get a complete meal."

"Well, I don't see how they can give nobody no food in that little old airplane up in the air." She raised a bony hand in a nebulous gesture, dismissing the subject. She shifted her body in the chair and sipped the coffee, pursing her loose thin lips into a funnel like the tip of an elephant's trunk. She swallowed the coffee, wiped her mouth with the back of her hand and pointed herself at him. "Mister Carl, maybe I oughtn't talk so much, 'cause it aint none of my business. But I been knowing all your family since Heav'n knows when, and I'm just going to speak my mind.

"That poor old soul laying in yonder, she don't like having to go on to her reward and leaving this house and her land here with no man to look after it. That's what's worrying her weary old mind more'n anything. Other'n that, she could just go in peace with nary a sorrow. She's lived a good life, Josie Brady has. A good life. Never harmed a soul. Why, I recollects way back 'fore your own Ma come into the world, long 'fore Miss Louise was thought of, Miss Josie worked all day in the white folks' house, cleaning and scrubbing, and all through the night, sometimes till daybreak the next day, working by lamplight, she was washing and i'ning clothes for the white folks. That's the way she got the money to send your ma and Miss Louise and your two uncles to school. Mister Wesley, he worked true, and he worked hard at the terra cotta factory till he was too old for that sort of work. But it was that poor old soul who was at it night and day, cooking and cleaning and washing and i'ning till her back was fit to break. And all the young'uns 'cept Miss Louise, they all went on up North after she done worked and slaved to give 'em a education. That's what they did. All 'cept Miss Louise, and she stayed."

Mrs. Henderson paused long enough to refuel her lungs then went on. "But, now, I might as well just say it, Mister Carl. I might as well speak my mind now 'cause it'll be too late after you gone. Miss Louise stayed on good and loyal to mind her ma, but she ain't got no man, and she aint no man herself, and so that don't help the matter none at all. That don't put that old soul's mind not a bit more at ease. It hurt her so to think this house and this land is going to be sold or somebody she don't know nothing 'bout will have it after she gone. It hurt her to her soul. And it just don't seem right she got to go away from here with no satisfaction in her mind."

The food stuck in his throat. He washed it down with the strong, hot, bitter coffee. He stared hard at the old woman unsubtly accusing him of betrayal. But, realizing that his irritation showed in his face, he glanced away from her toward the window. The pecan, wild cherry and peach trees were in rows on the lots behind the house. Weeds grew rampant on the uncultivated ground that had always been planted with vegetables when his grandfather lived. He turned back to his plate, but the sight of the food repelled him. He wouldn't be able to eat it now. He was irritated with himself for allowing the busybody crone to scuttle his equanimity. Carl drank the coffee and excused himself over Mrs. Henderson's objections. He left the kitchen by the rear door and went down the steps into the back yard. Crab grass and weeds grew everywhere, around the garage, between the rocks of the paths leading to the wire-enclosed chicken yard and to the peach orchard. He noticed several fat, listless hens waddling behind the wire. He recalled with a pang the flocks of white leghorns and Rhode Island Reds his grandfather had kept. He turned from that side of the house, as if fleeing the memory, and walked back in front of the garage toward the street.

At the edge of the driveway he stopped and faced the house. It was wide and flat, with a red roof that slanted at a low angle. A basement had been dug long after the house was built and the brick wall at the base was newer than the pillars. The hedges that hemmed the property were high and in need of trimming, as were the oak trees and the conglomeration of cedars and shrubs that obscured the porch. He recalled Aunt Lou, in a long ago fervor of landscaping, planting the cedars and later hanging them with lights at Christmas. The fenced-in vacant lots on both sides of the house and the rock garden, now clay-sterile and ragged with weeds and tough grass, belonged to his grandmother too. She had had the strength to gain it. Did her progeny have the strength to keep it?

Carl experienced a spasm of regret. He dug his hands in his pockets and gazed at the ground. In the distance children laughed, their voices mingling with the cackling of hens and the roar of motors on the busy street a block away. All the sounds seemed to converge and riot in him, catalyzing his private turmoil. Regret, kindled by a haunting, inadmissible guilt, burned into shackled rage.

He raised his face from the ground and swore, "Dammit, dammit!", and hustled up the sidewalk, angling in the walkway to the front steps. He sat on the concrete balustrade and nursed his simmering frustration. He could never live here. His grandmother knew he could never live here now. It had been different as a child. But even at ten, his mother had decided it was time for him to leave ("Why, the child can't even use the public library," she explained to his grandmother.) He had promised he would be back, but he did not know what a difference time would make. How could he have known? None who had left could return. Didn't she know that? Did she think his mother and his uncles merely callous and contrary? Didn't she know that they had made a step forward, a step nearer the goal she had herself set for them? Wouldn't it be betraying her not to seek a fuller freedom? (No, they were not free! Not truly free! But they were freer than they could be here.) And, after all, what could he do in that sullen, cheerless place choked by disdain and red dust? Nothing had changed. He still couldn't use the public library.

The screen door opened and Aunt Lou stepped into the porch behind him. He turned, greeting her appearance with anxious relief. He saw that her eyes were red as if from weeping and that a tight line angled down from the corners of her mouth.

"She's awake now," she said, averting her eyes. "She's still under the drugs but Mrs. Henderson will keep her from falling asleep for a few minutes. You'd better go now. I'll wait in the car to drive you to the airport. You can bring your suitcase out when you're ready."

Her voice seemed soft, tender, and he thought: "She's talking to me as though I am a child."

He stood up and went toward her, looking squarely into her face, searching it for a sign. For a moment their eyes met, and in that moment he raised his arms to grasp her shoulders and to pull her to him. But she moved quickly, clumsily, beyond his reach. He remained frozen in the half-completed gesture, looking foolish, and feeling it. After a moment he dropped his arms and shrugged in defeat. Then he opened the screen door.

"There's just this one thing!", she said suddenly, her voice strangled with emotion. Her eyes were riveted on the balustrade, her fists were clenched. "You can't *love* her into Heaven now. You weren't here when she needed you. There was no man here. It's too late to love her now, it's too late . . ."

She raised her face to confront him then, fury flaming in her watering eyes. But it was an impersonal fury, or an all-encompassing fury, flaring through him at some greater target. "Mama's going to die. Do you understand what that means? Nothing can keep her from dying, and you can't get any last minute stars in your crown by making her think you love her so much. . . . You come here now, with her on her deathbed, and you think you're going to get automatic redemption for all the years you didn't even come here to see her. I heard Mrs. Henderson. Yes, I heard her. But let me tell you. And you can tell your mother and all the others. You can tell them. I wasted my life here. While they were out in the world doing what they wanted to do, I was here. I gave up everything to stay here. I could have gone away too. I could have been a great singer. I could have married. Yes, I could have married many times. But I stayed here. I was here when Papa died, and I'll be here when Mama dies. None of the others will. You won't. You'll all come running back to the funeral, mourning and crying and pretending you cared so much. Well, it's no good. It won't make any difference. It's all over now."

Carl stared at her, appalled. He would not have been more shocked had she suddenly stripped naked before him. At first he did not comprehend. He could not believe. But then, watching as she fumbled in her jacket pocket for her handkerchief and stumbled toward the stairs in movements redolent of a weariness complete and profound, he understood at last the abyss between them. He knew now how her emptiness had been filled. She hurried down the stairs and out to the street, climbing in the car and slamming the door. She collapsed over the steering wheel, her body shaking as she wept.

Carl went inside the house and walked down the dim, musky hallway to his grandmother's room. He paused a moment with his hand on the doorknob. This was the moment he had dreaded. But now, somehow, inexplicably, it would be less difficult to face.

The Face

Pat Washington
(1975)

If I'm not careful, sometimes I see this hurt looking female thing staring at me out of mirrors and windows, not saying a word. Not a, "Hey, what's happening," or "How you doing?", nothing. She just looks at me with big brown eyes stranded in an ocean of pink, not blinking, just following me around with those big brown eyes.

No matter where I go, there she is looking hurt. Last week for instance, Wednesday afternoon, I ran into one of my men on the street. I put a quick smile on my face so my lies would look as real as they sounded, then I started rapping my usual shit about, "Where you been, man?", and "I've been trying to get in touch with you, when are we going to get together again?" Right in the middle of my rap I happened to look up and that female was looking dead in my mouth, shaking her head kind of slow like from side to side. My jaw dropped for a minute and before I could finish rapping to my dude he started saying, "I been staying close to the crib hoping you'd call me, because whenever I call you nobody's there."

While he was easing these words out of his mouth, that heifer had the nerve to try to look hurt. I moved my head to the side a little, looked her dead in the eyes, dropped my smile and said in a low voice, letting her know my jaws were tight, "I'm tired of this shit, I'm going to talk to you when I get home." Turning towards my dude, I straightened my smile that had cracked slightly, but it was good enough for him to answer it with one of his own. Damned if that man didn't grin like Billy Dee Williams when I told him to come over later on that evening. I wanted to talk to him in private because I didn't believe in putting my business in the street.

Besides, my other man was coming around the corner and I would have had to lie my way to China and back to explain why I was rapping to his cousin in the middle of the street. I just smiled and waved to both of those dudes as I eased my way towards the corner. As soon as I hit the corner, I was moving like a dog with a sore tail.

That heifer had really started butting into my business and I had to get her straight, quick, because the next thing you know she'd be talking instead of looking. I had worked too hard on those chumps, getting my game together, and I had no intention of standing still while that dumb fool messed it up. Yeah, I had a few choice words for her ears.

Just thinking about what I was going to tell her made me run up

159

the three flights to my apartment faster. I had to sit down a few minutes when I reached the top of the stairs before I could start to unlock my door. I was breathing and sweating just that hard. Couldn't sit too long because I knew she was waiting for me. Fumbling in my bag I found everything, matches, cab numbers, fingernail file, lipstick, eyebrow pencil, wallet— every damn thing (even my address book) but those door keys. When I reached in my pocket for a Kleenex to wipe the sweat off my forehead I felt the keys. I was really hot by now; sweat was pouring down my face, my hands slipping as I turned the key and unlocked the door.

I slammed it shut with my foot and stomped to the bathroom so she could hear how mad I was. Hollering with each step, "I'm tired of this shit, you just stay out of my business and get your ass out of my face, can't do anything without you and those buggy looking eyes staring at me."

"Do you hear me? I am taking care of my business and I want you to leave my business alone. There is nothing wrong with a little jiving, that is all those men understand. You try to be nice to them and they just walk all over you. The nigger ain't been born yet that could keep up with me, let alone walk on me!" I was at the bathroom door, my fingers were shaking just like a drunk's when I jerked the bathroom door open. I was at the mirror in two steps to shake my finger in her face. Sniffing and wiping sweat, snot-angry all at the same time. The mirror showed a small brown-skinned woman, sobbing.

The Saga of Sadfly
(An Adult Fairy Tale)

Nora Brooks Blakely
(1970's)

Once upon a time there was a dude named Sadfly. He was a *bad* dude, an awful dude, I mean he was *terrible!* And he wore some bad clothes. He had a maxilength coat with a big bright pink and white diamond pattern, with a superpink turtleneck sweater and white wool knit straight leg pants. He had an *awful* hat with a 20-inch brim! He had some *terrible* shoes with 2-foot heels. His hair curved like slick seaweed about his face.

Well, he was havin' a pretty nice time. Life was good to him and he was good to life—especially female life. Females—Sadfly had plenty. Women hung around him like fat on bacon. Well, one day he met his match. One day Ainteyephyn Goodbody came on the scene. She had on a *bad* outfit, with some *awful* shoes and a *terrible* hat. All were trimmed in chartreuse-dyed mink. Sadfly looked and he gasped! He dug her! He was sure of it! From her fuchsia and chartreuse stockings to her pink, yellow, red, green, white and blue natural. Well, Phyn saw Sadfly, she looked him up and down, then she got a big smile on her face. Phyn started toward him, she got closer, got closer, closer, she was next to him. . . . she was past him! He whirled! Another dude was standing behind him. Bigfish Littlepond. Biggie had on a silk maxivest with rhinestone flowers and satin brass-studded pants. *His* shoes were 4 feet high! His beard was seeded with rubies, onyx and emeralds. (Red, black and green jewels in his pink beard? You know he *had* to be relevant!) Biggie was *bad, awful, terrible* even. Big and Phyn walked off together, outshining the sunset. Sadfly tried to run after them but he tripped over his maxi.

Well, Sadfly was a changed dude after that. His brim flopped, he let his shoes stretch out of shape, even the tails on his maxi seemed to droop. He hung around his crib and wouldn't even stand under the lamp post to let the light shine on his clothes. It got so that his rags were . . . . . well they *were* rags!

This couldn't go on! Where was the *bad* Sadfly, that *awful* dude, that *terrible* man? Finally, one day—the worst happened! Sadfly's mirror broke. The last shreds of his old life lay around him on the floor. This was it! Sadfly decided to end it all. So he untied his shoelaces and jumped out.

What a bad . . . . awful . . . . terrible thing to happen.

Why The Wind Moans

Nora Brooks Blakely
(1983)

Once, a long time ago, the sun laughed. Its bright yellow beams tickled the birds as they danced on the flat, broad leaves of the chuckling trees. Everyone was happy, because Dalila was getting married. Dalila was the wind, and she was about to marry Moyo, one of the northern rivers. Dalila thought cheerfully of the great plans she and Moyo had made. Together they would bring cool breezes of comfort and refreshment to this hot land. As she thought of these things Dalila skipped and whirled, making her soft gold and blue dress whirl out from her delicate chocolate body, stirring the air gently.

Moyo was happy, too. He thought of the great treasures he was bringing Dalila: his cool waters, the northern plants, animals, and fish that would travel with him; things people in her land had never seen. As he dressed, he hummed and chuckled, the silver cloth flowing over his midnight skin.

Siwatu was not happy. He was Moyo's father, the Great Northern Sea. Although he had many sons, he was greedy and did not want any of them to escape, for that would weaken his powerful magic. Besides, Moyo wished to take gifts with him. Gifts, Siwatu felt were really his. This was more than he could stand! He brooded over this for a long time, his waters rolling heavily in anger. Suddenly he knew what he would do. So, the people of the hot lands wanted cool breezes did they? Well, they would see—yes, they would see.

Moyo was ready to leave. He began to flow in the direction that would take him to Dalila, but something was wrong. He felt as if he was made of soft, thick mud. Why couldn't he move any faster than this? And those sharp pains, what was happening to him? Fear began to grow; he realized his brothers had been right all along. His father would never let him leave. This was Siwatu's magic. Moyo was slowly freezing. What could he do? Dalila! Dalila was warm. If he could reach her, her breezes would stop this horrible magic.

All night he crept, more and more slowly, moving painfully toward Dalila's land. He was almost frozen solid when Dalila finally saw him. Moyo gathered his last energy and leaped toward Dalila in one great swell. But it was too late and he froze completely. Dalila shrieked and blew and blew, but he was so cold the cool breezes they had dreamed of became icy gusts that even froze her own heart.

Our days and nights are much colder now. Moyo tried so hard to reach the one he loved that it is only on the hottest days we do not feel his cold, heavy nearness. And Dalila? Well, now maybe you will understand. On these icy-grated days, and nights of frozen light, you will hear her screeching moans as she stretches and rips the rocks and trees, because she remembers. Yes, she remembers—and her song is as chilled as the glacier that was once her love.

a lil dribble drabble

Collette Armstead
(1982)

Zara wadn't always like this. Sittin up in the room. Stickin her head up under the pilla. Shakin and half-cryin then comin down to dinner, eyes all puffy, tryin to make like there's nuthin wrong.

Before, she didn't even like bein alone. She was always happy. Fun lovin and crazy.

Like that time her and her friends got caught in the rain on the way to the beach. And Zara said, "we can have the picnic on my living-room floor." She had them playin charades and fallin backwards into each others arms and dancin like they dance at home on Saturday mornin in the mirror when nobodies lookin. She even let me take part. Eventho I'm only thirteen and her friends don't want me hangin around cuz they fraid I'm gon tell somethin they do.

Mosta my friends think I'm kinda lucky havin a sister that'll take you places and fix your hair for you and even buy you clothes from the first check she get from her summer job. I guess so. I dunno. Nowadays she don't even comb her own hair. And she shole don't go noplace mus less take me with her. Seem like all she do is sit up in the room goin through that ol raggedy keepsake box a hers.

I don't know what that boy did to her but he did somethin. She won't tell me what happened. She told Momma tho, I suppose. When I askt Momma what was wrong with Zara she say that Zara is just languishin cuz she dun tasted a lil dribble drabble of love. So I guess Momma understands. But I don't. And everytime I ask Zara "what's wrong?" she just look straight down at the floor and say "Oh nothing" then go on back up to the room after awhile.

One night, I woke up and saw her standin at the window lookin like a statue with dark light layin on it and i askt her "why don't you just let it out, go crazy, stomp and holler insteada cryin so soft and only lettin a lil bit out at a time." She say, "Dessa, sometimes you have to be as quiet as you can, in your pain, to guard your dignity, because sometimes your dignity is the only thing you have left."

164

A Love Story Written in the Light

Judy B. Massey
(1987)

There are times when the Ancestors cradle us in their arms and open our eyes to a gift of God in expression. Held in their all-encompassing protection, images pass through our eyes and settle on our hearts. Gently the Ancestors encourage us to move toward what we see, holding our hands each step of the way and promising to stand near. This gives us the courage to open ourselves and hear the sound of the expression. A sound so sweet that we find ourselves dancing and losing control in the joy of the melody of the words as we find that the thoughts spoken bring form to the abstract ones of our own. We are swept closer and closer like a child in wonder and suddenly the image becomes clear and we see the face of a Warrior that is the essence of a beauty we hold dear. In it, we can trace a character, a spirit that has explored adventures similar to ours. And even drawn from them the same wisdom. Uncontrollably our hearts go out to them. Lay themselves bare before them and promise to love without question.

For the heart's main purpose is to love. And for too long it has been denied. It has wept many times out of loneliness. Many have passed before it but none of their notes has penetrated the walls our minds have built around it. The heart realizes it has been protected by the mind and appreciates that caution. But in the face of all it's dreamed of, becomes powerless to deny love's call. It has dreamed of a Warrior brought to it by the Ancestors. It has prayed for one such as this. One who in spite of all discouragement, looks upon himself and sees his Light shining brightly. One who will not dilute the wisdom of decisions found inside himself. One to whom God speaks and he listens. One who cherishes good and truth and love. One who believes in the wisdom of others. One who is still tied to the Motherland enough to revel in her beauty. And though transplanted, nourishes her ways, sounds, customs in his heart. Our heart recognizes this spirit as the perfect complement of itself and casts aside all doubt and fear and runs to embrace it—to hold it close—to love it as deeply as it can.

But the mind grasps tightly the hand of the Ancestors. Wanting this spirit so much but knowing not how to let go—to fully let go and drink in the magic of a kindred spirit. It has become used to things of logic—to seeing the ends of paths traveled—to walking ahead, not following. It has

165

become arrogant and powerful of the spirit. And, now the spirit too, rejoices. Moves to a different beat and threatens to melt into this gentle image. It begs of the mind to release it—to travel the road unafraid. It wants to be guided by and to guide this spirit—to be made strong and make strong with a union. The spirit yearns to stand close to this Black Warrior; the heart yearns to cocoon him in love.

The Ancestors understand the mind's hesitation. There have been many tests before this wondrous experience. The mind has learned them well. It is hard to forget past teachings.

The Ancestors whisper, "It is right. It comes from me. It is time. You must not be afraid to walk, for you know the answers. It is time you believed in the wisdom of your heart. For in its repairing, it has learned too. And you have learned to trust us—to trust us when you can find no words to explain. Trust us now. Move to this one. Fulfill yourself. After all, it is what you have dreamed of. It is what you have asked for. He understands for he has lived it too. He listens for he needs to hear. He knows the challenges of expressing a talent that will not be contained. And he's reaching out to you. Go to him. Fill each other's cup."

The mind moves beside the image and listens. This Black Warrior is strong but gentle. The mind speaks and the Warrior is made happy by its words and remembers them. The mind relaxes enough to express doubts and the Warrior presents answers that provide avenues to the mind that it has been searching for. The mind opens enough to release its own deductions, the wisdom it has found for itself. Wisdom that has been met many times with opposition. Wisdom many refuse to understand. Wisdom many have insensitively criticized. The mind makes ready to retreat, to prove to the heart and the spirit that there is no difference here. But the Warrior understands . . . even shares the same intuitive reasonings and there is no criticism. In fact, there is praise and compliments. The mind moves closer and is comforted for this Warrior is different. He has not allowed himself to be limited to things of this world. He, too, has opened himself to the Ancestors' profound nudgings and gathered unearthly wisdom unto himself. This mind, too, has stepped through much criticism and refused to stop believing in the logic of the unseen. And the mind begins to feel the glory of being understood and learns how wondrous it is to think aloud before this spirit. As slowly the wall around the heart begins to crumble and it loses itself in another.

A strong Black courageous Warrior has found another of a kindred spirit. The Ancestors smile and stand near. And two hearts, two minds and two spirits soar to new heights, new levels of understanding of the Self. They are made stronger by their togethertimes. They are made more powerful by their belief in each other.

■■■■■■■■■■■■■■■■■■■■■■■■■■

Shop Talk
(An Excerpt)

Judy B. Massey
(1985)

Characters

Emma: Attractive black woman about 45 years old. Always has a ciga-rette either hanging from her lips or burning in a nearby ash-tray. She is the owner of Emma's Coiffures.

Gloria: Pretty black woman of 29. Heavily made up and wearing very form-fitting attire.

Carol: Average-looking black woman about 34. Very feminine and dainty.

Michele: Slightly plump, jolly-looking black woman. About 32.

Scene is a beauty shop. One wall is lined with individual mirrors and adjustable chairs. The opposite wall is covered with four chairs topped by hooded hair dryers. One woman is under the dryer, another is sitting next to her, but dryer has gone off. The hairdresser is busy curling a woman's long, straightened locks with an electric curling iron. Both are turned away from the mirror facing the two women seated at the hair dryers. Magazines are strewn on tables. A couple of plants grace the open window that is lettered with the words EMMA'S COIFFURES. Outside the window the cold, unfriendly steel beams supporting the tracks of an elevated train can be seen. Now and then the roar of a pass-ing train is heard. It is summer.

Carol. *(waving her hands around her head)* Emma, do your stuff, girl. I got a hot date tonight. Want to really look good to this man.

Emma. *(balancing a cigarette on her lips and wrapping hair around the irons)* So what else is new?

Gloria. *(laughing loudly)* Yeah. Carol, it amazes me the way you get so excited about each and every one.

Carol. *(matter-of-factly)* Why not? I love black men. But this one is really special. We really could get something going.

167

Emma.   Right. Seems to me you said that about the last five.

Carol.   No, I didn't. Anyway, I ain't giving up. I want and need me a husband. So I ain't getting jaded like you.

Emma.   *(sarcastically)* Jaded. Is that what I am?

Gloria.   *(looking up from a magazine)* Yeah. That's what you are, Emma. Men ain't nothing to you but pleasure and dollar signs.

Emma.   Well, look who's talking.

Gloria.   *(smugly, lighting a cigarette)* Yeah, but I admit it.

Carol.   That's a shame. Ya'll don't take men seriously at all. That's probably why so many of them are turning to white women. Women like the two of you are messing them up for me. Just because you got hurt a couple times you gave up on *all* men. Not me. I'm hanging in. I know there's a good-looking, hard-working brother out there with my name on him and I ain't gonna be no hard-hearted Hanna when he comes along. I'm gonna be sweet and in his corner. Everything he thinks he needs.

Emma.   Oh yeah? Like the time you sweetly pulled that gun on what's his name? What was his name? You know, the one you found out couldn't keep his promise and marry you cause his wife would have objected. What was his name?

Gloria.   *(in total surprise)* What?

Carol.   *(somewhat disgusted)* Emma, you can't hold water!

Gloria.   Girl, you did what? Pulled a gun. You? Little Miss Sophisticated College Graduate. Pulled a gun?

Carol.   *(non-apologetically)* That was a long time ago. I was a child. I wasn't gonna use it. Just trying to make a point.

Emma.   Make a point or add a little drama to a dull situation? You just love drama, don't you, Carol? Come home from a dull day at the office with all them white folks and you need some excitement in your life. Some niggah drama. Need something wild and crazy in your life to be sure you can still feel. White folks too routine. I understand. Like my mama say, "If you ever been a niggah on Saturday night, you don't never want to be white again!" Poor baby. Don't worry. Emma's gonna fix this hair up so pretty, you gone be irresistible. Want a little hint of blonde in it?

Michele.   *(pushing up the dryer which has stopped whirring)* Talking about men again. I can tell by your faces. That's all ya'll do. Glad I got my Jimmy at home.

Gloria.   *(grabbing magazine from her lap and flipping the pages)* Aw, shit. Here we go with that storybook marriage of hers.

Michele.   Jealous, Gloria?

Gloria.   *(undisturbed)* Hell no. I ain't jealous of nobody that stares into the face of the same man every night.

Carol.   What's the matter with that? Especially if he's a good man that comes home to you every night.

Michele.   *(patting at her hair, feeling it to see if it's dry)* They're not all bad, Gloria. There's still a lot of good ones out there.

Gloria.   *(looking at Michele)* Michele, you been married 12 years. How the hell do you know what's out there?

Michele.   *(flirtatiously)* I'm married. I ain't dead. I talk to men.

Gloria.   *(looking back down into magazine)* Yeah, well, so do I and they ain't saying nothin'. That's why I use their bodies and send them on their way. I'm tired of trying to make sense of their conversations.

Michele.   Men come to you the way you come to them. I'm sure they can sense what you're thinking and that's all you get in return. They don't want to be used any more than you do. They've got feelings too.

Gloria.   Listen to you, Michele. You sound like a damn romance novel or Joyce Brothers or somebody.

Michele.   I think you want a husband, Gloria. You just cover it up with that slick talk.

Gloria.   Michele, you think everybody wants a husband. Besides, I had a husband. It was boring.

Emma.   *(almost under her breath)* You've had many husbands.

Gloria.   I mean one I was married to.

Michele.   *(placing her hand on Gloria's arm)* There comes a time when two people move into a different phase of love. They get comfortable with each other. But it doesn't have to be boring. Jimmy and I find ways to keep our marriage exciting. Little things.

Gloria.   Oh, Christ!

Carol   *(holding out her hand to examine her painted fingernails)* Gloria, some people do manage to have pleasant relationships. Some marriages are happy.

Gloria.   Really? Like the one that man that you pulled the gun on had? Tell us about that, Carol.

Carol.   I don't want to talk about it.

Emma.   *(laughing)* I bet he appreciated the hell out of his wife when he left Carol's house. See, I always say it's good for a man to have an affair occasionally. Makes it so much easier to tolerate his ole lady.

Gloria.   Most of them just filling a void anyway. Getting on the outside what they can't get at home.

Carol.   *(angrily)* Any man that plays on his wife is a dog. They got you psyched out, Gloria. How come it's always got to be something wrong with us that causes them to do wrong? Why we always got to be the ones to blame?

Gloria.   Oh, we ain't the ones to blame. They marry the ones hold back on the bed action because then they feel they can trust her. Only to their surprise nobody else can get any but neither can they. So they come out looking for women like me and Emma to fill the void.

Emma.   Don't put me in that bag, girl.

Carol.   Yeah, Gloria. And you're right there to take them in.

Gloria.   I perform a service.

Carol.   There's no difference between you and a prostitute.

Gloria.   Probably not.

Michele.   Gloria, how can you say that?

Gloria.   Just honest I guess.

Michele.   But how can you settle for that?

Gloria.   I can use the money.

Carol.   Cold-blooded. And you ain't got no shame.

Gloria.   (*gets up and walks to the window, looks out, then turns back to Carol*) Does Stevie Wonder feel shame when folks pay to see him?

Carol.   That's different.

Gloria.   What's different about it?

Carol.   He's entertaining.

Gloria.   And so am I. And if they pay Stevie to entertain, they can pay me. Besides, Carol, I noticed you said there was a hard-working brother out there for you. What if you meet a brother who's down on his luck. Between jobs or maybe just couldn't deal with the system anymore. Or maybe he's getting his own business together and needs to count his pennies. If you're so different from me, the fact that he ain't working a high-brow corporate job won't matter, right?

Carol.   (*almost inaudibly*) Don't know. Ain't met none like that.

Gloria.   Yeah, but if you do, money will be no object. You ain't like me. You'll dig him for himself. Besides, you working.

Carol.   (*snaps back*) I ain't giving no man my money.

Gloria.   Yeah, like I said earlier—only difference about me is I admit what I do.

Michele.   Gloria, who hurt you to turn you into such an unfeeling person?

Gloria.   (*sits in empty chair next to Emma and Carol*) Unfeeling? I've got bundles of feelings. That's why I had to get out of that brain-dead marriage.

Michele.   (*waves her hand in Gloria's direction as if brushing her comment off*) Well, all of them ain't like that. Jimmy and I talk to each other. We still act like we did when we were going together a lot of the time. Did I tell you he bought me twelve roses for our anniversary last week? He buys me one for each year. Been doing that ever since we got married. He missed last year but we laughed it off. Said he didn't want to spoil me or become too routine.

Gloria.	Tell me, Michele, in this storybook romance of yours, are there any flaws? This man can't be perfect all the time.
Michele.	Of course not. But he tries. Hell, I ain't perfect either. He puts up with my stuff, too.
Emma.	*(waving her lighted cigarette at Gloria)* Leave Michele alone, Gloria. That's why men keep their wives away from divorced women like you. You've lost your ability to believe in them.
Gloria.	You've got that right. They're pleasure and dollar signs. Let their wives watch them snore in front of the TV set.
Carol.	Humph!
Michele.	I still say that it's very possible to have a good relationship with a man and plus, I think everybody needs one. Men aren't the enemy. A little talking and some real listening to them without all the hangups could prove to be beneficial to some of us. *(looking at Gloria)*
Carol.	Yeah. Look, I've had my hard times with the brothers. Ain't trying to say that I haven't. But I've known a lot of them that think a lot like we do. I'm with Michele. We so busy scheming and plotting against one another—always trying to make sure we ain't the ones that get the short end of the stick—that we can't even hear each other no more. Well, I for one am gonna keep listening as hard as I can until I get me one all my own.
Gloria.	Ain't no such thing as one all your own.
Michele.	*(looking rather defensive)* I truly don't believe that's true.
Carol.	*(accusingly)* Gloria, that's downright mean.
Michele.	*(pulling at her skirt to straighten it)* Naw, girl, that's alright. I ain't taking none of this personally. Gloria don't mean no harm. Shame you so bitter though, girl. You'd make somebody a great companion.
Gloria.	I don't know. They don't seem to understand me. 'N fact, they don't seem to try.
Carol.	Don't nobody understand you, Gloria. So don't put that off on the brothers.
Michele.	Carol, don't be so insensitive.

Gloria.   Naw, she's right. Very few people relate to me. Ain't many people living at my consciousness level. Got to pay a lot of dues to get here. Most people go the safe route, Michele. Like you. Get tied up with some relatively safe guy and miss a lot of mind-expanding experiences. So they can't relate to people like me and Emma.

Emma.   Why you keep trying to make like my views just like yours, Gloria?

Gloria.   Cause they are, Emma, and you know it!

Emma.   In some ways, yes. But in a lot of ways, no. I've had some real good relationships with men. In fact, one was real special. That's how I got this shop.

Gloria.   Yeah, see that's what I mean. Little payment for services rendered?

Emma.   *(looking as if she's reflecting back)* Naw.

Carol.   *(pulling her head away and turning around to look at Emma)* Tell us about him, Emma. This the first time I ever heard you talk about a man. Give us some of your dirt.

Emma.   Ain't no dirt. The man was just real decent. That's all there is to tell.

Gloria.   Real decent, huh? He sure was if you trying to tell us he gave you the money for this shop without asking for nothing. Sounds unbelievably decent.

Michele.   There are some decent men around, Gloria.

Emma.   *(shaking her head)* Not that decent, honey. This shop cost a pretty penny to get off the ground. Naw, we were dealing but it was real. Maybe we even had what you call love. I don't know. Ain't never figured out what that is. And the way I've seen it do some people, I just kinda shy away from it.

Gloria.   Whatever. He was worth some dollar signs. In the end, that's all that really matters. You got this shop out of it. He's gone, the shop ain't.

Emma.   He ain't exactly gone. Least not like you mean it. Still checks on me every now and then just to see how I'm doing. Moved to another state shortly after I got the shop. And you know,

Gloria, it's funny. Sure he let me have the money, it's true. Lord knows I would never have gotten it together with that funky job I had. But what was more important than the money . . .

Gloria. Ain't nothing more important than the money.

Carol. Gloria, would you let her finish. Go on, Emma.

Emma. That money wouldn't have been half as important had he not believed in me. That's what really amazed me about him. He was always telling me how much potential he saw in me and how I should be doing something more than I was doing. Said I had a good head on my shoulders and I could go places if I'd try. I thought it was the regular rap at first. Didn't pay it no attention.

But one day he asked me what I'd like to do. Well, I ain't never been one for corporate life so going back to college held no interests for me. But I'd seen many a hairdresser get over real good. And I always liked to fuss over people's heads ever since I was a child. When I told him that, he insisted I enroll in Beauty School. I did. And he paid for it. Encouraged me all the way, too.

Yeah, when he got up off that money for me, I knew he was doing more than just rapping. And it felt real good to have someone believe in me like that. I finished with flying colors, too. Figured I owed him and me that. Shortly after I started working for this other shop, he suggests that I try to do my own thing. Said I was a good businesswoman. Should be handling my own thing.

Gloria. Yeah, probably trying to get back his investment and some profit. He suggest getting into it with you?

Emma. Naw, Gloria. And you know what, he ain't never let me pay him back either. I tried many times. He won't take it. We eventually drifted apart but it sure meant a lot to me how he thought I could be something more than I was. I think if he'd given me that, without the money, it would have been enough for me to make it.

Carol. See, Gloria, there are good ones out there. Sometimes I guess they just respond to what they got. If they ain't got nothing to respond to, they don't.

Michele. Don't be insulting, Carol. Gloria's gonna find hers one day. I still say everybody needs a man. Then you can encourage one another. Ain't no telling how far we can go if we start believing in one another again. Think about it, Gloria. I got to get outta here. Brenda's ready for me. See ya'll later *(getting up to go to chair of another hairdresser off stage)*.

Masque Etude

A Performance in Four Movements

Mike Cook
(1980's)

Production Notes

Performers:

    Principal—Feminine Dancer/Actor
    Principal—Masculine Dancer/Actor
    Supporting Dancer/Actors (4)
    Musical Ensemble

Set:

    Cabaret Style

Props:

1. Rocking Creature;
2. Largish, fabric Pterodactyl that can be made to come alive; *e.g.*, can be lowered from ceiling and made to move like a marionette.
3. Largish sack of mixed flowers and silver coins.
4. One live cock per performance.

Performance

Movement One: Masque Etude
Movement Two: Pterodactyl
Movement Three: Black Alms from the Golden Purse
Movement Four: Gospel Totem

Note: the Pterodactyl can also be a human dancer.

Part One

> *(Stage Dark. Drums are heard, slow and deep, as if in pre-lude to sacrificial rituals. Lights up, and a man and woman are sitting opposite one another at a small table. Their faces are painted in magical stripes and markings. The offstage drums end as the lights come up and three musicians with in-struments bracket the table. The musicians begin playing plaintive blues and jazz fragments in minor keys.)*

The man and woman are joined in strong mutual need and irresolution. This is underscored by look, movements, action. The man looks intently at the woman but she looks away. The woman looks intently at the man but he looks away. He reaches to touch her face but she leans away. She inclines her head towards him and purses her lips, but he stands up. She stands and they engage in a choreographic duet expressing: Attraction—Arousal—Titillation—Hesitation—Suspicion—Fear—Desperation—Alienation—Parting.

The woman begins a dance of withdrawal from the stage. The music becomes more abstract, faster. The woman and the musicians EXIT. There is silence.

The man begins a dance of disappointment and isolation.

He lies supine on the table.

LIGHTS go down.

> *(A high trumpet note sounds, is held, and the lights go up. The man rouses and sits alert atop the table. The trumpet note gives way to a rousing number associated with Louis Armstrong, and done in his style; such as: "Mahogany Hall Stomp," or "Strutting with some Barbecue.")*

Six dancers appear on stage. Each dancer wears a head-enclosing mask inspired by the traditions of various cultures: North American, African, Asiatic, Oceanic. The dancers circle and court the man, as they flow with the elegance of Louis Armstrong's music. The high spirits contrast with the elegiac blues played earlier. The man atop the table swirls and spins to the movements of the dancing around him.

The Armstrong melody ends and the ritual drums resume. The character of the dancing changes from the melodic to the hyperrhythmic, inspired by the insistence of the drums. As if in a salute of encouragement, the dancers in turn approach the man, then spin offstage. The last hesi-tates and the man holds her by the wrist. She snatches away from him and removes her mask, showing herself as his partner at the beginning of the scene. She tosses her mask at him and he catches it. She spins offstage. He holds the mask and it is spotlighted as lights go down.

Part Two

PTERODACTYL

Lights are down. Lights go up and the man and woman are again sitting at the table. Now, the woman is wearing the clothes and coiffure of a banker and the man conventionally but more sportively attired. The musicians are again arrayed around the space. They end the number they are playing and pause.

MAN
Music like this, with an exploding nucleus, requires faith, don't you think?

WOMAN
Requirements, yes; that's the subject that makes you boil, don't you remember?

MAN
Requirements must be questioned, but needs must be stated. You find that convenient to ignore.

WOMAN
I always liked the careful attention you payed to my feet and other particular areas.

MAN
At your best, your very best, my dear, you are the best. Forget the rest.

WOMAN
I shared my fantasy with you one time—and you used it as an excuse to be cruel.

MAN
You deliberately provoked me to an extreme. And you enjoyed it very, very much.

WOMAN
I granted you that power but right away you grew distant.

MAN
You could never tell me apart from the criminals you would use for your mutual frenzies.

WOMAN
Need, need, need. The worst thing would be to really need a character like you.

MAN
I saw the best in you, really, the part of yourself that you despise.

WOMAN

Once there was a giraffe, once there was a whale; and once a monkey with a wondrous tail.

The man stands in concentrated anger and dances offstage.

The woman then begins a dance passage delineating the tensions of her life as the musicians resume and interact. Her dance is one of urgency and the need for human contact. As the intensity of her dance increases she suddenly pauses, and the music changes mode.

ENTER the PTERODACTYL. The winged creature is flagrantly masculine with a codpiece and predatory headgear. She is fascinated as Pterodactyl begins his licentious version of a mating dance. WOMAN responds with as much fever as the Pterodactyl and they spur each other on to more erotic overtures. Pterodactyl suddenly seizes her and bears her backwards to the floor. As first she appears to submit and join him—then it becomes apparent that she is resisting. She is in possession of a long knife and taking whacks at Pterodactyl and his feathers fly. He whirls away from her but she pursues him until he collapses. Her dance changes character, becomes more lighthearted. She begins flinging off her business attire, seeming freer. The dance becomes one of enlightenment and atonement. She kneels beside the downed pterodactyl and removes the mask. It is the MAN. She becomes tender.
LIGHTS DOWN.

Part Three

BLACK ALMS FROM THE GOLDEN PURSE

(Stage dark. A single woodwind or brass instrument is heard. Then, human voices join the instrument, chanting: CARESS THE FIRE SILK HORSE, RIDE A FINE COURSE; CARESS THE FIRE SILK HORSE, RIDE A FINE COURSE.)

Lights come up slowly. Center Stage is an upholstered, fabric rocking creature. It is contoured so that its rider fits atop it in a carnal fashion. The creature is, in fact, being ridden to the music and the chants of two attendants who flank the moving creature, standing respectfully. The tempo of the music/chanting/rocking increases, then reaches a briefly sustained frenzy, then subsides. Then ceases and is still. The attendants reach to the creature and help the rider arise from it. She is the ALMS

GIVER, garbed in striking version of ritual regalia. She moves as if newly born or incarnated and rapidly increases in power and awareness. The attendants dance in homage and supplication. She takes command of her sacred area—the stage—and positions herself upstage of the rocking creature. She reaches inside a pouch of the Rocking Creature and showers handsfull of coins and flowers on the stage.

ALMS GIVER
Black Alms. Black alms.

ALL
Black alms from the golden purse.

ALMS GIVER throws more handsfull of coins and flowers into the audience.

> *(Suddenly, the lights go out. Music and voices are silent, and there is no sound, but the sprinkling of alms. But, when the lights go out, the alms are not flowers and coins but rice and gravel—which are liberally strewn. The lights go back on as a male voice hollers—*

MAN
What the hell is this?

The MAN is sitting in the audience next to an elegantly gowned woman. He is wearing a well-cut suit of a light color on which some sand and gravel have landed.

MAN
Huh? I come to support the arts and my suit gets splashed.

Menacing and streetwise, the irate MAN stands from his seat and advances toward the stage.

MAN
Who's in charge here?

ATTENDANTS
Take it off.

MAN
What?

ATTENDANTS
(chanting)
Take it off, take it off, take it off.

MAN
(turns to his elegant companion)
I'm only here because of you.

COMPANION
That's alright. Take it off. They know what they're doing.

MAN

Uh, think I'm not game, huh?

COMPANION

You, Chickie-Baby—game to the hilt!

MAN mounts stage, ALMS GIVER greets him with welcoming gestures and MAN undresses. The attendants take his suit and EXIT. ALMS GIVER remounts the rocking creature and the suitless MAN reaches into the pouch. He strews performance space with sand and gravel as the ALMS GIVER rocks on the creature. MAN chants to the rising voice of the instruments.

MAN

Black alms. Black alms from the Golden purse. Black alms.

Part Four

GOSPEL TOTEM

(Stage Dark. Drum figures are heard, played as if in prelude to rituals. The drums cease after this introductory figure. LIGHTS UP.)

ENTER two ACOLYTES, carrying between them a receptacle of black sand. They place the receptacle properly and cast some of the sand around the receptable.
ACOLYTES EXIT and REENTER, now carrying an altar on which is tethered a white cock. They secure the altar on stage and back off from it on either side. The drums resume in more urgent fashion, rising in tempo and volume. This drumming introduces THE SERVANT.
ENTER THE SERVANT, ritually garbed, highlighted. He stretches, flexes, prepares himself for the sacrifices to follow. Then, he dips into his receptacle of sand and cleanses himself stylistically, ritually, as if the fine sand was water. When the cleansing is done to the satisfaction of the powers, the servant suddenly thrusts high his knife.

(When the knife is raised, all musical instruments are heard up-tempo, except the drums. Music declares the power of the triad—the servant, the knife, the cock.
The ACOLYTES present the cock to THE SERVANT, and writhe in their supplication, in their passion to present him with what he needs. THE SERVANT moves in his responses

of inspection and acceptance, moving in his sacred obligation to the cock. He inspects the cock closer. The ACOLYTES move in to assist THE SERVANT and the cock. The ACOLYTES seize the cock in a manner that exposes the neck. The knife flashes high in the light and the music rises in tones of sacrificial tremor.)

The knife descends, cutting off the cock's head, and thunking into the board of the altar. THE SERVANT throws the headless cock into the air and the ACOLYTES pursue it.

(When the ACOLYTES chase the bird, the music resumes, music of pursuit and transition.)

The ACOLYTES catch the cock. They pluck him on the spot, moaning and shouting as they fling the feathers into the air. They all dance off-stage.

■■■■■■■■■■■■■■■■■■■■■■■■

SHANGO DIASPORA:
An African-American Myth
of Womanhood and Love

(An Excerpt)

Angela Jackson
(1979-80)

ACT I   SCENE 3

SETTING: *Smoke in the distance from a high place. That is Shango's lair/*
palace. The Girl is journeying. Again, trees walk and stones
move. Birds in flight. Bird signal songs. Flight from a big wind,
a movement.

Girl
(Watching the signs of animal flight. Worried. Muses.)
When Fire struts/bewildered beasts scurry. From miles away birds set out
a flurry of fear.
(A flurry among the trees. She cringes.)
I smell the skin of smoke. I sense his presence near. His teeth that mark
the barks of trees; his eyes peeling a path of leaves leaving the bones of
slow bedazzled beasts settled beneath his feet.
(Hesitantly approaches a gate at the foot of a suggested stairwell.
The stairwell has steps that are really landings. The steps curve.
The steps are in darkness. She listens.)
I hear his breathing. The soft rending of cloth. The soft tearing of the hair
of air.
(She looks around her, warily.)

Girl
A craziness of atmosphere, near his lair of brilliance and intrigue.
(Measures herself to meet the task.)
My heart wide as a child's. A woman's aroma at my wrists, at my temples,
behind my ears.
(Takes out perfume from her carrying basket. Carrying basket is
full of goodies.)
This craziness of atmosphere. I want to run. I want to stay. I'm wise
enough to fear. Fool enough to linger here.
(Girl, having decided to face Fire, prepares by dressing up. Adds
a skirt of bright colored veils, jewelry. All this from her basket of
goodies. A bowl is also in the basket.)

183

A Voice
(A warning voice, deep and stern, comes from nowhere and everywhere.)

Who enters his electromagnetic field is polarized, pulled apart, limb from limb, shocked, wild in the head.

(Girl pauses with hand outstretched toward the suggestion of a door/gate.)

Voice of Woman #3

You must go to him with a sacrifice. Go singing. If you don't, you'll never be free.

(Girl still hesitates.)

You want a good night's sleep, don't you?

(Girl opens door/gate. Girl mounts the long, wide steps that are more like platforms. Lights go up on Shango on high. He is close to a cloud. Clouds are stones. Shango Fire Diaspora sits in a Huey P. Newton, big backed, bamboo chair. He reclines. Arrogantly. He remains in shadow, although all around him is illuminated. Perhaps he is flanked by drummers who are at a distance. He has one soldier, at least. He is being fanned by a woman. All in Shango's palace wear African dress. Flamboyant fire colors. A great glaring light falls on the Girl's face. Blinds her.)

Soldier

Who comes?

Girl

Only . . . a girl sleepless with praises.

(Shields her eyes.)

Soldier

Then praise.

(Light softens as girl kneels and bows deeply.)

Girl

(Begins tremulously. Gains confidence. It gets good to her. She is downright cocky by the end.)

Most Excellent Lord Shango. You were a god before music/fell and broke/ into voices. Before the tribes were marked limb from limb, eye from eye, skin from skin, heart from heart, and brain before desire was formed out of hormone, mucus, and marrow. Before Osiris/you were a god. Before the market of salt, and spices and trade/beads before rice rose out of mud. Before bruteforce/you were a god before the deathhowl/before The Chain/ before The Coffle . . .

The Fan
(Bored and jealous.)

My. My. My girl is so extravagant. Sweet child.

Girl
(Loud and determined.)
You were born before Hallelujah, as old as Hosanna! Before the plain and orangebreasted lizard made marriage patterns in the sand./Before the funeral of justice, before mercy, before '27, the flood, when the house was torn from its roots and twins were birthed on the roof./Before the river ran wild before the anger of water/before the beacon, and the lighthouse.
> *(Is so excited she rises in her speech. Soldier and The Fan gesture her down. She ignores them.)*

You were a being before the Hawk and the Holy Ghost danced as one on the corner of Celebration and Sanctuary, before the women of the creme sachet and toilet water lay with porcelain gods and works of art./You were there in the time of the North Star/in the Time of Moss that hugs the Tree of Memory. You are as old as the longing for Messiah. Your lifeline equatorial and your heart bleeds back from the long tunnel of the First God. You have accumulated more pain than I. I have heard of you. I know that I am young. Magician of two thousand smoke screens, griot of light years, people say that I am aglow, a star has set upon me. And I am patient as the moon.

Shango
(In shadow. Bored. Matter of factly.)
You are a fool.

Girl
(Before he can get his out of his mouth good.)
Beyond a shadow . . . I am ready for giving. I have come singing. I know that I am young.

The Fan
Is that all, *little girl?*

Girl
(Feisty.)
I wasn't talking to you.
> *(To Fire.)*

May we have privacy? I have brought an offering.
> *(Shango snaps his fingers. All retreat to lower platforms. They watch and listen.*
> *(The Fan takes centerstage. She narrates the actions of The Girl and Fire. Fire and The Girl do dance actions in the shadows. A hot, hot, hot dance done in shadows with sparks shooting out.)*

The Fan
(Blasé. Delighting in the Girl's fate.)
She prepared a lamb for him. A sacrifice floating in herbs and blood and water seasoned with salt of camouflaged tears, onions, and three kinds of peppers, enough to kill a goat.
> *(She fans herself all the while.)*

Her mouth shaped half a plate of triumph. She held murder in her hands. He sat on his throne, a luxuriating storm. His neck was stiff as an eagle's. He watched the sway of her hips, heavy, widened as she walked with design. He took the dish and tasted it. He ground West African pepper with his teeth. He lulled his tongue inside the heat. Then he said, "This is not sweet enough. There is not enough salt."
(Gleefully.)
He crushed her eyes for salt. He opened her veins for syrup and let her laughter over lamb. Devoured it. *His teeth cracked bone.* Devoured it. *He sucked the marrow.* Then, he roared for more. She gave him her mouth. He pulled her kisses til she was gaunt. Her joints grew thin as spider tapestries. Still. He said he was not satisfied. She fell behind her mask. Inscrutable. Wall of water. Silent hieroglyphic of hurt. Reflecting, she watched his fine teeth glisten while he laughed.
(A deep bass growl-laugh descends from the shadow and sparks. The two figures now tangled in erotic, and subtly violent embrace. A low fade on couple coupling. Then Girl descends. Like a sleepwalker. She is off her center.)

Girl
(More to self than to others. Disoriented.)
Fire is absolute. You were absolutely right. I should have known. I had no ways. I had no means enough to know. I, who have always been water. More or less. Fire burns. Grates the eyes. Peels/flesh and sears.
(Gestures back toward Fire. Turns to shout to Him.)
Fire: you are absolute. There is no defense. A woman who loves Fire/who meddles with flame/who flirts with tongues/will burn/will be/consumed.
(On a lower platform the village women appear. They are doing a Fire Dance. Girl descends toward them.)
In the village, on the street corners, the women raised their skirts and only fanned the flame. Fire rose around their thighs. Went through them and blossomed between their breasts. Fire licked their ankles and they danced. Fire: you are music/nobody has business listening to alone. *And when I touched you you were warm. I cupped the heat and laughed into the colored shadows you cast across my skin.* I was laughing, people say. Not like a little girl. They say, I raised my skirts delicately, like a lady, and danced. Til they only saw the smoke.

(Girl goes up in fire and smoke. The Fan fans on like this happens everyday.)

Black out. Quick.

End ACT I   SCENE 3

The Gift of The Spirit

Debra Faye Anderson
(1984)

Eons ago. when black men molded iron for tools and raised the first civilizations and the great pyramids . . . carved art out of wood, fashioned ideas into spoken language and later still into written symbols on temple walls, charted unseen stars . . . practiced medicine, democracy and cooperative economics—other folk lived in caves.

Diggit.

and the tables were turned. they came out of their caves. took Afrika's suns and daughters and taught them to hate themselves and each other. but one escaped. yeah. and the Spirit hid the one and made a covenant with him. they said he would be the one to return and re/turn the tables. they blessed him and named him Ra. and he fled deeper into the jungle to prepare himself.

"Say! Say blood! I got some nice watches here! Men's Seikos and Charlie? Charlie Bennett! Say what's up bro', how you doing?"

"Jimmy B! Hey I'm fine man, how're you doing?" Much handshaking and backslapping. "Man I ain't seen you since . . . Shit man! I ain't seen you since Boys and Girls High! What'sup brother?"

"Jusout here hangin, y'know. Trying to rub two nickels together."

"I heard that."

"Say man, how's your moms?"

"She's fine," he nodded. "Fine. We were talking about you just the other day. You gotta stop by and see her sometime."

"Yeaaaaa . . . aah, I know man. I know. I shoulda been done stopped by to see your moms. Yall still on Prairie?"

"Yeah, she is. I'm over at Columbia."

"Really? You always was the smart one. That's hip. How long you been doing that?"

"Too long, my brother, too long!" They give each other five.

"I'mhip. I wasover at NYU for a semester, but I couldn't hang, so," he hunched his shoulders," I'mout here."

"Diggit."

"Say, whatchu doing right now man? Whyon'tchu c'mon round here to my lady's? I got some of that Joe Simon kinda smoke—the 'Choking Kind!'"

187

"I'd love to man, but I'm hoping I'll run into this guy for an interview."

"You looking for a job?"

"Naaaah. I'm doing some research for a paper. Say Jimmy, you haven't heard anything about a dude named Ra, have you?"

"Uh . . . nawl man, I haven't. Well ah . . . ah, take it light."

"Hold on Jimmy. I haven't seen him myself, but he's a big dude, about . . ."

"Yeah, wella . . . I don't ah . . . sniff . . . know no ah . . . Ray man. Take it light . . ."

"Nawl Jimmy, not Ray, Ra. See, he's supposed to . . ."

"Look nigga! I tolchu I don't know the muthafucka! Look . . . I'm sorry man. My nerves are bad. I'm sorry. Say man, say man, like . . . I'm sorry man, really. I didn't mean . . . say man, I gotta go . . ."

"Wait a minute Jimmy! What's wrong with you?"

"Hey muthafucka ain't nothing wrong! Why there gotta be something wrong with me? What's wrong with you? Look Charlie, I got some business I gotta take care of. You take it easy . . ."

"Jimmy this is me. This ain't no rooty-poot. What's . . . say man, you ain't on shit are you . . . Jimmy? Jimmy!", shaking him. "Jimmy!"

"Huh? Awl," dragging his sleeve across his face," nawl blood. Look, okay, I heard something about him, some ol' niggas was talking, but that'sall man. Look, you be eas . . ."

. . . And out of the East burst forth a . . . yes, a dunebuggy! BLAZING! GLAZING! Yellow-bright! like the sun. It seemed to ride down on her rays. It was so bright, you had to turn away . . .

"Damn! What was that?"

The blaze of light had been so sudden and so intense, that people had run frightened from the streets and into their homes. Slowly, the blaze began to dim. One by one, they stepped just outside their doors, or peeked out from their windows to get a good look at the ball of fire that had dropped into the middle of their Harlem.

Several minutes passed. and then, very deliberately, a figure stepped out of the dunebuggy. first a foot, then a leg. then the other, till finally, a very black Black man stood up, a full nine feet tall.

Nine feet tall and blackBlack! He was dressed in white silk robes and stood flat foot on the sidewalk, seemed to savor Harlem with his eyes. He started to walk away from the buggy. stopped short. looked down at the broken Thunderbird bottles and the fastfood bags at his feet, and reached back inside the buggy for a pair of leather thongs.

By now, a few more people had ventured outside, and a crowd of neighborhood hustlers stood not too far from the blackBlack man, watching him closely.

He wore a headpiece—a spiderweb of intricate Afrikan art. A worn and battered book rode low on his hip, strapped around and across his waist. As he approached the crowd, the wind whipped his robes behind him, and you could see that he was a bit bow-legged. a trail of colored stars flickered on and off behind him.

Being very sure of himself (women with curler-infested heads hugged their open windows and remarked, "that's a pureeeety black nigga!"), being very sure of himself, he didn't just walk, he kinda sauntered over, hips lean and fluid beneath broad shoulders.

And being very black too, his hand kinda fell back and forth behind him. Y'know, how cats pimpwalk and throw their hands behind them, to show how cool they are? Well, they aren't really being cool, they're really trying to fan away the gas they pass continuously (being cool all the time can cause a lot of pressure). But his wasn't a fake thing. Nawl. It was a natural movement. kept his ryhthm for you.

"My name is Ra. I'm pushing wisdom. Freedom." The air gave way and the tension snapped and the crowd broke out laughing.

"Ain't nobody buying that today brother!" a goldmouth pimp offered. "It take a quarter bag to get you high!" They broke laughing again. This dude was still weird, but it was a bit easier now.

"I'm here to show you brothers and sisters how to win your freedom."

"Hey baby! C'mon up here 'n free me!" a hefty, sausage face woman yelled down from her window.

"Even you sister. I'll help you find freedom."

"Where you from muthafucka? Ain't you a Venetian Lord?" A young and ambitious thug moved on Ra.

"Hey Benny, what it is?" Charlie greeted the thug. "Look man, I know this is going to sound like some insane shit, but this dude is Sun Ra. He was supposed to have been blessed by the Spirit in Afrika at the beginning of the slave thing. He's supposed to return to America and lead us to freedom."

"You right man, that is insane." Thug turned to Ra. "That right Ralph?"

"Ra brother, and for the most part, it's true. Our Spirit bore me and nurtured me and has finally sent me here to help you regain your rightful place in the universe."

"No shit!" said Patten Leather. "You a church dude, ain't you? Saintified I bet. Hey yall," he turned to the crowd, "this brother here to save us."

"Save us! Save us! Save us!" the crowd threw up their hands and swayed back and forth.

"How you gon save us blood?"

"I'm here to reveal your true selves. To help you discover your noble beginnings, and realize your choseness."

"Awl, we done heard that black shit before! That ain't in now brother," Vinyl offered.

"But I have wisdom," Ra continued, "that has not been revealed in its true light."

"Whatchu GOT in that robe?" Alligator Shoed stepped back. "A crisis or something?" They burst out laughing again.

A small, dark man, unnoticed til now, climbed out of the buggy and walked over to Ra. He was dressed in cream coloured robes, and if it is possible, he was blacker than Ra. This dark man reached up and whispered something in Ra's ear. His teeth were rotted black. It is said that he is the human manifestation of the Holy Spirit that blessed Ra. He wore a red, black and green belt tied loosely around his middle. This belt represented the highest rank in an ancient Afrikan form of self defense called Gnibbats-and-Gnittuc, otherwise known as cutting and stabbing.

Ra reached under his headpiece and pulled out a cigarette. "You got a light brother?", he asked Alligator. He gave Ra a light. He took a long draw . . . the crowd leaned in.

"Hey man . . . !"

"Blood what's wrong with you . . !"

"What the . . !"

"Say man! No you ain't smoking dope out . . !"

"Yes he is!"

Ra exhaled. "There's nothing wrong with gunja brother. But if anything impacts your life in a negative way, then you have a problem, and you're absolutely correct not to smoke. End of problem."

"You just another crazy nigga! That's all. Cop walk up on yo' badass, and to the jailhouse you go!", Vinyl snorted.

"Brother, you don't understand," Ra smiled. "But I hope to make it all clear," he assured, patting the book that hung from his hip. "This book, this book is the Book of Knowledge. Everything we need is here."

> Another streetcorner preacher
> > trying to reach ya
> We usually smile,
> > and pass on 'long our way
> But since he's so preeet-ty
> > we think we'll just sit here
> 'Sides, he might pass the joint our way

The cornercrooners did a three beat turn, harmonized in four parts, and moved in closer to the story.

"Hold 'Lickin' for me," Ra passed his gnarled stick to the small dark man. Ra unbuttoned the notches and slid the Book out of its leather strappings. He opened it slowly and put his face close to the browned pages. The smells of coconut and jasmine floated out. He closed the Book, turned it over to the binding and pressed a green button. A husky woman's voice spoke:

> ". . . where there is no vision,
> > the people perish . . ."
> "if ye have faith . . . nothing shall be
> impossible unto you . . ."

"Where did that voice come from?"

"How you change your voice like that?"

"Hey Jack, that sounded like Aunt Jemima!"

"That was the Voice of the Book of Knowledge, the voice of our Spirit," Ra answered all their questions.

"Wait a minute! Lemmee see that book," one of the hustlers reached for the book.

"It's for you brother," Ra handed it to him. He turned it over and over.

"Where's the tape recorder?" he asked.

"If there is a tape recorder brother, it's in your head. The Spirit of this Book is your Spirit."

"You the one come flying in here!" Alligator snapped.

"True, but you have the same powers within you."

"Reefer ain't that good!"

"No brother, you do have these powers, but you have neglected them. There is an old Ethiopian proverb, 'if you don't use it, you lose it.' There are strains of God within us all. That is why I'm here, to show you how to revive those powers, but above all, to give you faith."

"I knew it! I just knew it?" A gray haired, squat woman waddled to the center of the crowd. "I knew you were going to say you were God! I knew it! Fool out here just trying to fool yall! All right Mr. God, since you so bad, lessee ya do something. Do something! A miracle or something!" The crowd seconded the woman.

"A miracle?", Ra asked. "Why do you want to see me do something, when you have so much power?"

"Cop-out brother! Cop-out!", someone yelled, and people began to walk away.

"A miracle is commonplace. Life is faith, brothers and sisters. There are no 'miracles' with faith. Everything is always within your grasp."

"Then do something!" a wino yelled.

"When I speak of powers, I'm not speaking of magic, although magic is real. I'm talking about the power of your minds. I'm talking about the practical ability you have to complete any task. Brainpower. Willpower. Collective power. When I say you have the power to free yourselves, I don't mean you're going to make a giant white doll and stick pins in it . . ."

"Watch it!", a West Indian warned.

"No harm brother. But I do mean that if you prepare yourselves spiritually, and physically and mentally, then you'll have all the power you'll need to overcome any and every obstacle."

"Man, I swear you a church dude!"

"Or a civil rights dude," someone added.

The small dark man whispered something in Ra's ear. He walked back to the glowing buggy and climbed in.

Ra walked to the buggy and sat down behind the controls. "I'm going to leave you now. The time is not right." He pulled off and out into the sky, and disappeared in the distance, leaving a rainbow in his wake. But the rainbow stood vertical, on its end, with the bow facing neither heaven nor earth.

Suite for Queen

Oscar Joseph
(1980's)

His whole body shook uncontrollably. Behind him stands a schoolyard and two figures begin to walk his way. He wondered if they were just curious or intent on his harm. It didn't matter. Before they could get to him they had to climb the fence that surrounds the playground. "If they went through them changes, then they'd have me. I won't. I can't stop, not now, not now." DOODLEY DOO, DEE, DEE, DA, BOP!

He could sense the street, his surrounding environment, though he did not consciously see the dog mess, broken glass, and debris that is now a part of any city scene. As an artist he felt that he should always maintain an awareness of his environment, but not today, not now, not here. When he turned the corner a few minutes before, everything seemed smaller, more closed in, even more serene than he imagined it as a child. He knew that it was just his perception because this was the street he played on before he had to leave her. FA RA RA OO DOO!

Still it was all the same to him, just tinier. The houses still stood with their Victorian fronts. The church in the middle of the block separated the continuous progression of high stone steps leading to ornately carved, old and worn doors. At the bottom of those steps either a black iron railing or small stone gargoyles protected the entrances to the basements. High windows overlooked the street on the first floors. TA TA DEE OPP A DOP!

The first thing that he noticed when he turned the corner was that the city did the kids a favor by marking the street for a game of scully. When he was less mature, less worldly, he and/or some of the other kids had to draw the markings for the game in chalk. As an adult, it always took a summoning, almost an internal dare not to look at the window where she used to sit. This was the closest he ever came to a religious reverence—to look at the window where she used to sit and watch over him as he played on these streets. Once a few years ago, he saw her again and he saw that smile he had not seen since he was twelve. OOWEEE! OOOWEE!

Nervousness was what was crowding his insides now. He wondered if she would like it. Will she know what he was about to do? Did she know what his life had been like since she left? He wondered to himself if he was crazy, since he was about to serenade a ghost? He thought of Sonny Rollins who played over and over again on the Brooklyn Bridge. Rollins had just dropped out of the music scene and for years night after night played on that bridge because he felt he hadn't gotten his music right.

But this wasn't a copycat action because before he played here and served his music to a ghost he waited and practiced for years to make sure he had it right, then he showed on this street with his horn. He had made many pilgrimages here but never with his horn. He would stop just to meditate quietly on his life and where he was heading. It was on one of those trips that he saw her. No, he would never have dared to show up here with his horn until now. Unlike Sonny, this would be a one shot deal. This time had to be perfect. Because he wasn't sure if he was exorcising a ghost or saluting a memory, perhaps both. DOOODLE WEE DOODLE WAA!

Not even before live crowds did he feel so much tension. Munich, Brussels, Badden-Badden, Amsterdam, even Caracas, none of those crowds so far away from home had his insides so tied up in knots as this little one night stand in Harlem on an empty street. Will she know? Will she hear? The horn gleamed and sparkled catching the light from the streetlamp as he picked it up from its case. It seemed brighter than ever and once more he felt the heartbeat of that instrument as he lovingly caressed it. It was coming alive as it usually did but this time he felt as if there was a defiance in its touch, almost as if it was saying play me here and now if you dare. He put the mouthpiece on and blew some air into the horn; the valves seemed to stick and not move easily at his touch. He noticed that his mouth was dry and had very little spit. Not even before his first foreign gig in Sao Paulo did his mouth seem so devoid of moisture. The horn seemed so cold, colder than anytime ever in his love/hate/love affair with it. "It's like she's daring me to blow. There is still something inside her that maybe I haven't touched and can't control. Will it come out and attack me now?" SCREE SCREE DOO!

The two figures were directly behind him now, separated by the fence. The only sense of survival in him was just to note that they were there. "Perhaps they're wondering if I'm as nutso as my actions appear." In Harlem, the weak and different tend to die quickly. SCREEDLE SCREEDLY DOO!

It was one of those warm Harlem nights yet there was no life on this street. "Heat sucks people out their homes and makes them at least sit on the stoops if not wander the streets. But this street is deserted except for me, my horn and the two dudes in the schoolyard." TREEDLE TREEDLE TEE DO!

He wondered again if he was crazy. "Did I finally do it and go off? I recall what brought me here to this time and place. Maybe it's unfair to say that one thing can have so much influence in your life. Maybe from the first breath you take on your own dictates when—how—and where you take the next. Maybe it goes on *ad infinitum* until you take that last and final breath. Maybe." CREE CREE DOODLAP!

TWEEDLE CREE DOO WAH!

"Lady is what she wanted to be known as. Lady she was. There was a true love between us. Something that I've never experienced since.

On this block, 130th St., is where she held her court. She was more like a queen. Her friends from the islands would come over to see Ms. Lizabeth. She would entertain them in one of her long formal gowns.

"I rarely saw her in anything but those gowns. Mostly she would sit in that window which I'm facing and . . ." AHH CREE AH OOPA DOO TREE OO SWEE DOO!

It was in the middle of that thought that he suddenly realized that he had his horn and was blowing, playing his tribute to the love he had kept to himself for all these years. She seemed so tall and stately to him as she walked around the house with a slow and deliberate motion that now he realized must have been something akin to arthritis but then, as a little boy, just seemed to him the way someone with regal bearing should move.

The soft tones filled the air as he played the theme of an angel watching over a loved and innocent child. AH AH DOODLE WAH AH AH DOODLE WAH! She would sit and watch. "I believed then as I do now that she would always watch for and over me. I don't know how she did it but I know that she paid for my early lessons on the horn. She made sure that I practiced but she also made sure that I went outside to play and to hang around the kids in the neighborhood." DOOO WAAAH DOO WAAH DOO WAH WAH!

"We will name him Steve after his grandfather." It was something that his mother had always told him. She had no real say over her own son even to his name. It was decided by the "Lady," and the horn player imagined her looking at him while he slept in his crib as she sang a song of life and love to him. "Maybe she smiled and I smiled back as she said, "Oh, what a lovely son you have here. We will call him Steven Claire Anderson after his grandfather.'" And the horn player played that melody as he had heard it a thousand times and as he remembered it a million more in his mind. Now it was out and naked. It was now public. DOOAH DOO AHDOO DO DOOO!

UMP PA UMP PA PA DOOM PA! The beat picked up and the notes became more staccato as he pictured warm summer days and strolling through Mt. Vernon Park on a Sunday afternoon. All members of her court would be there after church and she would have her grandson dressed in his Sunday best to receive them. His manners were always impeccable because he knew that she would not tolerate anything less, and he wanted her to be proud of him.

"Nice day today Ms. Lizbeth, where you going wid dat one?"

"I take Stevie for a walk an' den, maybe if he good, we go to thee Automat."

The horn player continued in his mind as he began translating how he used to play under her long dresses while she wore them. Or how he would climb in her lap and tug at her hair, hug her neck until his mother would admonish him to let the Queen rest. TRREEOO TRREEOO DOO!

"The boy, he does nothing wrong. Go see to your husband."

CREEE OP CREEE DOODLE LO CREE LO! Then the walks in the park ended. The trips to downtown to eat the beans and franks at the Automat were no longer. Having someone watch out for you, pay special attention to you and you almost ignore that person because you're so wrapped in play and you knew you were safe, became that that was suddenly missed. FEE O FEE OO BALOO!

Harmony is no longer part of the security in life. SPLEE DUP! Not because of anything you did but because of things that others say is too hard for you to understand and does not really concern you. EEE OOOP EEE! But it does concern you because TEREEE! for the first time what you knew would always be there is now no TREEEO TREEEO TREEEO! longer.

The horn player begins to feel a loosening in his stomach that he had never experienced. There had been moments when he told himself that he could really feel what he was playing, but nothing like this, this new sense of himself made him play. He did not feel in total control of his instrument or music. It was now being taken out of his sphere.

It took him a long time to accept the fact that the Queen would no longer be a part of his daily life. At age eight, his mother moved to Connecticut, leaving the Queen and his father. Within a couple of years she had remarried and settled down to life in Bridgeport. For the next few years the young boy saw his Lady on special occasions and trips and he always missed her. For a few hours there was complete peace and freedom that he had never known since and it existed because he was in her presence. But the delight he had whenever they did meet came through the horn with a phrasing and tone he never knew he was capable of. AHTWIDDLE FROO AHTWIDDLE A FROO!

Tears flowed freely down the cheeks of the horn player as his tribute to the "Lady" tumbled out into the night.

SCREEE EEE AH SCREE OOP SCREE! The memory of that night became a vivid experience for him. CREEOO CREEEOO AH SCREEE! It was only a week away from Christmas and . . . "Steve, Steve get up." The floor and house were bitterly cold and the darkness in his room was accented by the luminous dial on his alarm clock that read four something, and he realized that he was not late for school but up too early in the morning. TOOODLE LOO TOODLE LO TODLE LO! He saw his father and knew that at the age of twelve he was entering a new phase OOOOH EEEE AHH OOOO! in his life.

Twelve and he was lost. That was when he took his horn seriously and began to play out of some comfort to himself and in hopes of maybe one day being able to dedicate some effort of his to her. The notes he played now were not as sharp and clear. He could feel a tentativeness in his playing that had not existed for some time. Yet he knew that he was playing the best he had ever played. Scales, scales up and down, up and down, they fought him until he became the master of them. Up and down, up and down he played them until his jaws and lips no longer felt as if they belonged to him. Up and down, up and down he played them until his fingers no longer required thought as to which keys they were to be placed over and how. Up and down, up and down he played until he was in a school for gifted children. Up and down, up and down the scales until at age nineteen he was on the road with a band playing what he felt was music. First around home, then in the south and then Canada, then South America and Europe. He played those scales until he thought he could do them in his sleep. And he did for a long while.

The sleep of drugs, that tells you you're doing it when all you're doing is sleeping. His brains fried, his feelings locked safely inside, he would practice those scales in front of crowds around the world and called it music. Whenever he came back to the states or when he was in or near New York, he made his pilgrimage to this spot to look at that window and remember her. But he never brought his horn until now.

DOOODLE LOO DOOODLE SCREEE! At age twenty-five on his way to Spain to play in a night club for servicemen, he stopped here on this spot one night to pay his homage and he saw her. Fear gripped him just as it was now coming out of his horn. She was sitting in the window and he could tell that she was wearing her lavender gown. Then he saw her smile and stand and hold out her arms to him as if she was going to hold him once more. Then a peace settled over him FREEE FREEE OOO! that he remembered when he was a child in a park on a Sunday afternoon. FREEEE AHHH FREEE OOOOO TERTERTREE!

The horn player did not go on that trip. Instead, the next day he found help to bring him out of his drug induced world. He began to use his horn not as an escape but as a companion. FREEEOOO FREEEOOO AHHH TREEE! His horn became a friend and not a crutch to lean on. The more he played, the more he realized there was to his newfound friend. It no longer was just scales but a relationship based on trust. He no longer mastered but co-existed with the knowledge that he had something to give and to learn whenever he and the horn TOOODLOO TEEE DOO LOOOP TOOODLOOLOO TEEE DOOOLOOOP! came together.

Now at thirty-five there was no longer a peaceful co-existence between them. They were one, and his scales were no longer just that: they became an expression of a personal experience. Tonight, tonight on a Harlem street on a very warm night he finally let go of himself and played his "Suite For A Queen".

DOODLEY DOO, DEE, DEE, DA, BOP!
FA RA RA OO DOO!
TA TA DEE OPP A DOP!
OOWEEE! OOOWEE!
DOOODLE WEE DOODLE WAA!
 SCREE SCREE DOO!
SCREEDLE SCREEDLY DOO!
 TREEDLE TREEDLE TEE DO!
CREE CREE DOODLAP!
 TWEEDLE CREE DOO WAH!
AHH CREE AH OOPA DOO TREE OO SWEE DOO!
 AH AH DOODLE WAH AH AH DOODLE WAH!
 DOOO WAAAH DOO WAAH DOO WAH WAH!

DOOAH DOO AHDOO DO DOOO!
UMP PA UMP PA PA DOOM PA!
TRREEEOO TRREEOO DOO!
CREEE OP CREEE DOODLE LO CREE LO!
FEE O FEE OO BALOO!
SPLEE DUP!
EEE OOOP EEE!
TEREEE!
TREEEO TREEEO TREEEO!
AHTWIDDLE FROO AHTWIDDLE A FROO!
SCREE EEE AH SCREE OOP SCREE!
CREEOO CREEEEOO AH SCREEE!
TOOODLE LOO TOODLE LO TODLE LO!
DOOODLE LOO DOOODLE SCREEE!
FREE FREE OOO!
FREEEE AHHH FREEE OOOOO TERTERTREE!
FREEEOOO FREEOOO AHHH TREEE!
FREEEOOO FREEOOO AHHH TREEE!
TOOODLOO TEEE DOO LOOOP TOOODLOOLOO TEEE
DOOOLOOOP!

The horn player had almost packed the instrument before he realized that he was being applauded. He hadn't known that there was anyone on the street with him. Then he remembered the schoolyard and saw that they were shaking the fence in salute to his efforts. The block was crowded with people on their steps or hanging out windows, and it seemed that all were either applauding or whistling and clamoring for more. "It wasn't the heat this time; it was us." In an unconscious gesture he held the horn in the air with one hand and gave a salute, then put it safely back in its case. The joints in his knees cracked as he started to wearily walk off. He dared not look at the window as he took his leave of the street.

"Wait, wait! Young man wait!" He tried to ignore the plea and would not acknowledge that he heard it until he felt a firm grip on his arm.

"You are him aren't you? I mean her son? No, you are her grandson right? Ms. Lizbeth's boy Steve?"

He turned to see an old man wearing baggy pants held up by suspenders with no shirt and a pair of worn house shoes on.

"Yes, I'm Steve." He was surprised at the strength in the old man's grip as he tried to keep moving.

"I thought so. You don't remember me do you? I'm Mr. Lee and I live just two doors down from you when you were here."

"Yes," he lied, "yes I remember you, sir, but I have to go now."

"I thought so," the old man insisted. "I thought so. You know, Stevie, once or twice I knew that it was you who would stand here and stare at that window. I—I started to come over too and say something but you always looked as if you were not here and maybe didn't want to be bothered. That thing you just did. Somehow, I know maybe it may sound like a silly old man to you, but Ms. Lizbeth came to mind and I just knew that for sure it was you. She would be so proud of you as she always was. You sound good, boy, you sound good."

"Thank you." Then inadvertantly he looked at the window. He half expected to see her standing and clapping too. But she wasn't there and he felt relieved.

"She was a lady, our, uh, your Ms. Lizbeth. It's been over twenty years but sometimes even today I think of her. There's a couple of us old folks left on this block that still 'members her. She was a real lady."

The horn player walked off that block knowing that he had closed one chapter and opened another in his life.

Mr. Gooden's House

Sandra Jackson-Opoku
(1986)

MENDEZ: Okay. This deposition taken on this 12th day of August, 1987, at the law offices of Rohm, Lipsholtz, and Barnes, of Mary Lee Wright . . .

ELLIS: That's Merilee.

MENDEZ: Correction. Merilee Wright, probate case 2112-6. Now. Are you comfortable, Mrs. Wright? Just relax and I'll be asking you a few questions.

ELLIS: Is she going to be copying down everything I say? All on that machine there?

MENDEZ: Yes, Mrs. Wright.

ELLIS: Well, I hope I don't talk too fast for her. People always tell me I talk real fast. I'll try to slow down a little bit.

MENDEZ: That won't be necessary. Just speak at your normal speed.

ELLIS: Well, alright then. The way I feel about it is this. I gave Mr. Gooden the best years of my life, and I gave him the best years of his life. I made that man's last days here the happiest ones he ever had. He used to tell me, say, "Miss Mella, you sure do know how to make an old man happy."

MENDEZ: Hold on, hold on. We seem to be getting ahead of ourselves. Now, I'll be the one asking you questions, and you will answer them to the best of your ability. Do you understand?

ELLIS: Well, hey. Ask me anything you want to know. I ain't got no secrets.

MENDEZ: We'll start with your name, then. Can you give your full legal name and your date of birth?

ELLIS: Merilee Ellis. And I was born on January 15, same as Martin Luther King. January 15, 1949.

MENDEZ: Ellis is your last name? Not Wright?

ELLIS: I go by my maiden name.

MENDEZ: Fair enough. May we amend the record to show that Merilee Wright is more commonly known as Merilee Ellis?

(Transcription stopped. Record amended)

MENDEZ: Now what is this name you say Mr. Gooden called you. Mella?

ELLIS: Well, that is just a name people give me. Years back they used to call me "Mellow Yellow," me being so light and all. It's just something folks call me.

MENDEZ: Like a nickname?

ELLIS: A nickname. But like I was saying. Mr. Gooden meant me to have that house. I don't care what Gina and them have to say about it. That was Mr. Gooden's house. And he told me time and again, "Mella, when I'm gone I want you to have this place and everything in it. It's not much but it's yours."

MENDEZ: Ms. Ellis, will you let me ask the questions?

ELLIS: Well, excuse me.

MENDEZ: Can you tell me how long you've known, or how long you knew Joseph Gooden?

ELLIS: Let's see. This September will make seven years me and Mr. Gooden been living together. But really, we had hooked up almost a year before that. So I guess it's eight years.

MENDEZ: I notice you refer to him as Mr. Gooden. Didn't you call him by his first name at all?

ELLIS: Well, no. It's a kind of funny thing. See, he had the same name as my ex-husband. Joseph. When I met him, I told him, "I sure can't call you that name if we going to get along. My ex-husband just ruined that name for me." So he say, "But you got to call me something." I say, "Why don't I just call you Mr. Gooden and let it be like that." He say, "That suits me. Just as long as you call me." And that's the way it went.

MENDEZ: How did you meet Joseph Gooden?

ELLIS: Oh, Lord. Honey, that was something else. See I was at Sears. You know the one on 79th? I was in the washroom, just coming out the toilet when this man comes in there. Come running in there. And I said to myself, Lord don't let me get raped up in here. So, honey, he ran up in the toilet, just talking away. Didn't even bother to close the door. "Oh, Miss. I sure hate to barge in on you like this. But this here is an emergency. When you got to go, you got to go."

Then I got mad. Man standing in the Ladies Room doing his business and chit-chatting. I liked to curse him out. "You sure got your nerve, mister. I could have been in here naked or anything. Come running in here on me. I got a mind to call Security on you."

He come running out looking nervous, zipping his self up. "Now, Miss. You know I'm sorry. What can I do to make it up to you?" Then he asked me what I come up to Sears to buy, and I told him an ironing board. So he said, "My treat." And do you know the man went and bought me an ironing board?

We laughed about that for years. Anytime Mr. Gooden want to get on my good side he offer to buy me an ironing board.

MENDEZ: You say that you and Mr. Gooden lived together for seven years. Yet you never married.

ELLIS: Well, it wasn't for him not asking me. Mr. Gooden was always on me to marry him. Wouldn't leave me alone about it. He must have asked me a hundred times.

MENDEZ: And why didn't you?

ELLIS: Now, I ain't come up here to answer no stupid questions. You know good and well why I never married to him.

MENDEZ: Just answer the question, if you please.

ELLIS: Me and Mr. Gooden ain't never married because I already was married and never got a divorce. Okay? It's just something I always meant to do and never did do. And then it was too late.

MENDEZ: So legally, you are still married to your husband. And how long have you been estranged?

ELLIS: Who?

MENDEZ: How long have you been apart?

ELLIS: We wasn't hardly together to begin with. I was just married for a minute it seems like and then it was over. I swear, I haven't seen the man in 15 years.

MENDEZ: How did you meet?

ELLIS: Who, Joe? Well, right in front of my house. My grandmother's house, really. She raised me up, me and my brother and some cousins of mine over in the Ida B. Wells Homes. You know, the projects over on Pershing Road?

MENDEZ: Your grandmother reared you? What about your mother?

ELLIS: Oh, she was around now and then. Mamma was totally out there. She did her own thing.

MENDEZ: What do you mean by that?

ELLIS: Big Momma, that's my grandmother, she was church. Curtina, that's my mother, she was street. You know. Always running some kind of game, whether it was policies or hot property or the con. That was Curtina. But like I said, Big Momma raised me up.

MENDEZ: And how long did you live with her?

ELLIS: Up until I got married, I was about seventeen. Oh, you want to know how it happened. Okay, I was sitting on my front step sucking on a strawberry snow cone. I always did like me something sweet. That's why my teeth so bad now. It was just hot that day and I was sitting outside trying to catch a little breeze. Here come this little man riding by on a bicycle and he shout to me, "Evening, sister." So I say, "Evening yourself." Next thing I know he turn around and ride back again. He stop and ask me, "Do you know the Lord, sister?" And I say, "Naw, but maybe you can introduce me."

I didn't really mean nothing by it. Just young and full of sass. This man, Joe Wright, he a short, skinny dude. Hair cut real short, and you know mens was into wearing them big naturals then. He was an old-fashioned man, just the kind that Big Momma liked. He got in good with her. He used to come ask her to let me go to Bible Study, or revival, or whatnot. Would ask her, not me. Just like she the one he trying to court. Big Momma just kind of pushed me at him. Thought if I couldn't get religion at least I could marry it. She wouldn't have been so particular about it if she had known the boy was pushing forty. He didn't look it, though. Always did have a young look about him, riding around on that little raggedy bicycle.

MENDEZ: So your husband was, would he have been 23 years older than you?

ELLIS: Was, and still is, I guess.

MENDEZ: And what led to your break up?

ELLIS: You getting mighty personal here, ain't you, Miss?

MENDEZ: Ms. Ellis, these are questions that I have to ask. Now, Mr. Grenshaw promised your full cooperation.

ELLIS: I came here to say my piece. I didn't come here to sit up and answer a bunch of nosey-ass questions. I don't give a damn, Mr. Grenshaw. This don't make no sense.

GRENSHAW: Excuse me, Toni. Can I have a few moments alone with my client?

(Break in testimony. Transcription resumed)

MENDEZ: Bear with me, Ms. Ellis. The sooner we get this over with, the sooner we can all go home. Now please answer the question. What caused you and your estranged husband to separate?

ELLIS: We was just two different people. Joe was what folks called a jackleg preacher. He pumped gas for a living and sang gospel sometimes with a little quartet. And he preached on Sundays, didn't have no regular church. He just went all over, church to church. He come from sanctified folks, real strict. You wasn't supposed to drink, you wasn't supposed to dance. You couldn't wear no makeup and you had to keep yourself all covered up, nothing showing. I was 18 years old and I felt like an old lady, sitting up there in those old mammy-made dresses. I couldn't have no fun.

MENDEZ: So you left him because of religious differences.

ELLIS: Well, yes and no. Really, Joe had put me out. He was always accusing me of stepping out on him.

MENDEZ: Your husband thought you were seeing other men. Were there other men?

ELLIS: I had acquaintances, yes. I mean, I was 18 years old and married to a dude who wouldn't even take me out for a hot dog. What was I supposed to do? Sit up and rot?

MENDEZ: And what about children?

ELLIS: What about them?

MENDEZ: You and your husband had children.

ELLIS: One little boy, name of John.

MENDEZ: Can you tell me about that?

ELLIS: Ain't nothing to tell. Joe name the boy, "John The Baptist Wright." Can you believe that? He was suppose to be premature. Anyway, that's the story Joe put out. Tell you the truth, I was pregnant when we got married but Joe didn't never tell nobody. I guess he didn't want the church folks to know we'd been screwing. Anyway, I had the baby and when I left, his daddy kept him.

MENDEZ: Why?

ELLIS: I just couldn't handle no baby. All that crying, those shitty diapers. Not a minute to myself. I didn't want to have the baby to begin with, okay? You know how birth control was back then. It wasn't shit. And those old rubbers, I wouldn't be surprised if Joe sat up and poked holes in them. He was always on the case about how bad he wanted a baby and how his first two wives couldn't give him one. So he was sure enough glad when he found out he was getting ready to be a daddy.

MENDEZ: Ms. Ellis, did you love your son?

ELLIS: Of course, I loved him. What kind of mother wouldn't love her own child?

MENDEZ: Then why did you leave him?

ELLIS: I just couldn't keep him. I was 19 years old. I was in the streets. I just couldn't give him a home life.

MENDEZ: What did you do for a living?

ELLIS: What didn't I do? I was on aid sometime. Worked in a liquor store. Was a crossing guard. A bar waitress. Shake dancer. That kind of thing.

MENDEZ: Did your receive money from men during this time?

ELLIS: Look. Why don't you just come out and say it. I know what Gina and them been telling you and it's a god-damned, chicken-shit lie.

MENDEZ: Please don't use profanity.

ELLIS: I never been a whore in my life. Any bitch that tell you different is a liar and the truth ain't in her.

MENDEZ: But is it true that you were accepting money from men?

ELLIS: I've had men spend money on me. Haven't you? That jewelry and clothes you got on, I know they cost you some money. You or somebody else.

MENDEZ: Who pays for my clothing is not the issue here, Ms. Ellis.

ELLIS: I'm just trying to make a point. You a good-looking chick, just like I was. Men liked me. They called me Mellow Yellow. I was young and had all my teeth and a good grade of hair. This ain't no jerri curl here, honey. This is the real thing. So what if men wanted to spend some cash on me, show me a good time. What's wrong with that?

MENDEZ: How many?

ELLIS: What the hell. Excuse me, but this is some shit. How I'm supposed to know how many men? You think I sat up and counted them?

MENDEZ: More than ten? More than twenty?

ELLIS: I told you I don't know. I couldn't even guess. Maybe more than ten, maybe more than fifty. But I will tell you this. Since I been with Mr. Gooden there hasn't been anyone else but him. And that's the truth. As far as I'm concerned I was his wife and he was my husband.

MENDEZ: Is that so? Well, tell me this, Ms. Ellis. Are you acquainted with a Mr. Wookie Hughes?

ELLIS: Honey, hush. You know that man gave his self that name after that old thing in the movie. You know. That big, shaggy, ugly thing. Look just like him, too. Yes. I've known Wookie since grade school when folks called him Wishes.

MENDEZ: Wishes?

ELLIS: And in high school they called him Alley. Alloysius was his real name. It's funny how a name can mess you up. That's probably how he turned out like he did. His mamma stuck him with that sissy-ass name and he was always fighting somebody about it. I know how it is to have an odd name. Kids was always following up behind me, singing, "Merrily we roll along."

MENDEZ: Are you aware of what kind of work he did?

ELLIS: Wookie Hughes ain't never done a lick of work in his life. He was a hustler, a gambler, a dope man.

MENDEZ: A pimp?

ELLIS: I wouldn't be surprised.

MENDEZ: And he was one of your acquaintances.

ELLIS: Look, girl. I know all kinds of peoples. Doctors, lawyers, Indian chiefs. If I go with a baker, do that make me a biscuit? Besides, Wookie Hughes is dead as a doorknob. Been dead. So what's the deal?

MENDEZ: Ms. Ellis, when is the last time you've seen your son?

ELLIS: Look, I don't get it. Why do you want to talk about the boy? The boy don't have nothing to do with it.

GRENSHAW: Just answer her question, Merilee.

ELLIS: We had him for awhile. It was about six, seven years ago. The boy was 12.

MENDEZ: And he stayed with the two of you? For how long?

ELLIS: It wasn't too long. Things just didn't go right. See, it happened one day I was over on the West Side. A girl I used to know say, "Mella, you better go see about your son. Joe can't hardly take care of him." I come to find out that old holy-roller had got the bottle near about as bad as he had religion. Same man that used to crucify me for taking a drink every now and then. He was in detox. So I went and got the boy and took him with me. I thought, well I got a man now. Maybe I could make a home for him.

MENDEZ: And what went wrong?

ELLIS: Mr. Gooden and Johnny just did not take to each other. You see, Mr. Gooden had already raised up his family. He had girls too. And girls is easier to raise than boys. He wasn't the youngest man, either. It was hard on him. Johnny's funky socks laying all over the place. Johnny's funky self all over the place. The boy didn't want to be chastised either. "You ain't my Daddy. You can't whip me." He sassed Mr. Gooden one time and Mr. Gooden liked to broke his neck. I tried to be a mother for that boy. I really tried. But he was too mannish. I couldn't keep him.

MENDEZ: And where is he now?

ELLIS: With his Daddy, I guess.

MENDEZ: You guess? A young boy with his alcoholic father?

ELLIS: Look, Miss. The boy is fine. He's the head of his basketball team at school and he's just as tall and good-looking as he can be. He's doing alright. He's like me. A fighter.

MENDEZ: How do you know that? Are you in touch?

ELLIS: Lord, have mercy. I'm sorry I brought this up. I keeps my eye on him, okay? I go to the games sometimes. I sit real far in back, so he can't see me. But I just watches him. He looks more like me than I look like myself. Hey, it hurts my heart that I couldn't keep him. Don't a day pass by when I don't wonder about him, and worry about him, and pray that he makes it. But you don't know how it is. You got any kids?

MENDEZ: No, I don't.

ELLIS: No, I didn't think so. But you try to see it my way. I gave up my freedom before I even knew what it was. First when I wasn't but 17 years old to an old freak hiding behind a bible. Then when I was 18, I had a baby. Johnny shouldn't have never been born. I'm like my mamma that way. I just wasn't made for no kids.

     I loved him well enough. I still do. But I swear, Miss. I sometimes used to walk around that stinky little place we lived in and that boy would just be hanging on my leg while I walked. Just hanging. I couldn't have nobody hanging on me. I felt like I was trying to keep my head out the water and this boy was a weight steady dragging me down.

     Anyway, he loved his old Daddy. He look like me, but he was his Daddy's child. Joe would be practicing his sermons around the house, preaching up and down the floors. "Sinners going to burn on Satan's barbecue pit." That kind of shit. And little Johnny couldn't hardly walk, less more talk. But he'd be following up behind Joe, just a preaching as he go. I was just something to hang onto when Joe wasn't around. That boy sure loved his old Daddy.

MENDEZ: Do you have any idea why Joseph Gooden didn't leave a will?

ELLIS: I don't know, Miss. Lord knows I don't. But Mr. Gooden meant for me to have that house, I can guarantee you that. When I come to live with Mr. Gooden he had the place jammed with dusty old tore-up furniture and whatnot. Didn't have but one or two dishes and looked like it hadn't seen a good cleaning since Gina and Coretta left home. I made that place a home for Mr. Gooden. And I made me a home.

     I ain't even forty and I've lived in every back alley, every little piss hole in every corner of this city. That place been my home for seven years. Mr. Gooden in the ground now. That's all I got left of us. You a woman, Miss. You ought to understand that.

MENDEZ: Regina Mathers and Coretta Gooden are women, too. You might consider their reluctance to give up the home they grew up in to a woman their father never even married. That home is the only thing they have left of their father.

ELLIS: Those womens is young womens. They got they educations, they got good jobs and good money. Gina is married into that family, those Mathers Funeral Home folks. You know that's some money. All I got is that house and Mr. Gooden's memory.

MENDEZ: That will be all, Ms. Ellis. Thank you for your time.

ELLIS: Hey, this is my story. I'm going to tell it now.

     I gave him eight good years and neither one of those girls was no where around. And I'll tell you this. When Mr. Gooden got so sick and he wasn't himself no more, I cleaned his natural ass. That's right. Cleaned his ass just like he was a baby. And neither Gina or Coretta showed they black ass around they precious house, less more their precious Daddy. Didn't bring him so much as a get well card. And when he died wouldn't let me sit in my rightful place as the widow. Say I wasn't family.

But I was his family and he was mine. As God is my witness, I gave up my son for that man. Mr. Gooden meant for me to have that house. And I mean to keep it. You tell Gina and Coretta this one thing. That there is my house. I ain't about to be moved.

Mama Just Didn't Like Thunder

George Leon Lowe
(1985)

Now so that you don't misunderstand why Mama didn't like thunder: Mama didn't like snakes (the kind that walk or crawl), bees, frogs, gnats, mosquitoes, cold weather, hot weather, Saturday night, cussing, whiskey, smoking, gambling, crows, red colored cars, loud talking, and children acting too grown up. Oh! I almost forgot, Mama didn't like lightning. And she really didn't like Uncle Otha's third new young wife!

Mama said Uncle Otha was a marrying fool, and a cradle robber. Uncle Otha had waited late to get married. His first wife was 24 years old and ten years younger than him. He left her after two years. His second wife was 20 years old and they stayed together five years before she left him. She went to Chicago on Easter Sunday right after church and he never heard from her again, except for the divorce papers mailed to him by her lawyer.

The day Uncle Otha received the papers in the mail he came by to visit us. Daddy had already warned us that we should not bother Uncle Otha because he was not feeling well. James and I didn't know what divorce meant, but we knew that it had to be pretty bad if it stopped Uncle Otha from laughing.

We were watching out of the window as Uncle Otha drove up. And sure enough he really looked sad as he got out, walked up the drive way, patted Tex, and came right up to the door. Daddy opened it for him before he could knock. He walked in and kind of tried to smile as he picked us up for his usual kiss and hug. But we could both see he was feeling kind of down.

We began to feel bad too as he and Daddy walked into the living room and started talking real quiet like. They had been talking for about five minutes when Mama came in and asked Uncle Otha how he was feeling. Uncle Otha said that things were pretty bad and he just didn't know what he was going to do. Mama said she understood but she had found something to help him get over it. Mama kissed him on the cheek and walked over to the record player. The next thing we heard was Jimmy Reed singing, "BRIGHT LIGHTS, BIG CITY, GONE TO MY BABY'S HEAD"!

Daddy almost fell off the couch laughing as Uncle Otha jumped straight up out of his chair and yelled, "Mildred you ought to be ashame of

209

yourself!" Mama just smiled and said, "I told you about them fast young women." By this time Daddy was laughing so hard he had to leave the room. James and I were rolling on the floor; we didn't know all of the story, but we knew it had to be funny if Daddy was laughing like that!

Mama sat down on the couch as Daddy came back into the room. Mama was laughing on one side of the couch and Daddy was falling out on the other. Uncle Otha just sat back down in his chair and tried to keep from laughing. Finally he said, "Mildred you got me this time," and all three of them waved at each other and began laughing as they described the look on Uncle Otha's face when Mama put the record on. Uncle Otha was feeling much better now. In fact he recovered so well that in seven months he was married again!

Daddy said that all of Uncle Otha's wives were pretty women. But that his third wife, who was only eighteen years old, was the best looking of them all. Uncle Otha would pat his stomach and say, "Pretty ain't good enough; if they can't cook, they got to go!" Then Daddy would slap the table and they would both rock back and forth with laughter. James and I would laugh too, but it was a long time before we understood all of the meaning of that one. Mama would just shake her head, and tell Uncle Otha he ought to be ashamed of himself, and that he should try marrying a woman his own age. And Uncle Otha would say, "I don't need nobody to swap Ben-Gay with!" Mama would laugh too and say he was enough to try the patience of Job.

Uncle Otha would keep on telling jokes until it was time for him to go. He would pick James and me up at the same time and kiss us goodbye, go over to Mama and kiss her as she tried to push him away, and burst into a big smile as he and Daddy walked out of the door. Mama, Daddy, Uncle Otha and us were real good friends.

The house was mostly quiet until he came around. Even old Tex liked to see Uncle Otha. He would start barking as soon as he caught wind of him, and we could tell by his bark who was coming. Uncle Otha would stop to pet Tex, and carry on a full conversation with him as though he was a grown man. Tex would just smile with delight as Uncle Otha called him a biscuit hound and told him the only thing he was good for was tracking down a day-old biscuit. Tex would bark three times at that one as tho he really understood the joke. Mama said that Tex and Uncle Otha understood each other so well because they were the same kind.

It didn't rain all of the time in East Georgia, but when it did rain, it made up for the times it didn't! I mean sometime it rained forty days and forty nights in one hour. Uncle Otha said the person who wrote "Didn't It Rain Children" must have lived in East Georgia. He said one year it rained so hard, the fish came out of the river and knocked on his door to come inside, and ground hogs had to climb trees, earth worms grew wings, and all of the local birds flew off to Oklahoma. Mama laughed and said he was the biggest story teller south of Atlanta and that he had better always keep his sense of humor, because he was going to need it when he shook hands with the Devil!

But Uncle Otha told Mama she didn't know about how bad it

rained because she left and went to Pittsburgh to get away from it. Mama admitted it really did rain hard that year, but it was too cold up north and she came back home after three months of visiting her children and their families. Uncle Otha said Mama came back home because she missed the thunder. Daddy and James and I fell out laughing. But Mama didn't think it was funny at all. She made us go to bed early, and put Daddy and Uncle Otha out of the house. Mama did not believe in joking about thunder!

Daddy use to say that Mama could hear thunder a hundred miles away even when she was a little girl. He says that Mama would stop playing and run into the house while the sun was still shining and there was not a single cloud in the sky. But in East Georgia, clear skies didn't mean it was not going to rain. In fact you could oftentime smell the rain when there was not a cloud for miles around.

Everybody knew that Mama didn't like thunder! She said that she didn't mind the rain as long as it did not thunder. Well, rain in East Georgia without lightning and thunder was about as rare as a catfish without whiskers, or a preacher who didn't like fried chicken. And so Mama never took any chances. When it rained she went inside the house, pulled down all the shades, closed the windows, the doors to all the rooms, turned off the radio and television, and waited for the thunder.

You had to be quiet and sit still if you was in the room with her, as she rocked while singing old spirituals until the storm had passed. And only when the echo of the distant thunder could be heard rolling far away as the dancing lightning lit up the darkened sky, would she get up, peek out of the window, say a little prayer to her Jesus for keeping her family safe, and finish whatever it was she was doing before the thunder came. But no matter how bad the storm and loud the thunder, she would never call it by name or ask that it go away!

It was something mysterious between Mama and the Thunder. She never tried to scare Daddy or us; it was her private thing, something we did not understand. You could go into another room and do whatever you wanted, as long as you didn't come into the room where she was, and not respect her ritual.

Most of the time James (who was a year younger than me) and I would leave her alone. We were both what Uncle Otha called her change of life children; there was ten years between me and the next oldest child. But sometime we would stay with her and sit still, watching her and wondering why she didn't like the thunder. I remember one time when I was about six years old, I stayed in the room with her during a real long storm. It had been going on for about two hours. Finally I got tired and got up and walked over to the window and peeked outside. The next thing I saw was a blinding flash of pain as Mama's open hand had met the middle of my behind. I started to cry but she said hush! And I stood there with a part of the storm flooding down my face. I walked over and lay across her lap until the storm had passed.

Mama got up and carried me in her arms over to the window and we peeked out. The lightning was flashing way off into the hills, and in the dying rush of winds you could hear the deep echo of the fading thunder, rolling back and forth in the distance. Mama whispered to me, "They calling names, they calling names, that's why, they matching up faces. They see with the lightning, that's why you have to be still, that's why you have to keep quiet. They calling somebody's name. And when they find you, they take you with them, way across the sea."

Her mother and grandmother had told her that same story many years ago. It had been passed down through the generations, through the centuries. I rested my head on Mama's shoulder and whispered I was sorry. Mama put me down and told me to go and play. The storm was over and James and I went out to catch worms and play in the puddles. I looked up at the opening bright high Georgia sky; I could still hear the thunder.

It was many years later when I sat in Mama's old chair rocking and listening to the thunder. Trying to remember all of the things Mama had said. Trying to bring back some of the memories of Daddy and Uncle Otha. Listening to the walls of the old house as they talked between themselves and to me.

I was trying hard to hear the Thunder rolling off into the hills. Straining so hard to hear the voices whispering to me of times gone, of time before time. I heard the soft deep roar of the way off Thunder; the story began to unfold before me. I could feel the tears forming. Mama had said that they were taking names. The story had been told by her Mother and her Mother's Mother. It had been handed down from Mothers in Africa and made its way across the long deep Middle Passage.

The hiding at hearing the loud noise. It was families, men, women, children, babies, hiding from the slave traders. The Lightning; the lightning was the lanterns, the torches, they used to stage raids at night on the unsuspecting villages. The Thunder; the thunder was the guns they used to capture and kill. And the Rain; the rain was the blood and tears, the blood and tears of the suffering.

Mama used to sing, "Swing Low, Sweet Chariot, Coming For To Carry Me Home."

That's why Mama didn't like the Thunder!

The Phone

Barbara Cochran
(1987)

Johnson picked up the phone after the first ring.

"Hello," he said.

"Hello, hello."

He pushed the receiver back into its cradle hard, while mumbling to himself. The red numbers from the clock glared at him. It was 3:30 A.M.

His eyes wandered slowly over to Mildred. She was so still. Her breaths moving in and out rhythmically—she acted as if she hadn't heard the phone at all. He reached for her, only wanting to pull her closer. Yet, the hand stopped mid air; she would never be able to get back to sleep. He rolled over and forced his eyes closed.

"It's gotta be day by now," he said, but knowing by some inner clock that only five minutes had passed. It was easy to push his legs out from under the covers. But he struggled silently to free his torso and not wake Mildred. The covers were like snakes, strangling him. Indiana Jones creeped into his mind. He'd seen that movie and all of those snakes. You had to get loose fast or you were dead meat. He forced himself to relax and gently unwound the covers—beads of perspiration were beginning to form along the bridge of his nose.

He sat on the edge of the bed—sank his toes deep into the thick carpet. At least the house is warm, he thought. In below zero weather, who needed to come home to a cold house. He looked approvingly around the room. Mildred kept a nice house. The lace curtains and ruffled pillows she placed around their bedroom were pretty to look at. His mother had always said, "Son, you got you a fine woman there—she's gonna make a good home for you." Johnson believed his mother then, and even now . . . 10 years later.

Tip-toeing cautiously, he opened the door to Johnny's room. His son lay sprawled across the bed, the covers on the floor. Johnson picked up the thick hand-woven blanket Mildred had made and placed it gently over his son's small frame. He's little for eight, but I was the same way—give that boy two years and he'll catch up. He stepped on a creaky floor board as he eased his way out. "Damn, I meant to fix that thing years ago." He crept stealthily into Jennifer's room. The soft warm, red glow from the night light cast a surreal quality around the room. At five, Jennifer still saw monsters in the dark. That round little face with soft brown hair crushed against the pillow brought visions of what angels must look like into Johnson's head. You could see one dimple even when she didn't smile. Her blanket was identical to Johnny's except for the bright yellow color. She lay snuggling its soft folds as if she didn't have a care in the world. Johnson touched her cheek softly and walked from the room.

The next logical step, he reasoned, was the refrigerator. Mildred always fussed at him for eating in the middle of the night. He had often tried to break the habit, but when he couldn't sleep, he ate. It was that simple. His stiff fingers fumbled with the last buttons of his shirt. Why fight it.

He made a big turkey sandwich, thick with lettuce and tomatoes—plenty of mayonnaise, and pickles. Then sat down at the kitchen table.

Johnson startled himself when he awakened. "What am I doing in this damn chair," he said out loud. There was an empty plate in front of him—he couldn't remember what had been on it. And like a shallow pond, shaking it only made things muddier.

"Honey, what are you doing up so early," Mildred said, as she came into the kitchen, tying the belt on her robe and patting her short afro into place. "It's only 6:00—you don't go to work today." Johnson stared at her with eyes unmoving. His mind raced as he tried to find something to say. He looked at her as you would a stranger.

Her big eyes grew wide.

"Oh, babe," he said finally, "I just wanted . . . ," he glanced at the plate, "a little something to eat. He finished lamely. "Oh, you should have woke me up. I would have made your breakfast." "I know, but your breathing sounded so, so steady. Remember when I played drums and kept the base. I held the rhythm—kept everything together. Your breathing was like that. And I didn't want it to end."

Mildred just stood there—her mouth wide open. "Where did all that come from?" A smile played at the corner of her mouth, but her eyes looked serious.

"Are you alright, Johnson?"

"Yeah Babe," I just want to go out for awhile, "could you get my coat."

"Your coat, but where are you going this early?"

"Just get my coat," he said through clenched teeth. The muscles in his neck tensed. He could feel his temples throbbing. Mildred backed slowly from the room. Johnson hurriedly put on his coat and left the kitchen. He felt awkward as he fumbled with the car door. For all the blood that rushed so quickly to his head, his hands were numb. The joints were stiff and cold, like they were bound by some invisible barrier. He flexed them out, then in. It was a feeble attempt to make the blood flow to the tips of his fingers. He finally stumbled into the car and fell heavily upon the seat, belching involuntarily as air freed itself from his lungs. He lay quietly for a few seconds listening to the sound of sleet hitting the roof—a pelting sound that carried deep into his head. The sound seemed to echo, reverberate—then disappear. It was a new sound. He listened closely, for a while, then started the car. Pulling out of the driveway, he headed left—for no real reason. It just looked as good as any.

The car moved slowly at first, deliberately—almost as if it couldn't pick up speed. Then with a roar, it burst into the street, nearly plowing down an old lady as she deftly jumped out of the way.

Johnson pulled to a screeching halt in front of the Blue Grass Tavern. "It'll be good to see Ray and Deak and Perry—them guys know how to have a good time. And what I need right now is a good time," his voice pierced the still morning air. He ran up to the door and instinctively pushed with his shoulder. It didn't budge. He tried again with a little more urgency. Finally noticing the blue and white "Closed" sign haphazardly thrown into the window, his eyes grew wide, glancing about like a predator away from its feeding ground. He backed slowly to the car without taking his eyes from the front of the tavern. He didn't want to be forced to concentrate on Lincoln Baptist Church with its golden steeple down the block, or Gordon School on the other side of Stevens Park. All places that he knew well—the names still registered. And for a quick moment, he remembered himself swinging high in that park, but that was all. Without warning, fear gripped his muscles. His throat was cold and dry. So he kept walking, backwards—staring at a blue and white sign in the tavern until he bumped the car. Turning quickly, he opened the door, slid under the steering wheel smoothly and headed home.

"Mildred, hey babe—I'm home." He casually walked into the kitchen. Hung his coat on the rack. "Where are you babe?"

He mounted the stairs, three at a time, heading for the bedroom.

"Why are you still in your robe? It's a beautiful day—we promised to take the kids to the museum. If we don't get there early, we should just wait and go another day." Mildred stared at him for a few seconds, her lips slightly parted.

"Are you alright?", she asked finally.

"Yeah, I'm alright—I never felt better. Let's get the kids up so we can get going."

Mildred slowly pulled herself out of the bed and headed for the bathroom. "Okay, Johnson—let's go. I'm sure we can all be ready in half-an-hour—don't you think?"

"Yeah, babe, that's plenty of time—we can even stop at McDonald's on the way—have some breakfast."

"Aw righttt!" Johnny yelled from the hallway. "That sounds good, Daddy, I'm ready."

It was January 15th and Martin Luther King had been in the news for days—"let freedom ring . . ." Martin's voice boomed through the television screen.

Ring. Ring. Ring . . .

"Daddy, don't you hear the phone," Jennifer said as she bounced into the bedroom and grabbed it. "Hello," her youthful voice rang through the house, "My daddy? He's right here."

"Thanks, sweetheart, give me the phone," he said, taking it from her. Jennifer rolled her eyes to the ceiling and walked out.

"Hey Beak man, what's happening? Yeah, we're taking the kids to the museum. Yeah, Science and Industry. We're leaving early so we can get a head start—beat the crowd. Come by tonight. Sure sounds good to me. I'll check with Mildred and call you back later."

The museum was big and spacious, Its tall pillars reaching toward the sky. It was more open than Johnson remembered. He walked slowly toward a brightly lit corridor; none of the signs were registering. Feet clanked loudly against the floor echoing through the large tunnel. He could almost make out the light at the end. Cleverly and deftly, dodging obstacles, he headed for it, a smile etched in his broad face. He pressed his legs farther apart, trying to get closer to the light faster. He pressed his hands to his chest, trying to slow his quickening heart. I'll catch that light. I will. Can't let it go. He broke into a slow jog. There, that's it. I'm covering ground now—making the distance. He held his head to steady the spinning room. Speed up, asshole, before you lose it. They are gaining on you. Don't stop. Don't stop. Gotta get a phone. Gotta get a phone. Hello. Hello. Can somebody help me. He spoke softly into the palm of his hand. Can somebody help me. Johnson could feel the screaming. Feel the cold, hard metal in his hand. His throat was dry and raspy. If only I could get a drink, he thought, something cold.

"Open your hand, Mister," someone shouted. "Open your hand, you're bleeding." Johnson slowly opened his hand and stared at the blood where his nails had cut into the flesh.

"What's wrong with you," another shouted.

He felt the binding pressure on his arms as they lead him down the long corridor. Johnson could still see the light, if he squinted. But squinting didn't erase the distorted faces of two children who stared after him. And that woman. She's so pretty. God, that's the kind of woman I want someday. He mumbled through the ringing in his head.

The Color Black

Jim Cunningham
(1980's)

He sat at his typewriter and concentrated. He concentrated on two seemingly unrelated things: the essay he was trying to revise for an unusually patient editor for a black literary journal and the upset, impatient wife in the bedroom he was trying to forget, for the moment. She had wanted to talk about his being what she called in her best moments an "unemployed writer." This was not one of her best moments, so she called him more choice and profane things.

"You're not writer, Tim!" Berdonia Johnson had yelled this at him and also at the fragile window facing their east neighbor's garage. Other neighbors would know they were at it again too. Tim believed in dignified arguments, so his usual response was to say nothing. When he wasn't able to ignore her, he simply grabbed his pillow and headed for the living room or started his day earlier than he'd planned. When he was weak enough to reply, he would say something like, "What you mean is that I never get to finish anything because of your crazy antics. You know you keep the whole house off balance with your bizarre scenes, like you were in some soap opera or something."

When he was weak enough to get verbal with her, there was just no contest. She scrambled his words up like eggs and burned them up to suit her mood. His mouth was no match for hers. She would simply say something like, "You would love that, wouldn't you? Love having some big time tv actress supporting you. That way you'd have me spending more good money on your sorry ass! Bleeding me as a librarian isn't enough!" No, there was simply no contest, even though she was no longer at the college because of her failing health. "I was a success at my profession. How much did *you* make this year?"

But he had been strong this morning and had said nothing. So she had switched to another mode. "You're no writer, Tim. All you really do is turn my living room into a library. Calling yourself a black literary critic. You're nothing but a lazy, no count library-hound, you black bastard! All you do is stuff yourself with ice cream and stick yourself in me to keep me quiet. This is my house and I want you out of it! I'm not spending another minute with a man who won't work and especially a man who turns my own son against me!" She delivered this last charge as close to his face as she could without biting him. He had pictured Lonnie listening from his

217

bedroom across the hall. Poor little fellow, he thought, trapped in bedlam like this.

Well, he was a writer, a step-father, and a house-husband. Early retirement had reduced a magnificent woman to something bitter, in-grown and sick. He was determined to finish this piece for the editor before leaving for graduate school in the cold North and before Berdonia's domestic fireworks burned him out and finished him completely. She had attacked the one thing that mattered, that still made any kind of sense, in all this uproar—faith in himself. The shield of his dignity was cracked and scattered all over the place. But his faith still had some kick.

But he also knew he should be worrying about what his mad, resourceful spouse was up to in the bedroom. She managed much of her mischief over the telephone. When he was working at this end of the house, in his garage-den, he could usually count on Lonnie to warn him about what was being plotted against him on the bedroom phone. But his step-son was probably trying to sleep. So Tim tried to concentrate on the essay. At least he was on better terms with his typewriter than his wife, who was in an especially ugly mood this morning.

He didn't get very far with his writing before he heard the door bell. He turned off the typewriter and tried to listen for voices. There were two. Male. He heard footsteps crossing the kitchen and watched the doorknob turn. Lonnie's worried face in the doorway to the garage gave him the bad news. The police again. This was going to be another one of those ruined working days.

He sighed and sat there a second before getting up to see what lie his wife had used this time to get the police there. They had become properly sceptical by this time. She must have whipped something new on them. She usually told them he was beating her. The last time she did that, he and Lonnie were trying to eat breakfast at the small bar in the kitchen near the garage door. The charge was so ridiculous that the two of them—father and son—just laughed, making things even worse. When he had gotten off the phone, she rushed to the bar and dumped cereal and coffee everywhere. What a mess! Now here was another.

As Tim approached the front hall where the two cops were wait-ing, one black and one white, he could see his wife looking self-righteous with her triumphant head held high and leaning back in her housecoat as though she were addressing the sandpainted ceiling or the sky-light. Her hands formed a kind of clenched fist. He suspected she was in the middle of her favorite I'm-tired-of-supporting-sorry-bastards story.

"I'm Mr. Johnson," he said to the two officers. "What seems to be the problem?" The white one gestured toward the living room, indicating they would like to hear his side of things without risking interruption from the fuming spouse. No one bothered to sit for this interrogation. The husband looked out the bay window toward the rose bed as the uniformed man recited the made-up charge. There was no charge, however. Berdonia had chosen a novel and especially self-destructive course this time. What was involved, it turned out, was a threat his wife had made over the phone about what she was prepared to do to him. The main statement came from the tall, slim cop who suddenly resembled Tim's oldest brother now that he was close enough to focus on the lean, dark face.

"Mrs. Johnson intends to shoot you if you don't pack up." This was said with a straight, expressionless kind of official thrust, but the tone bothered Tim for some reason. Usually the police immediately assumed the wife was the victim and he was the culprit. The burden of proof was usually on his shoulders. And naturally the difference in age made him look like a sponger. Besides, some of these men had been students at the college where Berdonia had been a librarian and had guided them through some of their first term paper library hunts. She was known to know her stuff. Some had even grown up in the church she used to attend before her diabetes got the best of her.

The black cops looked up to her as a sister who had survived the wholesale attempt to get rid of black educators and other professionals when so-called integration of the two colleges couldn't be avoided. Berdonia—or Mrs. Andrews, as she was called then—had slugged it out with the new racist regime like a real freedom fighter. She had been one of the few black survivors at the new "mixed" community college—others had been eliminated by any means necessary, especially the men. The black president of the former all-black Flora Beach Community College had been either framed or blackmailed out of the "new" school.

But Berdonia had a career to build and a son to raise and swore she wasn't going nowhere, no matter what the crackers tried to do. War was nothing new. She'd been fighting them all her life. So there was plenty of community sympathy for her. She was a veteran and a model. Tim, on the other hand, was just an outsider she had brought back from the North, just a young dude she had won like some kind of trophy. Now she simply regarded him as an embarrassment. But none of this history was reflected in the face of the cop who resembled Tim's brother. He too looked like a survivor. Black cops probably didn't go back that far in this racist town, Tim thought. And it was possible Berdonia had said something to belittle his survivalhood. Lord have mercy, if that's what happened. Not many black men would tolerate the sort of things Berdonia yelled at a husband.

What a way for a Saturday morning to start, he thought as he tried to anticipate the tricky bumps on this unforeseen path. He would have to reassure these men his wife posed no real harm to him. His wife's moods were like a see-saw. She hated and loved in turns. It had something to do with the imbalance in the sugar level of her blood. But he could sense a special challenge and a special inadequacy in his powers of persuasion. Had he been dealing with two white cops or two cops familiar with his wife's former position and standing in the community, his task would almost be a piece of cake. Now he wasn't sure about how to handle things, about how to handle this other black man in the house.

This was a race between time and ingenuity. His spouse's antics would soon convince them, if they hadn't already while he was still out in the garage, that she was really dangerous—to herself if not to him. And given the particular spicy brand of names she had called him this morning, the black cop could become a problem if she repeated them in front of him.

Tim simply yawned when Berdonia went into her let's-de-ball-a-black-male gear, but this brother wasn't about to put up with such insulting nonsense. The brother would need to save face in front of his white partner. And whatever swift or extreme thing the black cop chose to do, it would probably be in the mistaken spirit of Tim's would-be ally or mentor. There no doubt about it, Berdonia's special repertoire of epithets for "no-good black men" would trigger whatever this black cop did when defending his manhood—a constant battle in a place like this. And he didn't look like a compromiser. If Tim failed to get these two cops out of the house and on their way before the wife made the brother angry, matters could really take a bizarre turn.

Well, Berdonia put on quite a show at the expense of every black man in the world except her dead father. And the black policeman's uniformed face became tighter and tighter, and Tim had no way of shutting his wife up. He had to stand there and watch unnameable things shifting places in the man's cold, brown eyes as every digging, scraping syllable was flung from the bitter mouth of his foolish wife. She was oblivious to the murderous effect she was having on the hostile, stiffening cop.

Humiliating Tim in front of witnesses was one of her most single-minded pleasures these days. Not even discrete reminders by him that her son was also a black male seemed to touch her. But she was coming to view Lonnie these days as simply someone her evil black husband had alienated from her. Getting Tim out of her house was supposed to accomplish the magic job of reforming and transforming her errant son into his former loyal, obedient self. But these performances only taught him to refer to his mother as "that crazy woman!"

The two officers withdrew to a corner of the living room and whispered to one another in a huddle. This happened because Berdonia's performance convinced them there really was a gun in the house, a "loaded gun" his wife boasted.

"Show us where the gun is kept, Mrs. Johnson." This was directed at her by Officer Cold Eyes, whose very complexion spelled menace. Tim watched and listened like a worried but fascinated husband. Still in the grip of her performance, in her wrinkled bed clothes and with her hair still uncombed, Berdonia Johnson marched like a proud queen in formal clothes of state toward the filing cabinet in her small den and reached toward the bottom drawer. Then the low voice of the dark cop almost barked at her. "Just point to the right drawer, Mrs. Johnson. Don't open it."

She stopped in her tracks as Tim and Lonnie exchanged nervous glances. "Don't you want me to show you I mean business?", she said to both cops.

The black cop brushed his hand across his graying mustache and proceeded to look at her with eyes cold enough to cool the Florida sun outside. But she was still oblivious to the alienating effect of her behavior on this second black man in her house. Tim pictured the brother taking the gun from the cabinet and aiming it at her scandalous mouth. But he didn't, thank God! He just did the next best thing.

"Don't go any closer to that drawer, Mrs. Johnson. Just hand me those keys and move away." She hesitated a few seconds and Tim's heart went out to her. The confusion in her eyes was more like hurt.

The angry cop took the keys, using the one pointed out to him, and quickly opened the drawer, reached behind the storage boxes inside and brought out a revolver. He deftly checked it for bullets, confirming her story about its being battle-ready for getting rid of "no good black bastard men," and promptly nodded to his partner as he moved toward the living room. He whispered rapidly to the white cop as the latter shrugged his shoulder.

The two men returned to the hall area. Officer Cold Eyes assumed a dignity as exaggerated as that of the wife he was giving special treatment to, and Tim's heart dropped while his mind raced ahead to find the right words for calming him. He had been trying to think of him as a brother. But what they had in common was the source of this new problem.

"Mr. and Mrs. Johnson, there is a state law which permits us to take anybody in for psychological observation if we think they're dangerous enough to require examining. And they can be held for seventy-two hours or longer against their will, and the hospital expenses will have to be paid by the patient."

Tim was stunned, but Berdonia was simply angry. "What do you mean taking me to a hospital? What about him?", pointing at her husband. She asked this like a thoroughly outraged person. "I called you to lock him up for a little while so I can have myself some peace and quiet. Surely, the state can do that little service for me. I'm the one paying taxes here, you know." The cold-eyed cop had ears like rocks. He simply looked through her and suggested she get dressed for the trip. Lonnie followed his mother to the bedroom at Tim's suggestion to give whatever help and comfort he could. Then Tim turned to the two cops to keep this nightmare from getting any worse.

"Look, officers," he began, "there's no reason to take my wife anywhere. She's no real harm to me or anybody else. She's just upset. It's a matter of moods. She's diabetic, you know. A diabetic's disposition is like a see-saw. It goes up and down. By lunch time she'll be apologizing for all this nonsense. We just had a little argument this morning, and she's trying to get back at me. She knows I'm leaving for graduate school at the end of the month. She's had a lot of things to adjust to since her forced retirement. Health problems and medical debt and age as well as interfering relatives. She'll come around as soon as you two leave. You're like an audience to her. She's just feeding on the attention. And that gun's been there for over twelve years and she's never even touched it. It's there for security."

Tim was trying to keep up the fiction that he was addressing both officers, but it was clear that it was the black one he really had to reach. For the first time since this ordeal, the tall angry brother let a brief smile flit across his face. He gestured Tim to the side, out of hearing range of the other cop, put his moist face close to Tim's and between a hiss and a whisper assured him everything was cool. "Your old lady will have plenty of leisure away from us black men, strapped down to that observation table with them doctors and their rubber gloves poking her every which way. Doing you a favor, brother. She'll come back home real humble. It's obvious you don't know shit about handling sassy-assed women. I won't even charge you for this little service. Just hope you learn something from it."

Tim's mind shot out of his skull in a real panic. How do you talk a brother and a cop out of taking revenge against an embittered black woman who's not only wounded his pride but done it in front of a white colleague? He made no attempt to answer his own question. And all the profanity his wife had indulged herself in while attacking the image of black men didn't help matters. He did learn one thing. He and this uniformed hive of embattled male pride were brothers in the worst way. There was a violent boomerang quality to their kinship.

"We're taking Mrs. Johnson in," Cold Eyes repeated in front of his partner. "The rest is between them and the medical people." The unexpressed smile behind these last words was like the gleam on the edge of a razor blade, and it crouched like a funny pain in Tim's chest.

At this point, Berdonia came out of her bedroom on the arm of her son. She marched stiffly past her husband and climbed into the back seat of the police car with the help of the white officer. But not before shouting at the house and at the ears of any handy neighbors within range.

"I hope you're satisfied, you black bastard!"

Tim and Lonnie stood in the doorway. The father instructed his son to get out of his robe and wash up for the trip to the hospital. There would be a waiting room to wait in and social workers to talk to before he could manage to get Berdonia back home. Provided they didn't run into any more furious black men anxious to teach his sassy wife some bizarre lesson. And especially those bent on making him swallow some instruction in how to maintain brotherhood.

The Butcher's Wife

Eileen C. Cherry
(1987)

That afternoon, the people saw the sun pulsing on the shoulders of the bullish silhouette standing in the entrance to Larry's Get Down Lounge on the westside. Because the figure's face was blackened by the shadow cast from the room's dark interior, it took the bartender a moment to recognize the butcher. The butcher fussed with the top of a clumsy burlap sack he carried tucked into his broad black leather belt. The bulk in the sack bumped slowly, rythmically against his huge muscular thigh.

A big-hipped woman, tipsy and leaning on the jukebox, was also blinded by the light on the butcher. She rubbed her eyes and giggled at his shuffling feet encased in crumbling work shoes. Twisting the curl in her ten dollar wig, she inserted her quarter and bought a song: Al Green's "Love & Happiness." She gave the butcher a show, rocking her hips back and forth on the way to her table of beer sipping friends. Her hips disappeared into the dark caucus of muttering bodies. The butcher's gaze locked back into the bartender. Approaching, he bumped his belly against the bar.

"What's this weird, big nigger got on his mind?", thought the bartender.

"Jack Daniel with a water back," the people heard the butcher demand pounding his fist on the bar.

With a clean and practiced certainty, the bartender flipped out a glass and the whiskey bottle while never taking his eyes off his customer.

"And while you at it," said the butcher, pulling open his burlap sack and rummaging inside, "give this bitch a drank too!" Stunned. The bartender watched a curly cluster of black hair cascade from the butcher's foul fist as it rose up revealing two pink foam rollers bobbling against a yellow forehead and a pair of bulbous red and purple eyes. In the horrible seconds, in the low party light, the butcher's fist arched, grandly and victoriously dangling a fleshy and feminine head. Nose flared, mouth gaped with death, her neck was a quivering array of arteries and wounds. He rammed her rotting head on the counter.

All music ceased. The bartender collapsed against the shelves of booze. The people leaped, knocking over tables, spilling over chairs, without words or second thoughts, running like roaches, through front doors, back doors, side doors and trap doors, while the butcher calmly poured his own drink.

II

They heard paper crinkle and tin snap in the silent alley behind
Larry's Get Down Lounge. They heard the butcher's great knee press the
lid on the garbage can where he stashed his Medusa's head. He pushed
down with all his strength, but couldn't muffle the smell. But the butcher's nose had grown accustomed to the spices of death in the alley: rotting
meat, old wine and disemboweled fruit. They saw him, scuffling hastily
and crushing things under his massive feet: bottle caps, blood-stained
cardboard, their daughters' bashed-in plastic baby dolls; one-armed no-
legged blond dolls—hacked-up sugar baby brown dolls smeared with Vas-
eline and bold, bald patches in their synthetic hair held up with blond and
black bobby-pins. They saw him stumbling and entangling himself in
their discards and their untouchable things.

III

Dizzy with hunger, the butcher pushed himself up the creaking
back stairs to the one-bedroom apartment he shared with the corpse. He
ascended to the dark sour rooms thinking only of the screaming abyss in
his belly. In the kitchen the smokey brown shades were drawn. Water
dribbled from the wide-mouth faucet on the cooking pots cramming the
sink.

He walked carefully as if respecting the silence in their dark,
narrow rooms. He parted the plastic floral curtains separating the kitchen
from the livingroom. Cubes of light poured down the hallway from the
bathroom window to his right, making a pure white curtain where he
stood. It seemed to block his path. As he stepped into the light he could
see the blood speckled on his shoes.

She was resting in the shafts of crystal and silver between the
toilet and the radiator—enthroned in a room of grimy tile on the floor
splattered with blood, chipped paint and white pesticide. Her broad back
was propped against the old bathtub with its four graceful legs whose
elegant squat shielded a small gray victim crushed in the mousetrap beneath. The lacey breast of her floral frock was coated with purple blood
from the lump of her severed neck. Her hands, resting like two yellow
birds on her lap, were still dusty with the cornmeal and seasonings she
sifted to prepare their last meal.

IV

The people had heard screaming—heard the butcher's wife take
her last gasp. But it was a routine commotion. They were always comforted when, eventually, she emerged on the porch in her floral frocks and
foam rollers and battered house slippers of turquoise blue. She emerged—
always—yawning like a new sky after a storm's passionate passing. So on
that day—the day of her murder—nobody was even remotely curious.
They just turned up their TVs—occasionally banged on the walls—for

silence—to quell the serpents in her tongues—the roar of their tumbling among the plastic curtains and the varnished wooden floors.

So on this sunny afternoon, in the smokey kitchen light, the butcher gathered what remained of the pork chops on the stove—scooped his fork in the brick of cold buttery grits. He returned to the livingroom with a plate full of food and a TV table. He switched on the Cub's game and settled down to eat. With his fork, he mashed the grainy grits and seasoned them well with hot sauce, black pepper and salt. And from the corner of his eye he could see the shadows blackening on her defiant repose. She insisted on speaking. With no head and a bloody frock—she insisted on speaking. "Clean up this mess you lazy, low-down son-of-a-bitch!"

But the butcher was dispassionate. Having cut meat too long. Having made a routine of chopping and severing.

The Cubs were losing. He licked the cold well-seasoned steel he gripped between his teeth, forcing the food from his mouth down to the churning crematory in his belly.

■■■■■■■■■■■■■■■■■■■■■■■■■

Open Grave

Daniel T. Clardy
(1985)

They told me to keep quiet, that anything I say could and would be used against me. I'd been thinking they were going to kick my ass. I'd seen flicks where that's what they did. That's what I was scared of at first. But they acted like it really was in my best interest that I don't say nothing. They didn't kick my ass, didn't even act like they would. They just put me in a holding cell for the night. It was cold in there, but I was by myself and glad for that.

Seems like I remember someone saying, *Yo dude, what they got you for?* and the cop who'd just locked the door to my cage telling him to shut the fuck up and banging the bars with his nightstick. Like I said, it seems I remember that actually happening, but I can't be sure. You see, once they turned out the lights, it was so dark, I couldn't make out the bars or walls of my cell, and it was so quiet, all I could hear was that steady beep like when they test their emergency broadcast system on television. It was enough to make me wonder if I was really in a little jail cell and not some big black hole.

I figured that whoever asked me what I was doing there might ask me again now that the cop was gone. I tried to decide if it would be better to tell him the truth or a lie. The cell might've been bugged, so I started thinking up lies I hoped could be used for, instead of against, me. But when nobody called out to me, I asked myself what if any of these lies were actually the truth? And all those thoughts got mixed up so that even now, I can't be sure if I got them all sorted out.

It was hard trying to maintain a thought, lying there, my ass turning hard and cold like the floor itself. To concentrate, I had to think with one half of my brain while using the other to shut out the cold hardness of the floor. After a while, I felt myself split in two, part of me floating free in the darkness, the other part staying on the floor. The floating part felt good and would've liked to float away from the part on the floor altogether, to float away from the cold hardness that the part on the floor was feeling. Right then I heard God telling me: *This is it*.

My body was going back to the ground and my soul was either sailing to Heaven or drifting down to Hell. Now I was really scared, scared like I aint never been or could've imagined being. You see, I couldn't think of one reason why God would let me into Heaven.

I remembered something I used to hear in church about repenting your sins. I began praying only to find out that I'd forgotten how. I tried to say: *Dear God*, but I choked on the words, realizing how much like a faggot I must sound. I know now that what I wanted to say was: *Our Father*, but I couldn't think of those words for shit.

I saw a light and began drifting towards it. As I came a little closer, I could see that I was looking at the sky from the bottom of an open grave. As I came even closer, I saw that the opening was blocked with prison bars, but I could also see my tombstone, a short square block with a cross on top. As I looked at it, the cross broke and fell over towards me. It got larger as it fell, and I thought it would crash right through the bars to get me. I shut my eyes and hollered in the pain I thought would come; but no pain came—only a voice, *Say man, you alright?*

I opened my eyes and saw a man standing where the cross had been before it fell. I blinked once and recognized my dead partner, Sid. I was going to ask him what he was doing there, but he had his hand out to me, and I forgot my question while trying to slap him five. It was then that I noticed the crown of thorns on his head. "Hey man, I said, are you alright in there?"

I rubbed my eyes and looked at Sid again, but it wasn't Sid at all—only a cop standing at the gate to my cell. What I thought was a crown of thorns was daylight reflecting off the bill of his cap.

The dream fucked with me more than a little bit. It was good to see Sid, him having been my ace and all. But what the deal was with that crown of thorns, I don't know. I guess he was supposed to be some kind of Black Jesus. Maybe I did kind of look up to Sid. I wished I had his athletic ability. Sisters be giving up the pussy to athletes, athletes and rock stars. But I don't think I ever saw Sid as somebody's saviour.

They, the cops, brought me a bowl of cold-ass cereal that looked like bird shit. Since I was starving, I held my nose and tried to swallow without tasting it. The first spoonful had me gagging like I was about to violate. I wondered if all the food in jail is like this, and figured that if someone is in jail long enough, he'd probably get used to it. So I pretended I'd been in jail all my life and was able to finish the bowl.

I don't know why I'd seen Sid as a Christ in my dream. He didn't give a shit about Jesus. Once, when we were downtown, a moonie or something asked us if we know that Jesus loved us. *Yeah*, Sid answered, *He fucks me all the time.* The moonie dropped his mouth open like a dummy trying to talk while we just kept on walking.

Sid, I said, *I thought I was sinful, but you, you just got on the Hell Express.*

Sid laughed and said he didn't know what had made him say that.

Last year, when he got sick, he told me that he'd often think about what he had said to the moonie and wonder if the sickness was God's payback. I told him that if he was scared, maybe he should repent. Sid answered that he wasn't scared, just trying to figure out why he had to be dying at nineteen—and that if God can't take a joke, then fuck him.

They came and got me before I could finish thinking about all the things me and Sid went through together. It felt strange to be leaving the cell, to be out in the world again. Two cops took me out of the jailhouse and put me in a squad car. They talked to each other, but neither one said anything to me. That was cool because I was beginning to feel like you do when you be watching a flick and you know that the guy in the hockey mask is about to jump out of nowhere and do something. You don't want nobody talking to you, drawing your attention away from your heartbeat, your sweating hands. You don't want nothing keeping you from seeing the exact second that the shit goes down.

Like here I was in the back seat of a police car, one cop driving, the other sitting next to me. I began fantasizing that a van would drive up along the squad car and force it into the curb. Six or so guys belonging to some top-secret organization would then jump out, put the cops out of commission and take me to their hideout. There, they'd tell me where I went wrong and train me to perform some mission that will save a lot of people's lives—say, like there's this Hitler-type guy in the Cabinet or Pentagon who's planning to exterminate all the Black people in America.

And this group that rescues me knows of this guy and his plan but don't know who all are in it with him and how they're going to pull it off. That's where I come in. They send me to D.C., where I blend right in. I start hanging out at the bars and nightclubs where senators and congress-men be going. One time, I'm disguised as a reporter, asking questions on the sly. Another time, I'm a waiter serving Hitler and his right hand man their dinner as they talk about their caper. I'm eavesdropping as I work their table, but they never notice because they are talking in a code they think nobody understands.

But when all the intelligence work is done, I'm the one who picks up a submachine gun and singlehandedly blasts all those motherfuckers away. This time, when I'm arrested for murder, the guys who I was working with go to the President with the evidence of what was going down. He, in turn, orders that I be released and invites me to the White House where he gives me an award kind of like the one he gave Michael Jackson. By then, the story is in all the papers, and I'm a hero. Sisters be standing in line to give me some play. Brothers be ready to take your life if you badmouth me.

We pulled up at the Criminal Courts Building. Inside I saw a scene I'd seen bunches of times, but always from the other side of a T.V. screen. The hallways were lined by people with cameras. I was the picture they were after. I thought about how there must be millions of people at home who will watch me on the evening news, hating me, wanting to see me cover my face and cry. And strange enough, part of me wanted to give in to them—the same part that had wanted to pray when I thought I was dying the night before. But I nerved myself up by pretending that I was playing Scarface in the flicks.

When they called me to the bench, the judge had my gun on the podium in front of him. The cops who arrested me were there. They told the judge that it was the same gun they had found on me at the time of my arrest. They went on to tell him how I'd been positively identified in a line-up by the victim's girlfriend. I thought the judge would call her forward, but he didn't. I looked around the courtroom to see if she was there. I couldn't remember what she looks like and was kind of hoping that I would if I saw her again. It was while I was looking around that I saw my mother. She was sitting in the third row from the front.

The state's attorney came forward with preliminary lab reports showing that the bullets which killed the victim could've been fired from my gun. It's strange, now that I think about it, how I could understand so much of that legal yang-yang everybody was talking. I mean, I understood what was going on even though I didn't know many of the words they were using.

One word I did understand, though, was *victim*. They kept calling the guy I shot, *the victim*. I began tripping out on this idea for a movie titled, *The Victim*. It would be about somebody whose ghost comes back to haunt its old neighborhood in search of the guy who killed him. Since it's a black neighborhood, the ghost runs up on a lot of gangbangers, pushers and general cutthroat motherfuckers who freak out and go for their guns when the ghost suddenly comes through walls or up through manhole covers, interrupting their drug deals and shit. But when their bullets go right through the ghost, they drop dead from fear.

It doesn't take long for these strange happenings to reach the news. They send a T.V. newsman into the hood who ends his report by saying, *Although it is not known who or what is behind all of this, it seems that at least in this Black community, it is a day of judgment for the criminal, and justice for the victim.*

And from then on, everybody refers to the unseen force as The Victim. Everybody is talking about The Victim. Cops bet each other who will arrive at the scene of a crime early enough to learn the secret of The Victim. Mothers tell their kids that they better behave or The Victim will get them.

Meanwhile, the ghost is continuing its search. Now, this guy who killed The Victim in the first place has avoided being caught by the police. He's hiding out in an old, abandoned movie theater when he hears voices. He peeks out from where he's crouching behind a row of seats. Two men are arguing on the stage right in front of the screen.

Look, man, it's too hot with this Victim thing going around, I aint gonna do it.

The hell you aint, chump. You still into me for some long paper, and you gonna pay me off, Victim or no Victim. He pulls out a switch blade.

Motherfucker, you don't sell me no fear. He pulls out a longer blade than the other man. *I'm gonna pay you off alright.*

They start fighting all over the stage, cutting each other up some. Right then, the screen appears to start smoking—thick smoke that hangs over the two men. The smoke gets denser and denser and forms into a big, tall genie that has skin the color of reefer smoke. The expression on its face is like Satan waking up from a nightmare, but the guy who had killed him can recognize who he was.

The other two men stop fighting and stare in horror at the ghost.

With massive hands, the ghost reaches for the both of them. One man falls over onto his back, his eyes rolling up into his head. The other looks over at the dead man, then jumps up and runs for a door, but the door is locked. The ghost's hand reaches forward and is about to close around him when he takes his own switchblade and stabs himself in the heart.

The guy who's hiding behind the seats has reached that point that goes beyond fear, the point where you find strength and knowledge if you don't die from a heart attack. He stands up and walks towards the ghost.

Sirens begin wailing in the distance, getting louder and louder. Then, the lights from the squad cars are flashing into the theater. *Open up—police.* They begin ramming the door.

The guy looks to The Victim, expecting that it will do to him what it's done to its own victims. All expression leaves its face. It's not mad any more. The ghost looks like it's reading the guy who killed him. A natural, human color comes flooding into its skin. Then The Victim fades out. The doors come crashing open. I think this is where the flick ends.

"Yes, Your Honor, it's our intention to prosecute."

"Do you have a lawyer, young man?"

"A what?" I had heard the judge without really hearing him. He let out a deep breath like a teacher who'd been asked one stupid question too many, then spoke into his microphone, "Is this boy's parent or guardian present?"

"Right here, Your Honor."

"And you are . . .?"

"I'm his mother."

The judge looked as if he didn't believe her. My mom's still a fine, young sister.

"May I ask what you do for a living?"

"I work in a department store."

"About how much do you make per week?"

"I will get a lawyer."

"Please try to understand, mam. I have to ask these questions before I can appoint you a lawyer."

"I'll get my own lawyer."

They moved me to the county jail. My cell is smaller and nastier than the one at the police station. The first time Mom visited me, she told me that the court is going to try me as an adult. I though about how, when I was being taken to my new cell, the ugliest nigger I've ever seen had blown me a kiss from his own cage. He had no teeth—at least none that I could see—and a scar right under his nose that looked like a third lip. It sent a chill down my back, all the way to my asshole and I felt like I'd vomit my heart up.

For days after that, I had nightmares. Every time I closed my eyes, nightmares. And whenever my eyes were open, I was hoping to see someone with a gun and a badge standing nearby. After awhile, it got so I couldn't sleep at all. I couldn't get the toothless nigger's face out of my head until my mom came to visit. Just being able to sit down and talk with her made me feel like everything would soon be alright. Then she told me they'll try me as an adult and that face popped back into my head.

By the next time Mom visited me, I had almost gotten used to the face. It would still pop up from time to time, but it seemed to get less and less scary, provided that I didn't think about it too much. Mom told me that she had found a lawyer who'd be in to see me soon and that the first thing he'll do is to try getting my bail reduced. She expected me to be more—what?—excited, I guess, than I was.

You see, my mom's a fine young sister. She's halfway dealing with some nigger I don't like. She tells me aint nothing going on between them, but I know how easily that can change. If the judge reduces my bail to where this nigger can handle it, he'd probably give Mom the cash. He aint rich, but he's got a little money and acts like he's kind of stuck on himself. And a nigger like that be wanting you to kiss his ass if he does anything for you. A nigger like that be always trying to turn fine, young sisters into whores.

Two days later, the lawyer came.

"Let's start with your telling me what happened."

"Aint nothing to tell. I shot somebody."

"Killed him."

I didn't like the way he said that. I knew I'd killed him.

"Did you intend to?"

It was a hard question. I always carried a gun, never planning to use it any more on one night than the next. But I guess I must've always known I'd use it eventually. Does that mean I intended to kill somebody? I shrugged.

"Take your time. What was it that made you pull the trigger?

"I don't know."

"Sure you do. Come on, tell me."

"Fuck, man, I don't know."

"Why don't you know? You some kind of psychopath or something?"

That hurt; I aint even going to lie about it.

"I don't know, my man," he said, looking like he was almost sorry about calling me a psychopath. "I can't possibly know what's going through your head. And neither can any of the people who are screaming for your blood. All we know is that you killed a young brother much like yourself. Do you know that he was on his high school's hoop squad?"

I didn't. For the first time, I thought about how tall he was. But does that make him some kind of goddamn Jesus?

"They say he had a lot of potential—one of the nation's top college prospects."

The lawyer's going on about this motherfucker's potential was making me mad. Everybody's got potential.

"Some pretty big people showed up for his funeral. Personally, I wonder how many of them ever went to see him play. But that won't matter during your trial. What will matter is that your judge, your jury, your prosecutors and everybody else in the courtroom will have seen his funeral on television. They will have read about it in the papers. And when they decide your fate, they will be looking at you as a murderer, not a human being."

He stopped talking and stared at me for a long time. His face had no expression at all, just two eyes that went right through me. It was like being fucked.

"I have no idea how I'm going to defend you," he said after awhile. "If I were you, I'd try to think up something to say that could cut through public prejudice, something that would make them see me as human."

What am I supposed to say? For the rest of the day and the whole night, I tried to figure it out. When morning came, I still had no answers. I remembered damn near all the lies I had thought up during the night of my arrest—you remember, the ones I hoped could be used for, instead of against, me. But there's a big difference between selling another inmate a lie and selling the court the same lie. In short, the plain truth is that I shot and killed some brother for no good reason other than I was mad—and not particularly at him. What can I say other than that? How is that going to make them see me as human?

Mom visited me again. It seemed that my being in jail was making her pay me as much attention as she normally gives her boyfriend. I thought about how much her visits would mean to me if the courts send me up for life. I was sitting at the table across from her, looking into her face when I started thinking about it.

There was a guard checking out our conversation but trying to play like he wasn't interested. Mom was saying something about being strong, about holding out until the fury dies down. Her words were meant for me. *I* have to be strong. *I've* got to hold out.

"The lawyer thinks . . .," she choked as if trying to hold back a cough. She rested her forehead on her hand in such a way that shielded her eyes from me. Then she went on, "The lawyer thinks it best that we delay your trial as long as we can."

Suddenly, this strange feeling came over me like a firecracker that didn't go off when its fuse burned out. I felt like shit for having dragged my mom into this.

"Look, Mom," I said. "Don't worry about me. Whatever happens, I'll make it. But I killed somebody and there's no way in hell they gonna let me off."

"You made a mistake," she said, taking her hand from her face. "People have got to be made to see that."

"Momma, people see what they want to see."

I had sold my mom short. I began thinking about how it would be easier for me if she went off somewhere with her boyfriend and forgot me. That way, I could hate the world so much, it wouldn't matter to me whether the courts give me life, or the chair, or whatever. I fell asleep wondering how I'm going to make it through prison if they find me guilty.

That night, my mom came to visit me once more. She had turned into an angel and came right into my cell. A guard, hearing our voices, came by and shined his flashlight on us. Mom dissolved into thin air and sailed out through the bars of the window. I cursed the guard out and ran to the window, grabbing hold of the bars.

Just that quickly, she had completely disappeared. I strained to see some trace of her among the clouds. Then I heard voices from below. I looked down towards the ground and saw a basketball court. There was Sid and the brother I had shot playing some one-on-one. Sid was skying just like he used to when he was healthy and drawing "oohs" and "ahhs" from the ladies. Then the other brother got the ball and executed some moves that made Sid take note. But Sid was not going to be outdone. Neither one of them was going to be outdone by the other or by anyone or anything else, and now they had forever to prove it. I'd have given anything to be out there with them. Anything.

POETRY
1977-1987

Haki R. Madhubuti

Poet: What Ever Happened to Luther?

he was strange weather, this luther, he read books, mainly poetry and
sometimes long books about people in foreign places. for a young man
he was too serious, he never did smile, and the family still don't know if
he had good teeth. he liked music too, even tried to play the trumpet
until he heard the young miles davis. He then said that he'd try writing.
the family didn't believe him because there ain't never been no writers
in this family, and everybody knows that whatever you end up doing,
it's gotta be in your blood. It's like loving women, it's in the blood,
arteries and brains. this family don't even write letters, they call
everybody. thats why the phone is off 6 months out of a year. Then
again, his brother willie T. use to write long, long letters from prison
about the books he was reading by malcolm x, frantz fanon, george
jackson, richard wright and others. luther, unlike his brother, didn't
smoke or drink and he'd always be doing odd jobs to get money. even
his closest friends clyde and t. bone didn't fully understand him. while
they be partying all weekend, luther would be traveling. he would take
his little money with a bag full of food, mainly fruit, and a change of
underwear and get on the greyhound bus and go. he said he be visiting
cities. yet, the real funny thing about luther was his ideas. he was
always talking about afrika and black people. he was into that black
stuff and he was as light skin as a piece of golden corn on the cob. he'd
be calling himself black and afrikan and upsetting everybody, especially
white people. they be calling him crazy but not to his face. anyway the
family, mainly the educated side, just left him alone. they would just be
polite to him, and every child of god knows that when family members
act polite, that means that they don't want to be around you. It didn't
matter much because after his mother died he left the city and went
into the army. the last time we heard from him was in 1963. he got put
out the army for rioting. he disappeared somewhere between mississippi
and chicago. a third cousin, who family was also polite to, appeared one
day and said that luther had grown a beard, changed his name and
stopped eating meat. She said that he had been to afrika and now lives
in Chicago doing what he wanted to do, writing books. she also said
that he smiles a lot and kinda got good teeth.

POET: Gwendolyn Brooks at 70

as in music,
as in griots singing,
as in language mastered, matured,
beyond melodic roots.

you came from the land of ivory and vegetation,
of seasons with large women guarding secrets.
your father was a running mountain,
your mother a crop-gatherer and God-carrier,
your family, earthgrown waterfalls,
all tested, clearheaded, focused.
ready to engage.

centuries displaced in this land of denial and disbelief,
this land of slavery and sugar diets,
of bacon breakfasts, short suns and long moons,
you sought memory and hidden ideas,
while writing the portrait of a battered people.

artfully you avoided becoming a literary museum,
side-stepped retirement and canonization,
gently casting a rising shadow over a generation of
urgent-creators waiting to make fire,
make change.

with the wind in your hand,
as in trumpeter blowing,
as in poet singing,
as in sister of the people, of the language,
smile at your work.

your harvest is coming in, bountifully.

Always Remember Where You Are

For Zora Neale Hurston

1.
it seems as though she had been
planted outside northwestern high
next to the basketball court on 86th street
behind her weather worn blue buick
seated on a rusting folding
chair where she sold cookies, candies, history,
causes, chewing gum, vision, corn chips,
soda pop and advice to teenagers with
26-year-old mothers and grandmothers
under 40, most of their fathers music
ceased during viet nam and the f.b.i.'s
war against black men who dared to
question the saintliness of congress and the
imperial presidency.

2.
She sold wisdom from her weather
worn buick bought for her by her son,
a former NBA basketball star. he had
earned NBA records and money in new york
during the 60s and 70s flying high above
hoops and reality only to slip on a
nickel bag and later fall into deadly
habit of sniffing his breakfast, lunch
and dinner. eventually his snacks interrupted
practice and games as his place in
the world became that of a certified
junky circling a basketball that
he could not bounce and a mother
he could not recognize, nor she him.

3.
As his records faded and his money
disappeared quicker than shit in
a flushing toilet, he returned home to
mamma, a pitiful casualty, unable
to write his name or remember the
love that got him out of dusable high
with scholarship offers from 50
universities, no questions asked.
that his mother cared and he was 1st team
all american high school and college is

now history. this mother, in the august
and winter of her time, with eyes
and smile frozen in urban memories,
sells sugar and dreams now from the
trunk of destroyed promises in america.

The Great Wait

(it is possible that those persons who feel the need
to act against evil will be told to wait, be calm,
Have patience, don't get upset, be realistic, don't rock
the boat, you are not so bad off, etc., etc.)

conscious tire of
waiting on waiters who wait for a living
as movers perfect the reasons why
others must wait.

movers say that waiting is an ancient art form
perfected by negroes waiting on something called *freedom*

that will surely come
if the waiters wait patiently in the kneeling position long enough.
long enough is when the waiter's knees shine and
head automatically drops whenever waiters are in the presence
of movers that tell them to be grateful
to have something to wait for.

movers say that afrikans can't even clothe themselves,
that the major occupation in central america is the maintenance
    of cemeteries,
that the people of asia need to control their sex drive,
that the only people that *really* understand modern technology
are the south afrikaners and their brothers on pennsylvania
    avenue and
that the major problem for others is that they do not
want to wait for their time.

most of the waiters are poor and miseducated.
waiting, like cocaine, is addictive.
people wait on welfare, workfare, healthfare, foodfare,
and for businessmen and politicians to be fair.
waiters are line wise having spent a third of their lives
waiting in telephone lines, gas lines, light lines, bus lines,
    train lines, and unemployment lines.
waitin, waitin, tush, tush, tush.
waitin, waitin, tush, tush, tush.

waiters wait on presidents and first ladies to tell them
the secret of why waiting is better than
communism, socialism and hinduism.
why waiting is more uplifting than full employment
and is the coming tool to eliminate illiteracy and hunger.
waitin, waitin, tush.

western economist and sociologist have postulated that
waiting is the answer to family separations and ignorance.
that waiting will balance the budget and give waiters
the insight into why others care more about their condition
than they do.

the conscious world
waits on a people who have become
professional waiters.
the waiters' education clearly taught them
to aspire to become either the
waiter, waitee or waited.
for most wasted
waitin, waitin, tush, tush, tush.
popular consensus has it that
waiting builds character, cures dumbness and blindness,
waiting brings one closer to one's creator, waiting is intelligent work,
waiting is the fat person's answer to
exercise
waiting will be featured on the johnny carson show this week
    disguised as
black urban professionals pushing the latest
form of waiting, "constructive engagement."
waitin, waitin, tush, tush, tush.
it is documented that
waiting will save the great whale population,
waiting will feed the children of the sudan,
waiting will stop acid rain,
waiting will save the great amazon rain forest,
waiting will guarantee disarmament and peace.
the major activity of waiters is watching television, sleeping, eating
junk foods and having frequent bowel movements.
waitin waitin tush tush tush tush

consciousness decays from
waitin on people with plastic bags
on their heads waitin
waitin on negroes that live for pleasure and money only waitin
waitin on a people that confuse freedom with handouts waitin
waitin on sam to straighten his spine and care for his children,
waiting on six child sue to say no,

waiting on $300 a day junkies,
waiting on a people whose heroes are mostly dead,
waitin on boldness from all this education we got,
waiting on the brother,
waiting on the sister.
waiting on waiters who wait for a living
as movers perfect the reasons why
others must wait.
waiting benefits non-waiters and their bankers.
most people are taught that
waiting is the misunderstood form of action,
is the act that is closest to sex and bar-b-q consumption.
waiting. waiting. waiting. waiting. waiting. waiting.
a truly universal art is practiced
by billions of people worldwide
who have been confirmed by their leaders
to be happy, satisfied and brain-dead.

Debra Anderson

Gettin Back into That Swing
for b. c.

i used to be happy in this place
my mouth was full of memory

my body was a vessel
was a place we'd been before
was a dance
was electric
  and
    ion
set to stevie
and me and malcolm
  slowdragged
cross continent temptin' temptation
  we cut a hole all
    across
the
  face of
    this
land
i breathed the times
  through my skin
and came out
  jangled
and crystalled
beauty
  i was energy
    and life
shot up
  w/too much meaning
and love
  was no four letter
word
  for fuckin
    but

something
fragile
  and robust
    and shared
for some reason
my tongue is thick/white
and my stomach
  is a hollowed
    out place
that is hungry
not for food or liquor
    or even ice cream
but something . . .
lord,
  where is the
    exit sign
and how do
    you get
out of here?

Johari M. Amini-Hudson

Story for The Remainder

sometimes we could feel the impending close
as something about to descend
before we stopped dancing

we were body movements
which kept our minds silent in hunger and misuse
and the deaf dumb and blind were
just ordinary people
living a life of sliding uneasiness
almost
comfortable with their tissues and deodorants
at the base of the volcano

someone said loudly
     'can't we give love without
     stones'
     'cant we sense touches without
     descents into pain and gaping coldness'
     'can't we see and feel the beauty without
     becoming mechanized pleasures to each other'

but not many listened.

much went by without notice
while we spread our selves
to every invention and disease
which became common and expected at all ages.

we exposed our minds
to the embarrassments of idleness
and to releasing the present in smoke drifts
because we didnt want The Responsibility.

and we were encased in our tracks as the times
gathered tightly.

we would take no Understanding
until it became unavoidable

therefore we were surprised
that the journey to our Destination
was not through drifts of contrived and unusual colors.

No. as was revealed,
it was rather in peeling our hesitancy, our delay,
our unwillingness to assert Life.

*

But now that all has been washed
in the waters of our force
dont let that remembrance escape you.
hold the reflections of the past so
we will never go that way again

The land that bred us is at peace
singing
and has a sweet vibrant smell
it is ripe with the joy of bearing our lives
generous and fertile
in the quick blood of birth
and is not ashamed

we touch one another with sensible fingers
understanding arms
and an attunement to the Divine that we share

our children are wanted treasures
growing in the richness of our own
Creator's sun
altered with wisdom from our mouths and ways
and none of them have
syphillitic eyes

When we dance now we celebrate
and not decay

(untitled)

before
you was a slow rarified Blackness
moving dimly
around my heart
heavy

then indeed
you rose my Spirit with
fingers reading the river from my eyes
through my sides while we
learned a music

now this time in you
is as wine
heady about the cup
distilled welling tenderness
in our places

Sandra Jackson-Opoku

To Be Awakened by Birds

That cemetery back of our house
brims with life
spirits give witness to
miraculous flight

the earthbound scamper
of squirrels and rabbits
darting amongst the headstones
an occasional graveyard
creature spotted
burrowing into the plots
of our backyards

and the birds
oh, the birds
robins and sparrows
and birds I don't
know the names of
and then too, the cardinals
darting through the air
like bits of flame
and waking me in the morning
with their delicate song

In the night I am
also summoned up from sleep
by the raucous, sullen cries
of urban blackbirds
the lost ones
abandoned, motherless, flightless

busy in their nightly rituals
of bottled spirits
and white powders
and by loud music from
crippled cars
the soulless mating dance

the vulture cry of sirens
scatters the flock
but they always gather again

and blackbirds wake me
with their mournful song

247

Carolyn M. Rodgers

Touch

Poem 5.

> this is how it is.
> or can be.

a bird sits on the branch
of a tree
and perhaps
sings. this is not personal.
nor private.
but it can touch us.
the tree
has no leaves. only a
web of spiraling branches.
each branch is a level or degree,
a wavelength in the air.
we are building something.
a ledge. a liturgy in the sky.

Aunt Dolly

Sitting there on the
assembly line piecing
together frocks all alike
thousands by thousand for
millions to buy, the same
cheap pattern duplicated
all over the world, goes
home at night and sews
up a storm, a dream that
nobody has "ever" seen
who can deny, when "ever"
she steps out the door, any day or hour, after work,
after five, she is a *queen*.
She can sew anything you
cannot even imagine.

Wimmin

One woman say a good man make her want
to shout
He's my Lazarus, she says. we got UP together.
    Another one says, "a little bit of my
man's molasses goes a long way on my plate."
    What you say, woman?
                    I say—
    this discussion falls under
    the protection of grace.
                    oh yeah.

Melvin E. Lewis

Companera III

You are gold
I have come from
a slow march to death

There is magic in the silence of the sun.
There is silver in the content of your voice
I would like to mine it and spread it
over my world.

The night is simple in its raindrops.

Companera IV

Poet: Shader of light, caster of movement
         can you mold obsidian sand in the reflection
         of a hand running through phosphate.

Sculptor: Tell me the temperature and scent of the early wind,
           the taste of salt, and caribe lemon on the rim of a
           beer can.

Poet: In public she is an untouchable, very distant . . .
         a proper Puerto Rican lady. At dinner in an
         expensive restaurant in el Condado, she offers
         to help pay, and talks about being an
         independista and a feminist.

         After a second beer at El Obrero she stresses
         the clarity of Capital and attacks petit-bourgeois
         revisionism and the Party.

Sculptor: How has the earth revolved around the curls of
           her hair?

250

Poet: In a stroll along a midnight beach she
reluctantly discusses the thesis
she doesn't want to finish and avoiding
economic terminology.

Sculptor: Is there blue or green in the glow and
rhythm of her smile?

Poet: In Santurce and Loiza her shadows are outlined
by land reclaimers, azucenas, her lumpenness,
the fire of congas and the sugar of cane.

Sculptor: What are the lines and strokes of her cheeks?

Poet: In a quiet, open moment she told stories of
love and growth, while playing Nina's
"Black Is The Color of My True Love's Hair."

Sculptor: Why don't you write a poem about the
windspan of her echo, the brevity of rainbows
stroking her feathers in flight.

Poet: I want her image to weather a month of hurricanes.
In the still between night rain showers,
she remembers projects, warm and caring people
and hiding her talent.

Sculptor: Bronze can mold and hold images, it can't
outline spirits and shadows of complete dreams.

Jim Cunningham

Damani on the Hudson

Big-eyed
he holds on
to adult-fingered hands
while flirting with the wind.

Or touched by the morning tv's mirth,
in fact while sprawling on the floor,
he manages to crunch the cereal
into a universe of forms
and as though he had Medusa's hair
holds the morning shadows
stare for stare.

If hung in a museum,
he'd be anything
but a flat portrait—
perhaps a noisy mobile
with uncanny soft spots.

Though Damani settles down
for cartoons and cereal,
his submission—like his posture—
is a tentative thing.

II.

He is an optimist,
a stretch-artist
who moves with city-bred tension
who takes generous stock
of big city pavements
and big city heights

But whatever he savors
as he moves about the hurried
grown-up streets
in his child disguise
he keeps hidden
like secret voices.

Most of all
he savors the adult stride
with its pioneer stance no longer fresh.

III.

A small-pint creature
of cartoon mightiness,
Damani unscrambles
the electronic roar
of kitchen voices
long before his parents stumble out
in robes or underpants
to search for magic-rendering
coffee cups
or combs.

They tie yellow ribbons
around his wrist
and brush his hair
with reminders that parting
is a routine.

Routine assures him
that they will return to claim him
from the institutions of the world
that claim him too.

Being surrendered to his grandparents
is one routine:
they settle into space
like other landmarks.

IV.

Though he trusts nearly everything
but pain
he suspects that
he is wanted
that he is wanted more
for what he means
than for what he is himself.

He suspects
that no one is quite prepared
to want him
for what he is.

For what he is himself
is what we all are—
a mystery.

man wishing on a moon

a solid man
makes himself
a solid earth
somewhere
in this embattled universe

a solid man
hears himself wishing
for a solid woman
who could use
a solid man
but the only solid thing
he can make
is the unchanging clenched-mouth night

hold on
cries the solid man
to an unseen woman

hold on
to this big, round, solid arm of mine
and the woman asks
will it bend?

no, he says
it's too hard
and round
and solid

to reach me
the solid woman says
it will have to bend
and if you can't hold on to mine
for it is solid too
tell me then
why I should need
a solid man like you!

and they display
the wealth
of stone-shaped muscles
on their stone-shaped arms
and prepare to battle
through the night

Laid Back Blues

Your leg
was under the cover
out of reach
so my hand
caressed
what it could reach
without getting down
too far
into things.
It was a tame affair
and nothing growled
or barked
or moved
too quickly.

Collette Armstead

dream/9139

A brown child transcended
               translucent
    floats above the sparsely grassed lawn
            the water sprinkler
            ripples
            billows
            then gestures
Home
At the door
an easy whisper of welcome
I survey
  the air is waved heat
  the cottonwood tree invisible but there
The house is vacant like all dream houses
Perching on the corner stair
My life pours into my head
like a kaleidoscope let loose
Memory moves me and wonder strikes
The new residents breathe life sounds
in
and
out
The house is vacant like all dream houses
A malevolent spirit resides in the closet of the boys room—still there
it drove my brother to orange hair and a repetitive story of glory
I touch the doorknob of the closet door
Repelled
Sent from Home
I recollect
feel a tender regret
awake with a sigh
assimilate loss

On The Number 3

some people ride city busses & meet colored ladies
in bright blonde wigs & scarlet lips
who clutch at handbags & murmur
inane phrases in defense of their insanity
when i ride city busses
i meet angry women
in blues and blacks
with combs and brushes
and long black gloves with fingers gone
mad women
who pinch and pull at nappy edges
& hold thundering conversations
with themselves
when i ride city busses
i meet
wrath-full women
in blues and blacks
sent whirling into deep, dark, space
while looking for reflections of them
selves
in fragments of shattered glass

untitled

God is so weird
    She created dreams in technicolor and shadow
    Rain
    bowed
    through light and cloud
    good sex
    and on the
    edges of sadness and irony
    laughter.

Sandy Royster

Enchanted

I am
centered
on a vision
that is only that—
yet stronger than reality . . .

You fill my waking/sleeping spaces
easily
slipping effortless
between the daily grind
and restless sub-terrain
of dreams.

I play the wishing games
without a plan
blow out the birthday candles—
search for falling stars—
peruse the horoscope for fabricated clues . .

You are as near
as my breath
against the pillow
and as ephemeral.
we are a universe without a world
always becoming,
never become.

S. Brandi Barnes

Gentlemen at The Barber Shop

At the Barber Shop
men rehash dreams, settle wars & politics
and talk about mothers or ugly women.
They discuss the state of the Union,
joint around the corner,
and advise on law & child support.

Gentlemen in the Barber Shop
relive *the great love affair*
they didn't marry,
and always, always, give
instructions to the young.
Some talk about how they make women
scream from pleasure while
others exchange glances that
know better.

At times the phone rings—asking for
different ones to bring something home
and he knows, Mama was only checking.

At the Barber Shop, they brag
about female jealousy & insecurities,
and her checking up.

When I take the little one to get his
hair cut, they call him champ,
size me up quickly,
and change the conversation from
Men talk to small talk.

Prima Bopper

For nightmare knitters, sisters bop
for less than other boppers
so jamm, jamm, jamm the tambourines
when nightmare knitters:
poke her / force her to high jump
force her to hoola thru their hoops
they want more from her than the
other bopper / jumpers
so jamm the tambourines:
when they raise the bar / when she
starts over / when they brutalize her
nightmare knitters, will always
raise the bar. . . . .
so jamm, jamm, jamm the tambourines
before she readies for
tattered dreams & hazy day to daze:

celebrate blended browns
celebrate Gardenia Billies
celebrate African Violets
celebrate Simones
celebrate black brow, negroid nose,
celebrate pregnant raisin to ruby
                          lips
celebrate a watusi—her ballet
a blue bop—her jazz dance:
wave the banner for sister bopper
when she high jumps,
& nightmare knitters
the ignorant   the belittling
the racists   the anti-sister,
when they raise the bar
jamm, jamm, jamm the tambourine
before her frown freezes
keep her warm & praise Prima Bopper
(who must bop-better than the other
                          boppers)
Celebrate   and homemade jamm!
Hallelujah clap and homemade jamm!

Do you know a bopper?
Can you shake / shake / shake?
Can you beat a tambourine?

Sand Dance

With some there will be no empires or huts
yet if you call him, you for your reasons
he'll bring sea shells to catch your tears
& warmth for depressing cold nighties
he is not one to build with.

Magpies moan—beware—he is a pirate with
juju, and the gossipers rattle on
but if you call him, he'll bring sparklers
to your sadness.

With him futures escape, his history
a collection of nomad songs,
mink matings, litters of pain,
and questionable partings;
he is not one to build with.

He only offers
sea shells & warmth / cocoa kisses &
low lusty licks / sand dances &
balloons for his nomad ways.
But if you whisper to the darkness
& call him—you for your reasons,
he'll be there—he for his.

With some . . . there are only sand castles,
no empires or huts.

Walter Bradford

As Woman

For Gwendolyn Brooks

I place you in my heart
solid and perpetual as the march it makes

I am your soldier
your entire army.

You launch my dreams others rule incapable
pull from the shadows all my anxious secrets
turn them gifts the world sings back to me.

By and the by the sonic dust
records my past bleeps my vision
to a retreating flash of silver

Work, worry and advanced civilization
Binds me, ties my virtue in syllogisms
and I need a song to lift my trudging heart,

Come, my epic love
speak in single voice
bring heat, dreams and sermons
to heal and revive
my thirsting blood and dance
completely.

My Speech To A Casual Redeemer

For G. Brooks

In the hull of the moon
my life, as life in training
I have tried these words to you;
With skill and patience
I have learned to detect then convey
what really matters,
I have worked my heart muscular
for something, in a way never written
before this moving moment
A phrase, long and durable as silk
to fit around me, to shield me
from murder, sudden drafts, the heat
from the well of my dreams.
In the secret curve of the moon
I have searched but found no songs in the spinning air
What wisdom on this planet comes late
or not at all
The virtue or evil I perceive in others lives in me
So, my prescription is direct;
Drive my stake in the whirling snow
begin my speech here.

Nora Brooks Blakely

James T. Eldridge

He moves across a backlot of apathetic pavement
His chin leans out
And carries his body up the stairs
Against the worldweights that drag his knuckles
Across the ragged wood
Leaving twitchmarks of dusty defeat.

Vaguely entering his din, bleak cave
He drags disasters across the floor
To the turgid chili that has waited there listlessly all day
  Pepper . . . where's the pepper?
     no matter
  he should be used to the spicelessness

He leans on old wants with nowhere else to go
And slackly stirs his solitude and tea
He goes to the front room and surrenders to a chair
As dishes and despair sit in the kitchen
He rolls up his thoughtsieeves
Turns on TV and
Looks at living for a while

Philip M. Royster

You've Got It Made
(even in Manhattan, Kansas)

In early spring the winds blow in
tornado clouds and the scent
from hulking cow heaves.
Along a residential street
a slaughtered skunk forces
closed all windows, and in
the evenings, from the edge
of town, you may see fields
afire, searing the dark horizon.

The bus station closes before
midnight and after Ric's,
the town's only cafe
with style and good food.
A town bank sends personalized
congratulations when a
local poet publishes.
Strange folk smile and speak
as you walk the streets,
and most weekends are
cramped with parties.

Manhattan's a town where you
might forget for a minute
until your Jewish podiatrist boasts
he was the first town physician
to treat blacks, or your colleague
confides that many white landladies
want to know whether his new
graduate student is black.

People like them have made it sure
there is no real black community
in town. Poor blacks are scattered
uneasily along its edges while the few
comfortable ones clutch at their mortgages
perched in the midst of middling whites.

265

There is no black television, no
black radio, no black newspaper, few
black churches, fewer black concerts,
and absolutely no place of style
for a black man to buy clothes.

My blackness has survived this first year
here only with the help of my friends
and memories and dreams of Chicago:
One night I slipped off the pillow
and found myself back home watching
this sweet brown heartache petting
the plums and peaches at a vendor's
stand on Forty-third and State.
You could see all those strokes of love
her mama brushed into her long thick braids,
and she carried herself the way black girls do
when they know the whole neighborhood is watching
out for them. Never was a question
in her world that she had it made.

I watched this Chicago child
in my small town dream, and I felt
she was a promise the South Side
made me. She was every black woman
I had ever known; she was every black
woman. And she knew everything she did
she did for each of us: her thoughts
our insights, her smiles
our happiness, her touch
our blessing. Within her flesh
she held our generations
and because she knew all this
we had it made.

I woke trying to drag her out
of the dream and hoped she'd carry
the old neighborhood with her, so
when my hands came out empty, I sulked
at the loss of her sweet mama-made charms.
Then I despaired of ever finding Chicago
in Manhattan, despaired of losing street
after street of every thought and shade
of blackness, despaired of losing
the generations of loving and hustling

so hard and fine that black music is the only science
that fully describes them: like Miles, who captures
the flirting sass of a black woman's charm
with "So What!" Nobody talks like that
unless she knows she's got it made.

And with the sounds of Miles' head, I remembered
the wisdom in the voices of all black music:
You can have what you want by becoming it;
you become what absorbs you; don't clutch
what you become, and you can have anything.
And the promise is with practice
you'll have it made.

Master drummers teach to let the energy
of what absorbs you flow through your hands
without clutching; to ride the winds
of being with attention's wings:
So now my hands dance with rhythms of all
being with King George's steady African
drive, with 'Master' Henry's lilting quickness,
with Spencer Bibbs' consummate power,
with Ade's intelligence and compassion,
and with K'shkas precision. They taught me
the certitude and fidelity of Chief Bey's
tumbao, and to talk on the *quinto* with Mongo's
knowledge and Patato's wit. Above all, like Armando,
make every stroke touch the spirit.
My father told me that ofays think drums
are for beating, but, like Max Roach,
brothers play to speak and sing.
The energy of the world comes in vibrations, Man;
flow with that energy, and you've got it made.

And now in Manhattan when I visit black churches
and with eyes closed listen to small choirs
summon God, I remember Canaan Baptist
on Chicago's South Side, where Teeny and Willie B.
led the Gospel Chorus with "He's my light, my
guiding light, don't have to worry day or night,"
until the ushers had carried half the church
into the halls. Even when the Power of the Spirit
in others frightened me, the rhythmic call and response
of chords and lead took me on a flight all my own. Ah!

My man, when you were a child, you surely did have it made.
Now the South Side's promise is friend,
family, and work I love. And when I get homesick
I drive out to Tuttle Creek and search
for red-tailed hawks and bald eagles.
Three times last winter I saw the eagle
standing in a tree carefully eyeing a gaggle.
The last time his wings opened, and rising
with the wind he spread those wings and soared
across the heavens as if he know he had it made.

Enticement

The evening sun's
luminous curved
bright platinum
bottom
hangs
just below
the slate hem
of clouds.

Barbara Cochran

Life Lines

On winter morning
with dying dreams
like fallen oak leaves
brown around the edges,

kept in a wicker
basket near your
parlor door,

neatly wrapped
in red velvet scarf
stashed away for
sweeter times
for night-times

When you and your
pitch-black eyes
enter the market place
sporting a red-feather hat
silver-gray sash
and dancing to a tune
of Miss America
Pocket full of leaves
all wound up for a
good time

Staring eyes
concrete strong
carve your path
down Cleo Lane
Nearly bar your entry

On Cleo Lane
neon lights glowing amber
that's where your
sisters meet
soaked with Miss America Tears
Their brown-leaf dreams
covered with snow
and buried deep
in the pitch-black night.

You scrape, you claw,
you dig, you gently
gather them
careful of the wilted parts
and carry them home
to your wicker basket.

Memories At Mayrinna
(for baba)

I know a place
where love goes,
like light vanished
under toppled stones,
a place where hands
make signs and weep.

Red sands of Mayrinna
build you up to
places among the stars,
open spaces where
ginger grows
wild and sweet.

Where silver threads
bind memories
of dusty brown hats
and John-Deere tractors
of long waves in summer's sun
from ginger-brown girls
bare-foot and hopeful.

Stone turns to sand
even at Mayrinna. Home.

I know the pain
of missing you—
of settling your memories
comfortably around my edges,
of staring in the rain
and watching shadows move.

They embody you.

I know this place
where silver threads
bind memories
of crushed pillars
and missing dreams,
a lost smile,
of stone and sand,
of home—
a dusty brown hat,
a John-Deere tractor.

Sterling D. Plumpp

Speech

They
could tell
it was war.
By
the sound
it made.
If you beat out
memory on its
quivering palms.
People
would know
how to move heads,
twist hips,
or legislate feet.
By
the sound.
The
drum talked:
language, history,
myth, ritual,
and memory.
The
drum talked
if you planted
rhythms on its skin
and caressed it
with moods of
improvisation.

My grand
mother knew not
drums.
Her
pots and
pans talked.
If
she squeezed the dish
rag like wringing
off
a chicken's head and
pondered depths of
the image
less water
then

the old rooster
was crowing: a storm
was coming.
If
she held the pot
out
like it was a new
born
baby and screened
its rivers of dark flesh
through nets of her vision
then Poppa
was gon die.
Swooping
wings of the angel
was heard
clapping beneath
the geese.
If
she clenched her fist and
shoved it
under water in silence
then
some angel of
mercy was on
its way
to rain
down a little
ease.
If
she rattled pots and
pans like two cats
fussing and fighting
under the house
then
some
body
was messing with her man.
A low
down
rat
done brought the blues
in
to her happy home.

Alms

Home
less and no
where to go. I
am hungry and no
body to give me
food. Got / history
on my mind. Really / in
a bad mood. Tell me some
body, please,
tell me
some
good
news.
My head / breaking
open: out come
my troubling
blues.
Got / them
so bad. I need
a license
to sing. They / got so
much
power. Folks need a
vaccine.
Home
less.

Mister blues.
What
the crippled man
said.
Hungry.
Mister blues.
What
the crippled man
said.
Taste of
Chicago. He / ain't
even
half
fed.
Got / the
blues.
Need a
license
to sing.
Every
body pass him
by.
Don't give him a dog
gone
thing.

Big Maybelle

(for Angela Jackson)

She
parks her sorrows
near a curb, gets
out of
her skin and
stumbles
up steps of pleas.
Un
listening, at
tentive and calloused
hearts
tune in.

She
gets back in
her skin, cries off
down the long boulevard of
memory.
Her pain in
her voice/her
people in
her veins.

Official

(for William Faulkner)

1.
You
get your stamp.
Folks
pack in to
buy the honor.
But not
your words.

2.
They
can
not honor
a living witness.
The
pen would
get too up
pity. Claim blood
stains.
As signs.
Wanna
circulate among truths
nailed down.

3.
Dilsey
does
not make the occasion.
Though she
sent tales from yesterday's
letters.
She
mailed with fidelity:
with a tattered
thumb to in
form all:
your black
folks/exist in your novels.
Hers
rake leaves and
pick up paper a
cross hallowed lyceums.
Where Meredith
wrote a chapter
with his spirits
and
There
are no sanctuaries
here/for
memory

Jeanne Towns

The Specter

To them its simply a job

as the painter yields a brush to a naked canvas
and the sculptor molds clay giving it new definition

The specter clad in white
pushes a button, that putts and whizzes

and a life, gently woven/nurtured by the rhythms your lifeline
sheltered by the warmth of your womb,
is whisked into oblivion

A beginning is ended

and the specter moves with icy deliberateness

towards a new death

and

you are left . . . limp and crippled
with jagged memories of what might have been jutting out

a womb . . . once bold with promise,
harbouring a heartbeat
is now barren and empty

silenced by the hum of a vacuum

You gather up your hurt and prepare to live
with the voices of them that almost were
taunting you, crying out from their shallow graves,
clamoring for the breast that will never suck

faceless faces beckon you
in the midnight hour

and

the sound of their child-like giggles lay scattered in the wind
echoing your pain

you've walked them through their first hurts, and,
savored the sweetness of their victories
they dwell in the pit of your stomach/of your soul

and every time you look upon the face of another
the memory of your own leaps out from beyond

and you pray,
between the tears
while whispering condolences

that somehow they understood

as the specter in white moves on

When Morning Comes

And when morning comes,
raw and naked in its splendor

I watch you
as soft spills of sunlight gather
a pattern across your sleeping face
highlighting the whispers of
hair folding over your chest

the sharply defined curves of your
body etched like an artist's signature
in bold

And you a manchild

peaceful for the moment . . . like a quiet sea
all the pain of living given to rest

I am mesmerized,

silently drinking in the stillness of
your untutored, untamed beauty

AND

I dream as I have never dreamed before

If only I could barter with God
I'd ask that he lock us in now
and never let darkness descend

I want to capture you as you lay
(sculpture you in this moment)
to sustain me in my aloneness

AND

At that moment
I know if I met
you for no other reason
than to say I have loved
then that in itself is enough

for

GOD

knows I have loved.

Eileen Cherry

garfield/ 55th

they holler hey
sweet babies on
bubbles o/blues
& brew. wigglin
up wonderin at
the secret between
my thighs.

they make
the platform rock.

not the el roarin past
can still the snap o/
sweet thunder when
the wine nipple's passed
& the high pain & laughter
sparks bleed from they eyes

remindin
mine to see

them shamans o/streetcorner root
conjurers bound by shadow
dipping inguts of lust

dice dancin.

i offer
tribute to the brujos
o/pluck & pig knuckle
cruisin & cussin under the
shudder o/the el.

to the priests in chunk glass & high
water pants. piss puddles & runned over shoes.

i offer
tribute to the ways o/life
that grip the foot of great girders
tenacious
as the motion o/stone

unending
as the stumble of bones
thru time.

the trains will hustle on. over them.
gone.

africans sleeping in the park at night

"sistuh"
they asked me if i wanted to
lie on the grass and drink stout
and feel the warm fire in my belly
the heartbeat in my head
the dragon's breath pouring out of my nostrils.

they asked. "sistuh" if i wanted to dance
in the velvet shadows
wallow in cool leaves under a thousand
diamond eyes. hear my own cry over the lake's
burn herbs and musky scents.

they asked me if i savored the taste of rest. "sistuh"
i said yes
i use
some strong trusting brews that bring
the thickness of sleep that
release me to know—
my breath is inseparable
from the wind.

the mechanic

afternoons
lingering
gasoline rainbows
soak in the pork sops. the gravel lumps.
under the imperial.

she.   is shifting her feet and remembering
the light was moist
& whiffed of beige vinyl.   light was
lemon colored trim
taking its time
tracing the upper parts
of his lip while it
held & drew the narcotic
from the tobacco.   from the white stalk.
the golden tar that stained the pearl
in his teeth.   she is remembering him rolling
under the belly of the imperial.

she is remembering the green
speckled mint on his tongue.   his navel &
the way the blade of a toothpick jutted
from that parting of his lips
his   manhood panama hawaiian new orleans
yellow rican gold pecan bahamian pill
hill banana beans.
his fingertip smudges & smells.

she is remembering him & how he
rolled up under the iron
intricate belly of the imperial.

Don Ryan

Negroes in The Middle Class
Who Have No Class, But White Class

They're obsessed with Debutante
balls

with BMW'S
and Opera Halls

all white neighborhoods
And Un-integrated parks

rubbing noses with
white counterparts

Paris Fashions
and French Kissing

Eldorado homes
not to mention

with all the things they see whites do
They despise black people too.

The Fear of AIDS

She wears
a Psychological
Chastity Belt

What she use to feel
Is no longer felt
where there once was heat

the fire is out
what use to be a drive
is now a drought.

Bad Luck

Lady luck
Ain't No Virgin
She was never meant to be
But it seems
Everyone had her
Everyone but me.

Detmer Timberlake

August Moon

The days are short
upon an August moon,
time yields to no God.

pale clouds
harvest rain
heavy rain,
the August moon
is fully visible sometimes
and the rain fills
streets, mind and spirit.

where are my days,
those sun filled days,
such long warm days?
velvet sweet nights,
what will become of them?
nights filled with passion
when love was new
and OH what loves
will i remember,
what nights i shall not forget!

stars fall like amber leaves
across midnight's sky,
my days too
fall like amber leaves,
it is my autumn
racing against
an August moon
and time yields to no God.

Chicago

no stars tonight flashing
like diamonds
my moon, a streetlight
as i walk the lakefront
watching the skyline
lights reflect upon the water
as waves like lost souls
drift ashore,
like the water i take shape
to that which holds me,
i'm bound to this city
with buildings standing tall like tribunes,
it has given me form & reason
it's the architect of me.
i embrace it sometimes with a lover's love
or resent it with a lover's scorn,
it's not a perfect mistress
but always a breast filled matriarch
not denying its many children.
i as my mother & father
was borne here, made friends here,
fell in love, married & had children here,
this city may not always be my home
but i will return to live
my final days & have my ashes
scattered along the lakefront
becoming one with the waves
like lost souls drifting ashore

Antoinette McConnell

Brown Women and Sisterhood

Brown women and Sisterhood kindle heart round the cooking stove.
Heat strong, stretch kinks fall long, while
telling she heard bout one with short locks he got on the side.

Brown women's mother wit fills tilted shacks,
separated by clothes lines, amazing grace,
enough courage to pump love from water wells.

Sisterhood fixes dress hems,
freshly blocked hats,
starched handkerchiefs, that bring joy to swatting flies,
hallelujahs and amen cries.

Together, brown women and sisterhood
provides courage to fade gray, mend merciless way, unfold sight.
Remember Sojourner and Harriet did, Winnie and Maya do,
support brown women to sisterhood.

Odessa Johnson

She could leave you be and love you o so near.
I had never met anyone so skillful with love.
She was mother of twelve, every childs mama,
yet her soul didn't have a one.

Thought I'd never see Odessa past the grave
they placed her in; until a hazy day jogging
along the Sausalito Bay. I sat on a dock
stoop to catch my breath. Took a look in the distance
toward the mountains, there was Odessa,
after twenty years, she had come.
The same reddish complexion,
long slim torso, thin neck, oval chin,
same inflated lips, full chisled nose,
quick forehead and hair hanging long into the bay.

I stepped back to see her in view;
laid out, carved into the earth.
True enough, just as she lay across the bed,
after the last born;
just like she rested on a blanket, that day near the zoo;
just as she lay in a neat fitting casket,
here too, God strengthened her miles, beyond years.

My heart quivered; tried to take a deep breath before
I, again, looked toward my strength.
Odessa now wore fog, that draped like lace,
graced her red wear. There was green that ornamented
her hair, added accessories to her neck and ears.
I discovered while contemplating on what I saw
strengthened across the mountain, that Odessa was an
ancestral queen, reborn; her kind of love and beauty
to grace the earth, always.

(This is a tribute to the late Bulah McConnell, who inspired me
to see life and live!)

David L. Crockett Smith

December Requiem

for David Alexander Smith

Now we come again to the dregs of December.
Ice crusts from pebble to pebble
across the physiognomy of North America.

In December your brother called
in a cracked voice. You had gone
your own way for the last time.

Cancer crept into your body.
It scuttled sideways from cell
to cell, vein to vein and bone to bone.

Cancer nibbled your coiled guts.
Cancer raked its claws through your heart.
Cancer ate itself to death.

In December I listen for distant voices.
A salt wash filigrees the face.
Where are your words, father?
The deep December wind shudders in my ears.

Cowboy Eating His Children

Goya said it best
in a song without words:
Saturn devouring his son.

mad god with blood
on his lips and raw flesh
stuck beneath his fingernails.

weaver of words and illusions:
you command F-15s and television.
you try to bewitch us with your smile.

you try to twist back the arms
on the clock of history
just by flicking your tongue.

your unreal image
haunts us in our bedrooms.
we shiver at your voice
slithering through the air.

we hear you chanting:
"this bomb is a PEACE bomb."
"these dead children were TERRORISTS."
"we must fight the COMMUNISTS at all costs."
but someone's foot keeps sticking in your teeth.

Goya, they say, lived
in a darkened mansion.
his nightmare visions
hung on every wall.

you have the mansions, Cowboy.
you have the magic voice.
you spin these tales and visions.
we sit before our tvs watching you.

we listen as you croon
the words of war.
East against West, North against South.
we see the pieces of your children
dangling from your mouth.

Angela Jackson

Arachnia: Her Side of the Story
(Janet)

What Athena weaves best is
lies. Her and her whole
Olympus family. Wolfpack of
liars.

She said she was my teacher.
And I swollen imitator, ungrateful
student.
You believe that one?

My body is a busy dark flower
from the dark continent
her Daddy ran-
sacked. Plundered my pots,
my libraries, my stars, my
gods.

I wasn't from Lydia
either. Wrong girl's name.
I'm the dusky girl from
Memphis.

What Athena weaves best is
lies. Propaganda issued from Olympus.
A thread of deception.
Her stuff sticks to the history
books.
You believe that one?

I wove the real story
I only embroidered the
                    Truth.
Made it shinier
and it could be seen.
She embroidered seamy press releases
for the Wolfpack
that sits high on the mountain.

She called me blasphemer.
Purjuror. She slapped me
until I spun. She says she
sent me to the corner and I
hanged my self.
You believe that one?
That she cursed me and would not let
me die?
        It was a lynch-
rope, my Grecian girl wove
for me.
        It was a lynch-
rope, she spun and lay
and waited for me in a
spooky house.

Wolves bayed in the distance
but I didn't listen.
I was busy looking at the sun
god out of a dirty window
weaving his tapestry.
When she fell on me.

It was my murder.
But not my death.

You see this web?

You ever seen anything like it
in this haunted house world?

I am still working my charms,
                  quietly.

In Her Solitude: The Inca Divining Spider
(Ana)

It is dark in the pot
where he keeps me. The Inca priest
with gold rings on his golden wrist.
El Dorado. I smell the clay and the sweat
from the human hands that made
my bowl of solitude.
Where I wait in darkness,
captive, humming.

The priest, his hand trembles when he
lets in sun to look at me.
He squints
at the way I sit.
When I sprawl, legs spread,
extravagantly, loitering
in my pot—it's a good sign
and his teeth glint a smile.
When I sit
with even one leg folded
under me
like the woman that I am
with a bad attitude—he trembles
from smile to fingers—
tremors. I am a Bad
Omen.

He seals me in again
and prays and prays
for my legs to
open.

Hattie

Your mother outlived you by twelve children.
More's the pity the years spent on the rims
of someone else's jars of jelly or pot of greens.
What sweet or grease could a single woman fall into
with no education, no auspicious skin, and no money
but what she maid for? Only the visits home to Mississippi
—long and industrious—washing everything that would
wash, sweeping, and cooking and eating and gossiping,
done then in lucid harmony to look forward to.
The lovely lace lingerie lay in your drawers
crammed as flowers in Eden, redolent with promise
and sachet. Certain people give what they have
in skinned knuckles and cracking knees please and
thank you.

I keep expecting your just reward for you in this life.
The one you did the best you could by your sister-
dead-before-you's kids. I stick my hand out and
wait for your wages.

"Is this all?" I want to cry like a last minute virgin,
unsatisfied and raw, as I stand beside the marker
of your small grave life. Grieving the minority
of your simply tendered years. Regretting the tiny
kindness rendered to the huge spirit chastened
in your knuckled-under yet redolent flesh.

Only the air of this fine raiment day kisses my palm
like a lover and a prince.

What I Said As A Child

What I said as a child I say
as a woman:
      There is romance in common
          movement
      of sound and sand.
          Religion of a
          kind is
                true, affirmed.

      Ours is the worn water and ripe fire, leaves
      that burn alongside the road
      into
      smoke
      thick as Nigerian oil. A cover
      for
      magic and skill

      We balanced a house of extended families
          atop our heads.
      The music drifted down
          around our faces.
      Wind crossed our cheeks
          in scarifications.
      Spirits feathered around our waists
      and fell to our knees;
      a dance
      of prayers that I said as a child
I say again:

      We walked in the air of the ancestors, hot, and tight
      like
      the space between two breasts. A crossing
      of tongues
      in the middle of an African night

      The future is a quiet bed, a spread
          of hunger, and fallenwish
        is mystery to divine:
      a drug technique
          hidden in a man's hands.
      We sit on the edge of our own echo, and craft.

What I said as a child I say as a woman:

We are from a house of balance and control.
The road ahead is burning smoke and oils.
What comes after is an act of will.

REMEMBERING HOYT W. FULLER

Editor's Note: *The following tributes to Hoyt W. Fuller were originally submitted for a commemorative issue of* First World *magazine, planned to honor its executive editor, who died suddenly in May 1981. Material on other subjects was also received, including work by James Baldwin, Jeff Donaldson, Aguibou Yan Yansane, Peter Bailey, Carolyn Fowler, Eleanor Traylor, and John Killens. Unfortunately, financial problems prevented the issue's final production.*

Because of Hoyt Fuller's instrumental role in OBAC and his importance to others beyond that organization's local "family," current members felt it appropriate to reserve space in this volume for the unpublished First World *tributes. Though written in the Summer of 1981—under the weight of an imminent deadline and the recent death of an irreplaceable friend—these tributes offer fresh, long due insights into a remarkable man and his time.*

Hoyt W. Fuller:
A Capsule

Compiled by **Pamela Cash-Menzies**

PERSONAL—*Born:* September 10, 1923, in Atlanta, Georgia. Died May 11, 1981 in Atlanta, Georgia. *Education:* B. A. Wayne State University, 1950; advanced study at Wayne State University. John Hay Whitney Opportunity Fellowship 1965-66 for travel and study in Africa. [Note: Also wrote under the penname "William Barrow"]

PROFESSIONAL—*Editor-Journalist:* Assistant Editor, *Collier's Encyclopedia*, New York City; West African Correspondent, *Haagse Post*, Amsterdam, Holland; Associate Editor, *Ebony* Magazine, Chicago; Feature Editor, *Michigan Chronicle*, Detroit; Reporter, *Detroit Tribune;* Executive Editor, *Negro Digest/Black World*, Chicago; Executive Editor, *First World* Magazine, Atlanta. *Teacher:* Fiction Writing seminar at Columbia College (Chicago), Afro-American literature at Wayne State University, Northwestern University, Indiana University, Emory University, and Cornell University's Africana Studies Center.

NON-FICTION—*Journey to Africa* (Third World Press, 1971); Bigsby, *Black American Writer;* Long and Collier, *Afro-American Writing*.

POETRY—(Periodicals) *Essence*, November 1971; *Negro Digest*, November 1963 and March 1965.

FICTION—(Anthologies) Adoff, *The Poetry of Black America;* Clarke, *American Negro Short Stories;* Williams, *Beyond the Angry Black*. (Periodicals) *Negro Digest*, June 1961; February and March 1962, and January 1963.

NEGRO DIGEST—"Of Fondu and Faubus"; November 1961. "With Apologies To Pepito"; February 1962. "The Sun-Burned Soldiers"; March 1962. "A Haircut In Conakry"; January 1963. "Charles White, Artist"; July 1963. "The Big Black Burly Negro"; August 1963. "The Role of the Negro Writer in an Era of Struggle"; June 1964. "Just Throwing the Bull"; July 1964. "The Myth of the White Backlash"; August 1964. "The Negro Writer in the US Assembly at Asilomar"; September 1964. "Seravezza"; March 1965. "Perspectives"; December 1965. "Nostalgia in Pigalle"; February 1966. "The African Look"; September 1966. "The Defense of Black Poets—For Hoyt Fuller"; September 1966. "The Myth of 'The White Backlash' "; December 1966. "Happenings"; August 1967.

"The Black University"; March 1968. "Black Theater In America"; April 1968. "The Critics Will Learn"; November 1968. "Black Studies"; March 1969. "Black Theater In America"; April 1969. "Algiers Journal"; October 1969. "Some Other Hue And Cry"; October 1969.

BLACK WORLD—"Black Theater In America (General Report)"; April 1970. "A Warning To Black Poets"; September 1970. "The Alien Message Of The Wind"; October 1970. "Black Theater in America-General Theater Round-up"; April 1971. "Of Racism, Rationalization and Reason"; July 1971. "Houphouet-Biogny Onstage"; August 1971. "Focus on Negritude"; October 1971. "Negritude in Vermont"; October 1971. "Of Academics, Revolutionaries and Debts"; October 1971. "George Jackson: One More Martyr"; November 1971. "Black-White War for Control of Images"; November 1971. "Traveler on the Long, Rough, Lonely Old Road: An Interview with Chester Himes"; March 1972. "The Manufactured 'Feud' "; April 1972. "Black-White War for Control of Images—Continued"; May 1972. "Black America"; October 1972. "Notes on the Second World Black and African Festival of Arts and Culture"; January 1973. "Joseph Walker and the River Niger"; April 1973. "Tribute to a Black Man: Paul Robeson"; July 1973. "Second World Black and African Festival of Arts and Culture"; July 1973. "On Literary Colonialism—In Africa and America"; December 1973. "Literary Anthologies—Addendum"; December 1973. "Ed Bullins, Playwright"; April 1974. "On Black Studies and the Critics"; May 1974, "Another Fork In The Road"; October 1974. "The View From U.N.I.T.A./Angola: Unity and Struggle—Double Duty For Freedom Fighters"; October 1974. "Notes From A Sixth Pan-African Journal"; October 1974. "The Second World Black and African Festival of Arts and Culture"; January 1974. "Stage, Screen and Black Hegemony: *Black World* Interviews Woodie King Jr."; April 1975. "An Interview: The Original Hebrew Israelite Nation"; May 1975. "African Heritage Studies Association Meeting"; July 1975. "Second World Festival Notes"; July 1975. "Black Elected Officials: Is There A Measurable Difference?"; October 1975. "The Congressional Black Caucus: The Members"; October 1975. "The Nation: Cape Verde"; October 1975. "FESTAC '75"; October 1975. "Africa; Homeland of My Heart"; November 1975. "Festival Notes"; January 1976. "Pan-African Notes"; February 1976. "The Angola Crisis and Afro-Americans"; March 1976.

OTHER PERIODICALS—*New York; The Nation; New Leader; New Republic; Midstream; Southwest Review; North American Review; Chicago Defender; Black Position; Chicago Jewish Forum; Book Week* (N.Y. Herald Tribune); *Book Week* (Chicago Sun-Times); *Books Today* (Chicago Tribune); *African Forum; Detroit News; Christian Science Monitor; New York Times Book Review; Arts in Society; NOMMO* (OBAC Writers Workshop, Chicago); *Jet; Ebony; Journal of Black Poetry.*

BIOGRAPHY AND CRITICISM OF FULLER—*Arts in Society* 5 (1968); *Black Books Bulletin* 1 (Fall 1971); Llorens, "Two Busy Writers Who Also are 'Real' "; *Negro Digest* 15 (December 1965).

Hoyt W. Fuller's Challenge

Robert L. Harris

Very few Black Americans navigate this country's seas of racial intolerance with purpose and determination. All too many bob aimlessly like rudderless boats with no course to guide them. The currents of American society easily sweep and toss them about. The tragedy is that they do not know who they are nor who they want to be.

Hoyt W. Fuller lived as a beacon in the murky waters of race that challenge the identity, if not the sanity, of every Afro-American. As a young man, reared in the relative security of Detroit's Black middle class, he noted the rituals of race that required self-abnegation, compromise, and accommodation. He vowed not to sacrifice his integrity as a Black man to become successful. He knew that Black people had a proud heritage both in the United States and in Africa. He recognized that Afro-Americans would never alter their condition as an oppressed people until they developed a sense of their own history. They were almost hopelessly divided because they did not value their past. Too much energy was wasted trying to escape from themselves and attempting to imitate their adversaries, who denied their very humanity. They could not see the promise of a new day as some brave Afro-Americans struggled for freedom after the Second World War and as African nations demanded their independence. He later observed that, "They (were) like weary strangers in a forever unfriendly land who cannot return to the home they long ago abandoned now that it is joyous with hope."

Fuller gained this remarkable insight from his mentor Fred Hart Williams, his vocation as a writer, his expatriation to Europe, and his travel in Africa. Williams, who founded the Hackley Memorial Collection of Black Arts at the Detroit Public Library, was a prominent supporter of that city's Association for the Study of Afro-American Life and History branch. He inspired Fuller to appreciate Africa and introduced him to the history of Black people in the Detroit and Windsor, Canada areas. Fuller sometimes accompanied Williams as he interviewed old-time residents and recorded their recollections, especially of the Underground Railroad.

As an editor, Fuller defended the legitimacy and value of Black literature. He held that Black critics should have primary responsibility for evaluating Afro-American writing. They brought a sensitivity, an acuteness, to the well-springs of Black literature that only the exceptional white critic could muster. Fuller steadfastly resisted the idea that Black artistic expression of merit had to conform to white standards of beauty and taste. Through the pages of *Negro Digest/Black World*, he stimulated Black consciousness. In many respects, he fostered the Black Consciousness Movement which transformed Afro-American thought during the late 1960's and early 1970's as much and perhaps even more than the New Negro Movement at the beginning of the twentieth century.

When Johnson Publications terminated *Black World* in 1976, Black artists and intellectuals from across the country rallied to launch *First World* Magazine. They knew that silencing Hoyt W. Fuller's voice would have dire consequences for all of Black America. As editor of *First World* and Professor of Black Literature at Cornell University's Africana Studies and Research Center, he continued to address the issues of Black identity, unity, and liberation. Until his untimely death at age fifty-seven from an apparent heart attack in Atlanta, May 11, 1981, he still tried to persuade the Black middle class of its duty to advance the cause of Black people. He maintained that the Black bourgeoisie was a party to the oppression of the Black masses. The hesitancy, vacillation, and fickleness of the Black middle class confused the bulk of the Black population. The Black bourgeoisie conveyed mixed signals as they tried to play both ends against the middle by accepting key positions in the Black community but seeking to identify with white America.

The Black leadership stratum was a special target of Fuller's analysis. He held that Black leaders by and large had become estranged from Black people. Proponents of the white status quo promoted those Blacks whom they considered safe and who would protect white interests. Fuller excoriated establishment Black leaders for not being serious enough about freeing Black people. They did not demonstrate the patience or perseverance to nurture the Black masses. More often than not, they geared their messages to white America. For Fuller, it was the common Black folk who held the potential to change once and for all the status of Afro-Americans. He knew that there was strength and dignity within the Black folk, that they possessed the virtues to sustain Black people. Their kindness, compassion, unselfishness, and faith in each other were traits to emulate instead of the greed, coolness, egotism, and suspicion that characterized white America. Fuller embraced a strong sense of propriety, of respect for himself and others. This quality came from his background, the Black middle class, from which he recoiled because he saw them betraying themselves. He did not condemn comfort and security, but he rejected people denying their identity to achieve it. At base, he judged it uncharitable for Successful Afro-Americans to turn their backs upon the less fortunate. In fact, those Afro-Americans of some means had the greatest obligation to the race.

Self-assured without being strident, confident but not condescending, Hoyt W. Fuller knew who he was and who he wanted to be. He was a consummate Black man with a profound sense of his people's past, a fervent attachment to Africa, a tireless devotion to the Black Aesthetic, and an unflappable dedication to the integrity of his people and their culture. He intensely yearned for Afro-Americans to know who they are and passionately desired that they determine who they wanted to be instead of thoughtlessly accepting the society in which they found themselves. He knew that Black people with faith in themselves could shape their destiny. Much depended on the Black middle class, his own formative milieu, to make a choice, to devote itself to saving the race. Fuller once wrote that, ". . . the most enduring monument a man can ever have (is) the faith and tribute of the new generation." If we neglect his memory, fail to consult his wisdom, or ignore his example, we damn the present and future generations of Afro-Americans to the abyss of self-destruction.

Mari Evans

For Hoyt

I

(May 1981)

Brother, comrade, confidant
how the fabric of life is rent
How do we keep on keeping
without you our rugged rock
our cornerstone
How do we sing the song
with your indomitable voice
no longer lordly no
longer loudly raised
How do we wage the wars
Where will we find the strength
in the absence of your sure concern
If you had known the measure of our unrestricted grief
The bottomlessness your going left
That time could never heal our
anguish at your passing
Being you, you would have
put the day on hold and labored for
another lifetime yes to shield
all those who keen and mourn you
from this lacerating pain
Brother, friend, confidant
how the fabric of our lives
is rent
We say your legend
See! Even now
there is a rainbow of our tears
in full pursuit

II

(Aug. 1982)

and now
this sudden quiet
your name whispered
in the mind it
is not as though we
loved you not enough
but rather that our pain
is more than sanity
can bear do not believe
the myth that Time will heal
Time moves us on but
. . . single file
irrevocably
Alone

III

(May 1985)

past colloquium and celebration
past academe and argument
there is this crevasse, this abyss
down which our love stands looking . . .

Brother, comrade, confidant
the fabric of our life is rent
in the absence of your sure concern
who has the strength and
which of us will say
"This, is the fine
direction"?

Glimpses of Hoyt W. Fuller

George E. Kent

The selves of Hoyt W. Fuller that I in varying degrees knew are of profound meaning for our community. Most prominent and most clearly sustained was the self of the man-engaged-by-history. But also visible were the man of individual aspirations and the private man who had put himself together in his own distinctive way, a fact recognized by those who habitually addressed him as *Mr. Fuller*.

Though modified by the occasion and presented in different forms, Hoyt's historical response to existence in America and in the West generally was a single message to the community. In *Who's Who in America*, the elegant Hoyt put the dedication of his life into the following terms: "As a Black man in America, my life's work has been devoted to awakening Black people to what I see as the evil in the fundamental character of the nation and of the inescapable responsibility of Black People to alter and improve the nation's flawed character by rejecting the destructive ethic and the propositions embraced by the naton's rulers which are inimical to a decent and humane existence for all people."

At a Southern college conference, the blunt Hoyt put the matter in terms chosen to shake up his Black audience. *"You,"* he began in measured tones, "are not white. *You* are Black. This American system was not designed to release you—but to *do you in*."

Consequently, Blacks would have to revitalize relationships with each other, re-group offensively, abandon the individualistic values associated with making it in someone else's terms, and make use of history and Africa for birthing the self as a totally functioning man or woman. The alternative was acceptance of zombie-hood.

Thus, Hoyt was the keeper—necessary updatings being allowed—of the Black conscience and consciousness which were firmed up during the 1960's and early 1970's. As sentry, he unvaryingly stood firm at the last outpost, whether release of triumphant feeling or tearing tensions resulted.

The November 1971 *Black World*, for example, carried on its cover an announcement of the martyrdom of the revolutionary prisoner George Jackson and contains within tensional responses that would recur at this outpost. Surlily introducing the poetry occasioned by Jackson's martyrdom, Hoyt denounced white racism and Black cowardice as two roles necessary for the continuation of a humiliating game:

> White people will, as they always have, heap insult, degradation, violence and contempt upon Black men, as a manifestation of their American-given rights, their ordained status as superior human beings and rulers in this appropriated land; and Black men will, as we always have, protest against their brutalization, plead for justice and equality, and organize our lives and our views of the world in line with the models white men have established for us, accepting the implicit proposition that we will become more 'acceptable,' more bearable, to the degree to which we approximate the white ideal from behavior to appearance. We diminish ourselves in this way, playing that game, mangling the psyches of our children, robbing them of images of manhood.
>
> And everytime a Black man falls, his death flinging before us the absolute intolerableness of our situation here, we resort to an outpouring of emotional prose, of angry rhetoric, of cathartic poetry. It is a sad release.

According to Hoyt's statements at a recent conference at the University of North Carolina, the heart of what he had had to say in this historic role was in the "Perspectives" section of *Black World* and the editorial comments of *First World*. He stated that the files he had left at Johnson Publishing Company were rich and historically significant records dealing with writers and issues. He hoped that they would be acquired by the DuSable Museum of African American History.

So much for the man intensely engaging the historical imperative.

A brief word about the other selves, which Hoyt valued but kept subservient to the historical. The self of individual aspirations involved his desire to fulfill his identity as writer. One gains a strong feeling of Hoyt's talents from stories and sketches which had appeared in his book *Journey to Africa* and in the *New Yorker, Black World, Ebony*, and other publications. In such publications his outstanding mode is that of a well-modulated irony which registers the values, the hopes, and the betrayals, forming the responses of contrasting worlds undergoing upheaval and change. He is thus able to release fully the sensibility of a cosmopolitan narrator (himself), through whose responses unstateable feelings are often registered. He had hoped to receive a grant from the MacArthur Foundation, with which he would complete a novel-in-process and bring other works together in a unified whole. He was unable to gain such an opportunity, but his published works show that his talent was outstanding.

As might be expected, the private man was human, contentious, generous, passionate, and contradictory. A foe of the "bourgy" world, he would, on the surface, appear to cling to its symbols of elegance; yet he transcended such matters in a creative and cosmopolitan style.

Fortunately for us, the selves also fused their qualities in Hoyt's historical role, a fact which gave us the latter years of *Negro Digest* and *Black World*. They also gave us *First World*.

And the challenge to sustain it.

Seeds for the Coming Hell and Health Together

Gwendolyn Brooks

Missing Hoyt

Hoyt Fuller, innovator, scholar, persuasive influence, never presented himself as a god, never wished to stand away from the rest of us. Multi-talented and enacting, he involved himself with youth and age. He was cleanly committed. He subscribed to the quality of Afrikan glory. In the interests of its preservation, in behalf of its regeneration, he Watched, he Warned, he Warded Off.

> He hammered us high,
> he hoisted us
> in Black self-believing.
> He was hinge and hi-fi and Home.
> He was hunter-host,
> hope.
> Is.

Never was Hoyt-missing so intense as at the recent Black Writers' Conference banquet in Chicago. Ivan Van Sertima was there. Ivan Van Sertima—poet, critic, record-correcting author of the serious and solid "They Came Before Columbus." He offered us an important speech. It should have been the feature of the evening. But Robert Bone, white critic fierily deplored by Hoyt for many years, was allowed the last speech.

Bone opined that times are different now; that in the late Sixties Blacks (he prefers calling us "Negroes") were hostile to him, that it was *dangerous* to come into the Black midst; that *now* he could come into the Black midst—and be *cheered*. I was told that at an afternoon Conference session where he delivered at length his overseer's messages, a dashikied Bone got a standing ovation from the Blacks before him—which suggests we are not only still in chains, but are hungrily licking them.

Hoyt, you left too soon. There are still these people here, felicitously bulwarked by little Black aides, telling us that our work must not be "politically burdened." It's really better if we just play baseball or do hair, but if we *must* write, we must Write Nice or Mastuh won't like—Mastuh won't give us any *prizes*.

We have, still, these carefully organized soldiers sent from their Generalhood ("the World-Runners" is Haki's phrase) to keep the continuing slaves in line—to whip the errant ones back into chains, back into position.

Bone tells us that Derek Walcott is acceptable to the white literary Mafia. Derek Writes Nice, Bone would have us believe. James Alan MacPherson, according to Bone, is "*non*-politcally-burdened." As a matter of fact, both are Black people who have suffered Blackly and are Blackly burning. Bone classifies Black literature as "politically-burdened" or "non-politically-burdened." What is "politically burdened" is dangerously regrettable. What is "non-politically-burdened" gets a bored OK because—what *harm* could it do? Bone knows that the Black Majority won't read it. And Bone and his fellow-soldiers *know* that *they* are not threatened by "*non*-politically-burdened" Black writing: they *know* that imitators of whiteness are not likely to out-do Shakespeare or T.S. Eliot. These white soldiers feel safe from "non-politically-burdened" Black writers. The "politically-burdened," however, must be crushed at all costs. Not only is *organic* Black writing, because it deals with real-thing-Truth, likely to be vibrant, vital, richly thrilling, more nourishing emotionally and mentally than the latest sex-mad, violence-vaunted white excuse for a novel, for example, but it is actually likely to CHANGE something (if "only" a sleepy Black mind)—and that AINT all upinheah.

We had better remember Hoyt's warnings every day, and understand that our enemies are still out there, trying to break into our living places, to poison our Rooms. Some of us make home-invasion unnecessary—we send engraved invitations.

We had better remind ourselves, as I've said before to the Diaspora, *of our work*, that was done, to be done to be done to be done.

Requiem Before Revival

We still need the essential Black statement of defense and definition. Of course, we are happiest when that statement is not dulled by assimilationist urges, secret or overt. However, there is in "the souls of Black Folk"—even when inarticulate and crippled—a yearning toward Black validation.

To be Black is rich, is subtle, is nourishing and a nutrient in the universe. What could be nourishing about aiming against your nature?

I give whites big credit. They have never tried to be anything but what they are. They have been and will be everlastingly proud proud proud to be white. It has never occurred to them that there has been or ever will be ANYthing better than, nor one zillionth as good as, being white. They have an overwhelming belief in their validity. Not in their "virtue," for they are shrewdly capable of a very cold view of *that*. But their validity they salute with an amazing innocence—yes, a genuine innocence, the brass of which befuddles most of the rest of us in the world because we have allowed ourselves to be hypnotized by its shine.

In the throat of the Town Crier throbs the Power.

If you yell long enough and shrilly enough "I'M GREAT!", ultimately you will convince your listeners. Or, you will be thrown into the insane asylum. The scant Caucasian race has escaped the insane asylum and has gone on to *virtually* unquestioned "glory"—has achieved virtually unchallenged italics.

Swarms of Blacks have not understood the mechanics of the proceeding, and they trot along to the rear of Pied Piper whites, their strange gazes fixed on, and worshiping, each switch of the white rear, their mesmerized mentalities fervently and firmly convinced that there is nothing better than quaking in that tail's wake. They do not see that the secret of Supremacy success is—you just go ahead and impress yourself on the world whether the world wants you or not. They have not seen some Announcements register just *because* they are iterated and iterated and iterated—the oppressed consciousness finally sinking back and accepting the burden of relentless assault. Though eager to imitate any *other* property of the white compulsion, much of the Black swarm has refused to imitate the efficacy of Iteration and the fruit of that Black refusal in chaos, is vertigo, is self-swallow, or self-shrivel and decline.

I continue my old optimism. In spite of all the disappointment and disillusionment and befuddlement out there, I go on believing that the Weak among us will, finally, perceive the impressiveness of our numbers, perceive the quality and legitimacy of our essence, and take sufficient, indicated steps toward definition, clarification.

Making the Most
of the Middle Passage

Kalamu ya Salaam

*The admission price to the world of life is not only an entrance
through the portal of birth, but also an inevitable exit through
the doorway of death.*

Hoyt Fuller was my literary "main man," my beacon and arche-
typal embodiment of commitment to promulgating a "Black aesthetic"—a
frequently misinterpreted concept which, nonetheless, critically impacted
the work of those of us who sought to produce a creative and engaged
literature anchored in the African-American experience. In many ways for
many years, Hoyt was our preeminent emcee as well as critic. He championed as well as published our work, first in *Negro Digest*, then *Black World*
and finally in *First World*, an amazing span of over 15 years of constant
literary activity.

A male midwife for countless poets, fictionalists, essayists, dra-
matists and critics, Hoyt delivered the first writings of many of us to the
world, helped bring them to life: washed them off with his critical editorial
eye and slapped our fledging scribblings into print.

Hoyt was our father-figure in a world which routinely grinds good
Black men down to mean nubs, pulverizes us into a bitter blob of human
hamburger. Somehow this strong man remained tender enough to spend
time talking with us about whatever we wanted to talk about; remained
knowing enough to be conversant about the whole Black world (his knowledge of Pan African events, personalities and issues was encyclopedic);
and he was caring enough to correct us when we were wrong. We all knew
his disdain for mediocrity, especially among those of us who, for one lazy
reason or another, declined to work hard at developing our potential. He
was hard as true love; he never led us on. His smiles and compliments
were genuine, *and* ditto his criticisms.

Unlike the way literary lengends have it, there was no Oedipal
conflict between Hoyt and those of us of younger generations. That is not
our tradition (no matter however much the Wright/Baldwin disputes have
been badly misinterpreted). Our tradition is like Coleman Hawkins re-
cording with Sonny Rollins, Pharoah Sanders blowing with Trane, King
Oliver tutoring young Louis. I recall now, with a clarity I didn't have then,

that publishing under Mr. Fuller's tutelage during the Sixties and the Seventies was a maturing (w)rite of passage.

Hoyt was also a very important role model for me. The integrity of his work was impeccable. His example fashioned the markings I followed in my attempts to become an editor—I knew of no other person who was as editorially competent as he. Other than Alain Locke, I can think of no other Back person of letters about whom we can say their major work was as an editor and that their editorship was important to the development of African-American literature.

Hoyt gave me hope and vision; he never stopped, nor whined about having to wade through the slaughter of Black literary life in white America. He spent his last years not in a retirement he justly deserved, but rather commuting back and forth between his office/home in Atlanta and classes he taught at Cornell University in Ithaca, New York; back and forth every week, reading manuscripts and correcting papers, conversing with writers and counseling students, publishing a magazine and preparing lesson plans—as he never stopped.

If you asked him about it, he would acknowledge that it was hard, and on some few occasions during his last two years reveal how physically and emotionally draining his lifestyle was. Like 99 percent of us, Hoyt had to work to make ends meet, but what he was tying together was not personal comfort nor material aggrandizement, but an African-American literature. Once you come down off the slopes, after you have climbed all morning and worked all day, there should be some rest at night, but Hoyt, at over fifty years old, was still travailing under the hot sun in the fields. Hoyt knew from experience, that for our people, when you get to the mountaintop, you not only see the beautiful valley below, you also clearly discern the next mountain to climb—and there was always a next mountain.

I don't have anymore to say, except I am blessed to have shared time, space, struggle and many hours with this "simple African man," who, to paraphrase Amilcar Cabral, "simply did his duty, in his own time." It is true: if you live, your time will come. What is important is what you do along the way. Although I am sorry that Hoyt is dead, a greater and more important part of me is glad that he lived, is strengthened by this man's passing through.

Hoyt Fuller. Simply said: he did what he had to do and moved on. Our world is a better place because of him.

OUR WORLD IS LESS FULL
NOW THAT MR. FULLER IS GONE

It is always difficult to measure
and undeniably impossible to replace
the vital space
that a friend's
final passage leaves

At the funeral site
i viewed the corpse
—and that is what that was,
undoubtably the man we knew
was not lying there
silent, still and accepting
of circumstance
that was never Hoyt,
striding, stirring, agitating—

From somewhere
Hoyt's dead reached me
the evening of the notice
of Marley's dying, i remember
i muttered an obsenity,
the certainty of death
for us all does nothing
to lessen the impact
when fighters fall
however, it is our way
that only the forgotten are
truly dead, the remembered
live always inside of us
simply moved to another
plane of existence

I know it is an appropriate
occasion for brilliant phrases
and praise poems
describing his work
and worth, but i don't
feel that right
now, as i watch writers
relatives and friends
view the remains
sadness aches my head
and tastes dry in my mouth

Let us transform this touching grief
before we return to the front
(and hopefully that is where
we all are
headed from here),
let us work as hard as he
stopping only at the
time of our going,
let us retain his memory
chew it like mint
swallow and make muscle of it
fill and satiate ourselves
with Hoyt's indomitable spirit,
and resolve, each of us, to
secure a portion equal
to our capacity and create Hoyt
whole again rising within
the community
of our necessary
carrying on

Hoyt Fuller and the Black Aesthetic

Addison Gayle

In the fall of 1972, a well known Black critic spoke to me concerning remarks about his integrity attributed to Hoyt Fuller. "I don't believe that Hoyt said those things. He is honest enough to have told me himself." The critic, no friend of Hoyt's, was acknowledging some of Hoyt's major characteristics: honesty, integrity, and a fierce dedication to principle. Less than three weeks before his death, at a gathering in Chapel Hill, North Carolina, he reaffirmed these basic tenets: "I insist upon telling the truth, regardless of what the personal consequences might be." Such a dedication to principle and truth was almost an obsession, and was the theme of his book, *Journey to Africa:* "I had quit *Ebony Magazine*," he wrote, "for the magazine did not seem to be moving in any direction that it seemed important for me to go, and it was extremely difficult in 1957 to find meaningful work that also would not threaten my sense of racial integrity in the white publishing world. . . . I could not play the game of 'making it,' when the cost of winning was my self respect."

Such sentiments were alien to Black literary figures in the 1950's. Then as now, dissimulation remained the predominant characteristic of all too many. When, in a 1954 essay, Richard Wright wrote dispairingly of Black people as consumate actors, he was simply footnoting a tradition that had survived since the days of slavery. In the early stages of our history, telling white people the truth or things they did not want to hear meant uncertain punishment and sometimes death. In later years, death was minimized, though punishment took on the form of loss of income, status, and position. The governmental actions initiated against Paul Robeson and W.E.B. Du Bois in the Forties and Fifties demonstrated obeisance to the old tradition and served as a warning for many Blacks of the consequences of adhering to principle. For many, Du Bois' words of warning went unheeded: "The thing we have got to face is that when for the sake of principle we take a radical position, we have got to pay for it."

The risk of taking radical positions and facing unpleasant consequences was foreign to most Black critics before 1950. Those acceptable to both Blacks and whites were primarily Professors of English, who practiced the art of dissimulation with a skill that would have astounded even Richard Wright. Langston Hughes's "The Negro Artist and the Racial Mountain" was written in defense of the younger writers of the Harlem

Renaissance against such academic critics, and Claude McKay's autobiography, *A Long Way from Home,* indicates his displeasure with the reigning academic critic of the time. To read the criticism of most Black professors, then and now, was to be in a netherworld of inarticulate discourse, where attempts to analyze Black literature by the aritificial standards of graduate schools predominated. Such critics had learned, to paraphrase Hoyt, to divorce art from life and in so doing to avoid censure from their white colleagues and possibly loss of status as well.

Such critics were likely to be incensed—and many of them were and are—at statements like those recorded by Hoyt Fuller in "Towards a Black Aesthetic": "The great bard of Avon has only limited reference to the revolutionary spirit raging in the ghetto. Which is not to say that black revolutionaries reject the 'universal statements' inherent in Shakespeare's works; what they do reject, however, is the literary assumption that the style and language and the concerns of Shakespeare establish the appropriate limits and frame of reference for black poetry and people. . . ."

"Towards a Black Aesthetic" is one of the seminal works in Black American criticism. The essay had two fundamental objectives: First, to encourage the efforts of new and younger writers who were motivated by the rebellion in the streets to produce a literature different from most of that of their predecessors, and second, to warn the Black and white critical establishment that Black critics would no longer evaluate Black literature by white standards. Whether the end result of such rebellion would be success or failure, Black writers and critics were embarking upon a journey: ". . . revolutionary black writers have turned their backs on the old 'certainties' and struck out in new, if uncharted directions. They have begun the journey to a black aesthetic."

The journey would lead into heretofore uncharted fields. Such an exploration had been initiated, here and there, by a minority of Black writers and critics, including Langston Hughes, Du Bois, and William Pickens, but their undertakings had been stifled by the combined power of the Black and white literary establishment. The present undertaking would be dangerous also, for those who had achieved status, some recognition and, in many cases, money by perpetuating the fiction of a non-Black literature, would not suffer this challenge to their authority very lightly. Black and white critics, who may have been segregated in every other walk of life, would join in an integrated assault upon a critical system that suggested the irrelevancy of much of Shakespeare to Black life and culture.

"Towards a Black Aesthetic" demanded revolutionary change in the perceptions of Black literature in terms of form, language, and content, and few of the academic critics, past or present, were capable of making such changes. They had been nourished on the various schools of Western criticism: Platonic, Aristotelian, Classic, Neo-Classic, Romantic, New Criticism, and some had become proficient in applying the tenets of those systems to literature. Thus they had become special people among academic circles and in the scholarly journals: they were black Aristotelians, black Neo-Classicists, black New Critics, strange breeds of animals indeed, stroked now and then by their white counterparts with words of recognition and praise. The courage to break with all they had learned and known required an effort they were unable to make. Hoyt often attributed their inability to do so to cowardice, but this was not necessarily the case. More likely, the journey towards a Black aesthetic demanded the kind of intellectual commitment and willingness to take risks that, given their own self-denigrating attitudes concerning Black people and culture, they could not take.

Not out of cowardice then, but out of limited intellectual curiosity and the lack of daring to confront the new and uncharted, few of the academic critics emulated the courage, honesty, and intellectual acumen of Hoyt Fuller. For it is here, in his vast display of these qualities, as much as in his salient social, political and literary commentary, that Hoyt becomes as much a paradigm for modern Black critics as Du Bois was to a generation of social scientists and historians. As a writer he evidenced the kind of intellect that comes only with immersion in the literature of the world. No literature was outside of his intellectual curiosity. He read the works of Shakespeare, Pushkin, John Killens and Gwendolyn Brooks. He read the African writers, the West Indian writers, and the European writers. His intellect was strengthened by trips to almost every continent. Few political, social, or critical systems were foreign to him. Such sophistication was demanded of the proponents of the Black Aesthetic from those who would attempt to evaluate Black literature, and—with the exception of George Kent, Houston Baker, Stephen Henderson, Carolyn Fowler, and Eugenia Collier—few were to be discovered among the ranks of Black academicians.

The strength of intellect that Hoyt Fuller brought to his writing was necessary for structuring a radical, revolutionary critical system. Equally important was the strength of character he possessed. He set high standards for those seriously involved in the articulation and analysis of Black culture. Thus Hoyt Fuller the writer and Hoyt Fuller the man complemented each other. Honesty, integrity, unswerving devotion to principle were the hallmarks of both the man and the product. He looked at our literature and our life and wrote and spoke honestly, with passion and conviction, about both. He criticized the shortcomings of Black writers and offered praise where praise was due. He criticized and admonished Black people, even while tenaciously defending us. And he challenged the white authorities on Black literature, when it was unpopular to do so.

Hoyt continually reminded us that there could be no dichotomy between politics and literature, that universality rested in the eyes of the beholder, that every literature and every critical system rested upon a superstructure—whether nationalism, as it was for Dostoyevsky and Daniel Webster; religion, as it was for Ignazio Silone and Saul Bellow; Marxism, as it was for Bertolt Brecht and Adorno; or race, as it is for the younger Black writers. That system of morals, ethics, and values that contributes to the growth of the human animal, contributes also to his perceptions and visions which form the foundation for his artistic output. Thus those who argue, derogatorily, that race forms the superstructure for a Black Aesthetic, are not suggesting, though they may think so, the absence of any superstructure at all, but rather the absence of one formed by those morals, values, and ethics of the American society which any sane Black writer should summarily reject.

To suggest that Black Aestheticians have replaced the Marxist superstructure with race is to confront the Tom Sowells of Black literature head on, those men of little vision and far less courage who seek to divorce literature from life. They would return the evaluation of Black literature to the academies, where it would either die a natural death or be bludgeoned beyond all recognition through senseless jargon, intemperate analysis, and confusing rhetoric by those seeking to accrue status, a book contract, or a promotion.

Black literature belongs to Black people, and Hoyt Fuller spent a great deal of his short but productive life propounding this fact. He did so in the face of many enemies and former colleagues, who, having grown weary of the struggle even before his death, had attempted a revision of the Black Aesthetic. Yet he held fast to his principles, realizing that the battle waged historically by Black people for humanity and decency was not yet won, that Black children still went to bed hungry at night, that Black people were still gunned down in the streets of America, that the per capita income of Blacks was only three-fifths that of whites, that the United States still waged warfare against Black people from Mississippi to Angola, and that no manner of self-serving rhetoric from Blacks at Harvard or Yale could obscure the fact that we remained oppressed, brutalized, and victimized. Given these realities, our literature must be revolutionary, must be anti-oppression, must wage warfare always against the forces of anti-man.

These were the bricks and mortar out of which Hoyt Fuller erected his cathedral. Those who would worship there were asked to bring nothing less than commitment, honesty, and dedication to truth and principle. His most memorable epitaph was actually written long before his death and was carried on the fly-leaf of *Journey to Africa:*

> I would imagine that his strongest assets are the ones least known—those of stabilizer and teacher. This is to say that his influence as a black man and his quiet movements throughout the world reflecting such have pushed writers to dedicate books to him, artists to paint his portrait and poets to write lines of him. By the force of his personality and seriousness, he demands of others who are in his context to face themselves and their predicament. . . . Hoyt W. Fuller is . . . *A Black World.*

Moonlit Chambers and *Sibylline Leaves,* or, How 'The Black Aesthetic' Changed My Life

Houston A. Baker, Jr.

I

Three months prior to a Saturday morning in early-September of 1968, I received my Ph.D. degree from the University of California at Los Angeles. The vision that came to me on graduation day was lifted—unabashedly—from a John Updike short story. I envisioned myself teaching in ivy-covered buildings, resonantly instructing "Yale men" on the nuances of literary masterpieces by Homer, Chaucer, Racine, and Donne. I imagined that I would work brilliantly and die some calm evening in a moonlit chamber with a copy of *Sibylline Leaves* spread on my chest.

The ring of the telephone that Saturday morning broke my latest rehearsal of the fantasy, and, thus, prompted my very curt "Hello!" I was immediately embarrassed when I discovered that the caller was a graduate school acquaintance from whom I had not heard in two years. He and I had been friends and comrades during our first year in the UCLA doctoral program. But he had decided not to return after that first year. Instead, he had assumed a teaching post in New York, and had completed two books. One was a collection of essays on the Black arts written by Black artists, scholars, and critics. The other was a collection of his personal essays.

I was astonished at the news of his publications. Not because I doubted his ability to write books. What surprised me was his choice of subjects. I wondered who would be interested enough in his topics to grant them serious attention. It was somewhat mysterious. I congratulated him, nonetheless, with as much enthusiasm as I could muster. And we promised to get together soon—either in New Haven, where I had assumed my own first teaching job, or in New York.

II

I entered my first classroom at Yale expecting instant silence and significantly-awed nods in my direction. I was, thus, taken totally aback by the students' indifference to my arrival. I asked two of them to make room for me at the head of the table, and they gave such venomous stares that I was tempted to flee. Searching my mental inventory of rationalizations for the acts of white people, I came up with the following: "I look so young that they don't realize I'm their teacher." I cleared my throat, pushed into the miniscule space grudged by the two students, and said: "My name is Baker." There were movements of the head, but they were not ones of significant awe, rather they were shakes of consternation, or perhaps, utter disbelief.

In addition to instructing the affluent, future leaders of America, I was expected by Yale to publish with a scholarly vengeance. My plans were well formulated. They included a series of articles on poets of the British 1890's and a full-length biography of Oscar Wilde. So convincing was I as a Black Victorianist that the *Yale Review* asked me to write an unsigned critique of David Daiches, and two journals in the field of Victorian Studies accepted my articles for publication. I was well on my way to moonlight and *Sibylline Leaves*.

III

New Haven work crews, it was reported in the Spring of 1970, were welding down manhole covers in order to prevent the underground passage of looters bent on pillaging merchandise from downtown stores. Drugstore owners and liquor outlet managers were frantically covering the windows of their establishments with sheets of heavy plywood. National Guard troops and Federal Bureau of Investigation agents were expected to arrive in awesome numbers. Undergraduate students were hastily packing expensive belongings and heading for the safety of parents and suburbs. The most amazing phenomenon of all, however, was that people were referring to me in 1970 as a "Black leader" of the Yale faculty. It was not at all clear what had happened to produce this nomination.

It just seemed as though my wife and I were suddenly in touch with Black people—Black graduate students, Black professionals, Black Panthers and members of other community groups in New Haven. The word "Revolution" became a vital sign in our day-to-day conversation. And the music sounding in our apartment changed from Western to Afro-American classics. My hair raised itself from "stocking-cap-flat" to natural heights.

I was born and reared in the American South, but, in a very real sense, my first contact with a world of *genuinely Black* activities occurred in 1968-70. When New Haven was under threat of "leftist" domination, and when May Day was brewing, I joined men and women who called for a total shift in the nature and function of the American academy and an alteration of its relationship to Black America.

May Day passed—not with the expected bang, but with a carefully-controlled whimper. There were so many hired guns (National Guardsmen, FBI Agents, Federal Marshalls) in New Haven on May Day that I am sure no one even dared to trespass an eighteenth-century ordinance regarding grazing on the public green. With the passing of May Day, the corpus of faculty, graduate students, and administrators who had found refuge (and a reason for being) in a hastily-constituted Black assembly, disappeared. When the Director of Afro-American Studies called a follow-up meeting for late May, three people attended. So much for the building of Black revolutionary institutions at Yale University.

The Black faculty and student group that we had assembled had furiously condemned the racist designs of Yale and had drafted a 10-point program to ensure a more humane and pluralistic course for the university. At a general meeting of the Yale faculty in the spring of 1970, the proposal had been unanimously adopted. By the following year, not only was the proposal forgotten, but both its drafters and its contents had been pre-empted by another vital university issue: *i.e.*, Should the junior prom continue to be held each year?

IV

For me, the most significant aspect of the disorders and disturbances in New Haven in 1970 (which were triggered by the arrest of Bobby Seale on trumped-up murder charges) was not my activity as a member of the Black assembly. The most significant aspect was the reorientation of my professional life that resulted from my participation.

The revolutionary social trends of the 1960's and 1970's found Black people in the vanguard. In fact, from the mid-1950's to the mid-1970's, the demands of Blacks were more dramatically foregrounded than at any time since the abolitionist movement. What happened in my life during these years was equivalent to what has happened to thousands of Black men and women in America from 1619 to the present: social events, in a racist society, claimed my voice. The codes of America have always kept the *majority* of Blacks from obtaining even the barest essentials necessary for a satisfying existence in a complex, modern, technological society. One of these essentials is education, literacy. My Ph.D. gave me the letters of Black spokesmanship.

I am told by a noted historian that Martin Luther King, Jr. was fond of saying when civil rights protests broke out in unpredicted and unpredictable areas of America: "Well, let me go and catch up with my people!" What happened to me in the decades of activism marked by the Sixties and Seventies was that my people demanded that I catch up.

Catching up meant re-directing my career. I effectively abandoned the Aesthetic Movement, Oscar Wilde, Chaucer, Racine, and John Donne. It was a miraculous time. I was surrounded by people bent on setting Blacks in a high place in American society. Each day, I read not only works by Black authors whom I had previously neglected, but also the pamphlet literature of the era such as *Muhammed Speaks* and *The Black Panther* newspaper.

It was difficult to go anyplace in the country without encountering among Black people ideological debate concerning the degree of violence that would be required in order to correct the longstanding abuses of American racism. No one doubted that violence (which was ever-mounting on the Establishment side of the Sixties and Seventies equation) was the *only* effective response to oppression. Frantz Fanon was the frequently-invoked prophet of the era. Anyone who believed that violence was not the *sole* answer, or who felt that street-corner thugs were not necessarily the best of all possible guides for Black people, was deemed a strange thinker, indeed. The naiveté and excess that prompted such evaluations were, of course, also responsible for the exotic primitivism that curiously extolled poverty and remoteness from power as signs of "Black Beauty."

It was difficult, during my glorious days of discovery, however, to see any of these activities of Black people as naive or excessive. I was enthralled by a utopian prospect of Blacks coming into a substantive American power. My role would be that of a teacher, and I would prepare for this role by placing myself under the guidance of "The Black Aesthetic."

V

I cannot remember when I first encountered the phrase "The Black Aesthetic." Perhaps it was on a New Haven afternoon, tucked away in a corner of Sterling Library. Or maybe it was far less medieval than that—a telephone conversation with Addison Gayle? I do know that the phrase signalled an entirely new train of thought for me. It was, in the words of Frederick Douglass: "a new and special revelation, explaining dark and mysterious things, with which my youthful understanding had struggled, but struggled in vain." I came to understand through "The Black Aesthetic" that at no time, under no conceivable set of circumstances, and at no place in the modern world would white men and women ever acknowledge the genuine power of Black creativity and concede to Black people the absolute right to generate, define, and perpetuate this powerful creativity.

Hence, it was left for Black people ourselves to organize institutions and to promulgate programs and critical projects that would break the monopoly of whites in the creative arenas of America and give rise and prominence to Black creativity. According to the dictates of a leading spokesman, "The Black Aesthetic" signalled war, a no-holds-barred conflict designed to give birth to a New Man through the agency of a new creativity. The function of the artist and the critic alike was to craft and to celebrate inspiring images of Black life.

In compliance with the injunctions of "The Black Aesthetic," I compiled my first book—an anthology of Black American literature from folklore to the present. I went on to write a series of critical essays as part of a course on Black American literature that I substituted for Homer, *et. al.*, in my second year at Yale. The essays appeared in 1972 under the title *Long Black Song.*

VI

It is difficult at this date in time (summer of 1981, Ronald Reagan and the moral majority in firm control) to explain the factors that brought about the dramatic surge of Black people and Black creativity during the

Sixties and Seventies. The movement of the Black masses was surely one cause of positive action. Surely, too, the efforts of writers, thinkers, and intellectuals who allied themselves with the movement of the masses had much to do with this surge. An anomalous blend of white liberal sentiment and control at the uper echelons of national power in the 1960's combined with an outgoing Black activism at local levels of America to produce a breach in the stony walls of oppression. Some fair number of Black citizens slipped through.

The sealing of this breach came with devastating swiftness, however. Few, it seems to me, can disagree that our present Chief Executive is but a geriatric avatar of President Richard M. Nixon, who was blown to power on the "law-and-order" winds of 1968.

The combination of liberal sentiment at the national level and local Black activism would not have been possible at all, however, had it not been for the courageous dedication to change of Black spokespeople like those who instituted "The Black Aesthetic." Of these, none was so influential and dedicated as Hoyt W. Fuller, the editor and journalist responsible for *Black World* and *First World* magazines. Hoyt was a man who quite literally gave voice to hundreds of spokespersons seeking a world in which Black people could claim our just rights and privileges. He gave a striking legitimacy to my own work and to that of many other Black academicians. A concluding anecdote will perhaps suffice to give an idea of the seminal role he played *vis-à-vis* the established literary-critical and creative codes of America.

VII

I remember sitting in an elegant dining hall at Yale listening to the white man who was in charge of English department lectures for the 1969-70 academic year: "I don't think we can act on your request to invite Mr. Fuller to speak," he said. "I have now read some of his writings, and he really seems to me more a literary policeman than a critic." The man's condescension and smugness were comically enlightening. They enabled me to recognize exactly how Hoyt must have appeared to white onlookers and to Black shuckers-and-jivers for the *bourgeoisie*. He loomed menacingly as a formulator and defender of a new law that said Black people and black interests were to be served prior to the interests of any other group. He demanded a halt to white cultural aggression and suggested that cultural criminals (those who perpetrated stereotyped and negative images of Blacks) should be forcefully apprehended and exiled.

I felt comfortable, indeed legitimate, on joining the initial stages of labor of "The Black Aesthetic." One law for the ox and the lion (especially if you happened not to be a lion) did seem to be a form of rank tyranny. I was enthusiastic about the new dispensation proposed by Hoyt Fuller. It allowed me to envision an entirely different future for myself. In those wonderful days of the late Sixties and early Seventies, the Black poet Etheridge Knight's injunctions seemed far more appropriate than the fantasies of John Updike.

"Black poets," wrote Knight, "should live—not leap/From steel bridges (Like the white boys do." "The Black Aesthetic" constituted a vibrant *building of bridges* for a Black tomorrow. If its work has never been completed, and if its original intentions were perverted by hustlers, false rhetoricians, and neo-conservative apostates, still its work was well begun. A truly modern criticism of *Black* American literature began with its work. Such labor saved me from the enervating prospect of moonlit chambers and *Sibylline Leaves*. In the late Sixties and early Seventies, and under the prospect of "The Black Aesthetic," it came to seem far more fitting for me to conceive of my ending in terms projected by Knight:

Let All Black Poets die as trumpets,
And be buried in the dust of marching feet.

■■■■■■■■■■■■■■■■■■■■■■■

Some Thoughts on The Black Aesthetic

Eugenia Collier

The concept of a Black aesthetic is so simple, so obvious that the fact of our questioning its validity is a monument to our eternal devotion to Ol' Massa.

A Black aesthetic is based upon the conviction that Black people share a complex of perceptions that do not have the same meaning for other people. While it is true that all humans have certain basic physiological and emotional traits, socio-historical experience divides us into ethnic groups whose members have more in common with each other than with members of other groups, even though there may be overlapping. We all belong to ethnic groups. Ethnicity is inescapable. There is no such thing as a "universal" person.

The problem which limits American Blacks is our confused definition of our ethnic group. We still believe, in spite of the unheeded lessons of history, that we are Americans who happen to be Negro. A more realistic view is that we are Black people who happen to be Americans. Now, lest the patriotic accuse me of some weird kind of treason, let me say quickly that this concept does not preclude loyalty to the nation of one's birth. Instead of Negro Americans as opposed to white Americans, we need to think of ourselves as American Blacks as differentiated from, say, West Indian Blacks or Latin American Blacks.

The difference is profound. If we are Americans, aspiring to acceptance by our "fellow" (white) Americans, then we are lost. The no-color people emanating from Europe, spurred by madness, have subdued this world and convinced the oppressed that white is the source of all things bright and beautiful. The white world has rejected our humanity totally and completely from the day when the first white man set foot upon soil occupied by people of color. Moreover, their power is created from the ashes of other peoples' cultures. Unchecked, they will destroy the world and themselves with it. To define ourselves as an integral part of them is to embrace our own destruction.

We are not Americans who happen to be Negro. We are Black people who happen to be Americans. We are blood kin to Black people all over this globe. This is the perspective of the Black aesthetic. It is a perspective which strikes terror in the hearts of those who cling to the status quo, for such thinking—as simple and obvious as it is, is revolutionary. It is revolutionary simply because the status quo, based as it is upon racial oppression, is wrong. If Black people everywhere accepted this view *and really believed it*, our oppression would end in one generation. And our children would be free.

I did not always think in this manner. I was reared on all the self-destructive myths that have ever haunted Black people. For most of my life, I really thought that Negroes had to prove to white people that we deserved our civil rights; I thought that the key to it all was ultimate acceptance by white people. Meanwhile, those other dark-skinned, crinkly-haired people from Trinidad and those places, with their funny accents and weird ways, had nothing to do with who *I* was. I was going to work hard, be intelligent and moral and upright, and someday I and other such Negroes would be granted our status as full-fledged, one hundred percent Americans.

(But what about the Bigger Thomases? And the Sister Margarets? . . .)

The Black aesthetic was the pathway to my own personal enlightenment. And since I am not only a unique individual—as all of us are—but also a part of the community of Black folk, perhaps my experience is shared by others and therefore significant and worth the telling.

For me the Sixties were years of terrible personal upheaval. At the end of the Sixties, I was facing life as a single-again mother no longer young and as lost as a pebble in a whirlwind. Realizing intuitively that my only anchor was my own Self, I decided to begin on a scholarly project. I wrote to my old friend Richard Long for help in getting started. Richard suggested—and for this I will bless him forever—that I prepare a monograph on Black American literature of the 1960's for Atlanta University's Center for African and Afro-American Studies,which he had developed. The nucleus source material for this project, he said, might be *Negro Digest.*

That work was the star that guided me out of the desert. The monograph was never published. It was so dreadfully naive, I'm glad it wasn't. But the research behind it changed the direction of my thinking, my values, my Self. All at once, I was confronted by a whole body of writing that addressed *my* world, that portrayed the people *I* knew, that gave me perspective on *my* Self. Fiction, poetry, drama, essays—all cleared away the debris in my mind and replaced it with a far different image of my/our Self. I was like a half-blind person who, for the first time, puts on eyeglasses. Blurred and formless things became clear. Menacing shadows yielded up their secrets, and I was no longer afraid.

Understand, I had studied literature all my life. Since childhood I had been an avid reader. By now I had my Master's degree in American literature from Columbia. None of my courses had included any Black authors; none of the criticism had assessed Black literature; none of the works had portrayed Black people except as inferiors. By the same token, most of the literature I studied had only a vague, general relationship to me and mine. Few of the characters resembled anybody I knew. Few of the themes dealt with any of my concerns. Most of the criticism was so otherworldly that it was little more than some kind of intellectual puzzle to be solved. On my own, I had studied works by American Blacks and had, indeed, published a piece or two. But my context was still this (WASP) American literature, which in my blindness I had thought was the only standard.

The writers of the Sixties freed me. Beginning with *Negro Digest* and working outward to books and periodicals, tracking down the works of specific authors, attending conferences, meeting the writers themselves and rapping with them, I became a different and much wiser person. The process was gradual and continues today.

In the summer of 1969, I met Hoyt Fuller. Richard Long had invited us both to be consultants at a workshop in Atlanta University. I was anxious to meet Hoyt, for I greatly admired his work as editor of *Negro Digest*. For some reason, I pictured him as a short, squat, hyperactive little man with piercing eyes behind round gold-rimmed glasses. The moment I saw that tall, beautiful man in the black turtle-neck, his quietly intelligent eyes gazing at the students, his smooth voice sharing with them the products of a brilliant mind, I knew that Hoyt Fuller would be a friend and a positive influence on all my life. And so he has been. The force of his personality, the depth of his convictions provided a dynamic which, perhaps more than any other single factor, nurtured the Black aesthetic. Certainly the fact of his existence was a pivot on which turned the entire direction of my life. This change in direction accelerated immediately after the Atlanta meeting.

Five years earlier, I had written a story. Since childhood I had written stories, sporatically, but I never had any faith in their quality. With good reason: they were terrible. The characters were always the kind of people I was reading about—white people. As I grew older, the characters (I realize now) were white people with Black accents. The themes dealt with the petty conflicts of individuals, not with the destiny of a people. The stories did not grow from the soil; they were spawned by my own misconceptions.

But early in 1964, drowning in a personal crisis, I wrote "Marigolds." One evening, rather than commit murder or suicide, I wrote. All night and all the next day, I wrote, compelled by some life-force that would not let me stop. The story leaped from so deep inside that there was no room for white folks or for the racist myths that had undergirded my warped vision. The story was about a Black girl in rural Maryland during the Depression and how, out of her own pain, she committed a destructive act which ultimately taught her compassion. I couldn't stop writing until the story was finished. Then I slept.

Having no clear idea what to do with the story, I sent it to an agency advertised in a writers' magazine—along with a fee for an assessment and, hopefully, placement. The agency responded that it was nice that I had made an effort, but really, the story was hopeless. There was neither plot nor conflict—after all, the poverty of the people provided no conflict, because the people had always been poor and always would be. The (Black) characters were not particularly interesting. The dialect was pretty good, but the story had little else to recommend it. Good try, girl. Thanks but no thanks. So I stuck the story in a drawer and forgot it. Another failure.

Four years later, exploring *Negro Digest* with a feeling of *deja vu*, I realized that the fiction bore a family resemblance to my story. I exhumed the story and, without changing a word, sent it to *Negro Digest*. Months later, when I met Hoyt in Atlanta, I hinted that I had not heard anything about my work. With apologies—they were understaffed and had a back-log of manuscripts—he said he would look it up.

"What a fine and sensitive story 'Marigolds' is!", he wrote some weeks later. "Why have you not been writing all these years?" The story received the Gwendolyn Brooks Award for Fiction that year. It has been reprinted often, and I have received many letters from people who read it. Most important, Ruby Dee did a reading from it; she read it exactly the way I "heard" it on the frenzied night and day of its creation.

Since then I have developed as a writer and critic, as a Black *person*. The concept of a Black aesthetic freed me of the notion that art had to be legitimized by white critics' approval, that I am a "colored" person in a white world. Consequently, I am no longer an alienated person banging on locked doors; I am part of a community made beautiful by generations of strength and wisdom, a worldwide community which can, if we are wise and strong, prevail.

We American Black intellectuals have a lot of problems with definitions. We expect neat, objective, codified definitions of things— otherwise those things do not exist. "I don't bother with Negritude— nobody's ever told me what it is!" . . . "I get so irked when these people talk about 'the Black experience.' What does *that* mean?" . . . Some definitions come from a soul-deep area of the Self which recognizes Truth. These definitions don't need codifying. If you see the Black aesthetic and don't recognize it, then you're not ready to deal with it.

David Dorsey, in his definitive essay "Formal Elements of the Black Aesthetic in Poetry," has defined the term "aesthetic" as "the syndrome of factors within a work of art which govern the audience's perception of, and appreciation of the work, that is, the sum of factors with disparate relative importances which are noted consciously or uncon-sciously, by the audience and prized or disparaged." He goes on to say, "A black aesthetic therefore would be the syndrome of internal factors gov-erning a black audience's perception and appreciation of a work of art." In literature, music, drama, painting, and so forth, Black art has certain characteristics that make it differ from the art of other peoples' in theme, form, and impact. Others can, of course, be moved by Black people's art. For art, ultimately, is a gift to the world, a contribution to humanity's pool. But our contribution is recognizable as Black, emanating from a nuclear culture and a diaspora.

The greatest enemy of the Black aesthetic is Black artists and critics who believe the myths of the establishment. We cling to the oppres-sor as a child clings to an abusive mother. Sixty years ago, when Du Bois and other Black thinkers suggested that there was a Negro literature, other

Blacks complained vociferously that there was one standard for all, that Blacks must prove to the world (apparently the white world) that we could meet that standard, and most important, that "Negro-literature" critics were stifling Negro writers by confining them to "Negro" themes. This short-sighted argument persists today.

The Black aesthetic is not confining but liberating. Nobody is telling artists how to create. Would that be possible? As a writer of fiction as well as criticism, I KNOW that when you create, you are alone with your deepest self and with your history. No critic can tell you what to write. That's just the point. This great white "standard" has told us how we must write, has tried to fit us into its mold, though our historical experience has given us a different contour. Though white criticism itself, certainly in America, has disparaged our work or ignored it. The Black aesthetic does not prescribe how one must create—it describes creativity which has issued from a Black perspective. It emphasizes the validity of our historical experience, which began not in bondage but in freedom, in the place where humankind began. It enlarges our vision. It enables us to be ourselves. Our Black selves.

I am not minimizing the fact of our dual heritage. All Americans except the original inhabitants have a dual heritage. But there is a difference. Europeans came here voluntarily, seeking an easier life. Africans were torn from home and family and were brought in chains to build this nation for the Europeans. These are historical facts which we forget at our peril. They define the nature of our dual heritage. Any Black artist who chooses to create according to current white critical standards is certainly free to do so, and may the gods be with him. He is simply not creating from a Black aesthetic.

The impetus of the Sixties, which thrust the Black aesthetic to the foreground of creativity, died in the Seventies. For reasons complex and incomprehensible, at least to me, we stopped talking about a Black aesthetic, got into a whole different kind of writing.

But endings are also beginnings. We have lost our friend and mentor Hoyt Fuller, whose convictions were a vital dynamic in the development of the Black aesthetic and whose great personal sacrifice made *First World* a reality. It is time for reassessment. I would like to see the current crop of writers and critics return to the ever-recurring concept of the Black aesthetic, not to make it slickly popular, but to grapple with basic, centuries-old concepts of what constitutes art. I would like to see us deal with the fact that white publishers pander to a white public and to view this conservative, racist time as an impetus to support our own publishing companies and to satisfy and enlighten our own public.

Make no mistake: The Black aesthetic goes beyond this time and this place. Whether or not this generation considers it valid, it will surface in times and places undreamed of by us who struggle to keep afloat in this age. For if, as I believe, the Black aesthetic is grounded in the experience of Black people from the dawn of mankind, then it will exist regardless of the wisdom or folly of this moment.

People are what they believe they are. If we believe that we are

Americans who happen to be Negro, who must deserve our freedom, whose "progress" is measured by our acceptability by white Americans, then that is what we are. If we believe that we are Black people in a Black world, who happen to be Americans—and better ones than those who soil the American dream by oppressing others; if we believe that we are people whose labor built this nation and whose grace and fortitude and wisdom are an inspiration to the entire world—then that is what we are, and freedom is within our grasp.

We have the power of self-definition. We are what we believe we are. The Black aesthetic taught me that.

■■■■■■■■■■■■■■■■■■■■■■■■

Watching Just The Same: Some Recollections of Hoyt

Richard A. Long

Inevitably, in agreeing to a suggestion that I sketch in something of the range of Hoyt Fuller's interests, his "renaissance" quality if you will, I have to prepare a personal and personalized account, in part because many of those interests were rarely indicated in print, in part because we shared a large number of these in common from 1967 to his death. Such an account has also to be replete with the names of persons and places.

Hoyt relished people, whether he approved of them or not. Consequently he was always eager and anxious to know not only the product, but also its creator. He was also much more tolerant than his acerbic public statements would have led one to expect. He was often genuinely delighted by the personalities of those whose political or esthetic postures he was prone to abhor. This sprang in part form his tendency to ascribe to people positions rather more rigid and less nuanced than they in fact held or could have held, given their intelligence, circumstances or background. By the same token, he was often troubled by unsatisfactory traits among those with "correct" positions, and suffered much discomfort and disillusion because of them. Hoyt also enjoyed travel to new places, though he was rather more inclined than I to be distressed by inefficiency, negligence, and diffident hygiene.

The Festival of Negro Arts held in Dakar [Senegal] in April of 1966 presented many of the facets of Black life and offered many of the challenges and paradoxes which were to occupy Hoyt during the years that followed. It was at Dakar that I first encountered Hoyt. He was vaguely attached to the group from Chicago who were covering the festival for the Johnson Publications. The attachment was vague, since he did not in fact identify himself with the general tone of the Johnson Publications.

The result of the vision of Alioune Diop and his associates at *Presence Africaine* in Paris and of the patronage of President Senghor, the festival brought to Dakar during that month, beginning with a colloquium which preceded the festival proper, the largest group of Black scholars, intellectuals and performers ever gathered on an international scale. For Hoyt it was at once an affirmation of the direction that he was taking in editing the revived *Negro Digest* and a dramatization of the issue of cultural colonization as he was beginning to define it; it was a special grief to him that the chair of the United States committee was a white woman. He further argued that the festival had in effect been "closed" to the larger Black public by the elitist American Society of African Culture, headed by John A. Davis, since little publicity about it had been circulated in the United States and no appeal had been made to the Black public for financial support or participation.

Hoyt later brought his perspective forcefully into the United States Committee planning for Festac '77, and while he never relented in his critique of the stance of AMSAC in 1966, he developed an understanding of the problems they would have encountered had they adopted his strategy.

In spite, however, of the various reservations about Dakar which he ventilated fully in the pages of *Negro Digest* subsequent to the festival, the event itself was profoundly exciting to him as it was to most of the Afro-Americans who attended. Their numbers included Etta Moten Barnett, Zelma George, Benjamin Quarles, James A. Porter, Millicent Dobbs Jordan, James E. Lewis, Hale Woodruff, and Frederidck O'Neal. Two honored elders singled out for special honors by Senghor were Langston Hughes and Duke Ellington.

Mercer Cook was, appropriately enough, the United States Ambassador to Senegal at the time. A brilliant reception given by him and his wife Vashti featured music by the Duke Ellington Orchestra. Another reception, offered by the U.S. chair, Mrs. Virginia Ennis-Jones, presented Martina Arroyo and the Marion Williams Singers. The festival brought Lavinia Williams from Haiti, John Akar from Sierra Leone, and Marpessa Dawn, still in the flush of her triumph in *Black Orpheus*, from Paris. Katherine Dunham moved like a presiding presence through the festivities. There was capoeira from Bahia, Nubian dancing from Egypt, a pageant at Gorée with a script by Jean Brierre. The crowning moment of the festival was the appearance of Alvin Ailey and his troupe.

A year later, in April of 1967, I met Hoyt at a weekend forum, "Conversation with Africa," convened by Dr. Frederick Patterson, then president of the Phelps-Stokes Fund, at Capohosic, Virginia, not far from Hampton Institute where I was then teaching. The conference center at Capohosic is located at the summer and retirement home of Robert Russa Moton, overlooking the James River. With absolutely no distractions in the vicinity, conferences at Capohosic are always serious morning-to-evening affairs. Apart from Dr. Patterson himself, the most impressive person at this "Conversation" was Richard B. Moore, whose Barbadian eloquence and dynamism were still in full vigor. Both during the group discussions and in casual conversation during the intervals for meals and general conviviality, Hoyt and I discovered mutual interests, mutual friends, and mutual concerns about the direction of Afro-American life and its relations and interfaces with Africa and the rest of the world. We also discovered that we would both be going to Europe that summer and exchanged notes about where our paths would cross.

In June, both Hoyt and I were in Barcelona, where we met and talked. I do not now remember whether he went to Mallorca, where at an earlier period he had spent a year writing, before going to Guinea to live, drawn there by the excitement and bright promise of that nation's independence. We met again that summer in Paris, where I introduced him to Beauford Delaney.

When I went to Atlanta University in 1968 with the idea of holding a conference on African and African-American Studies in response to the burgeoning of interest in the topic, Hoyt was available to participate. And he did so enthusiastically each year down to the last full conference in 1977. The CAAS conferences became, indeed, a principal focus in his busy year of editing, writing, speaking, and occasional teaching. It was an occasion for meeting regularly a number of persons such as George Kent, Eugenia Collier, Eleanor Traylor, John H. Clarke, Lucy Grigsby, and occasionally Sara Webster Fabio, Toni Cade Bambara and many, many others. Hoyt made other visits to Atlanta in the course of the year to visit his mother. I usually saw him on these occasions and met him also in New York and Washington, where we both found ourselves frequently. I rarely went to Chicago.

In 1971, Hoyt and I, along with a number of other Afro-Americans, were invited by President Senghor to Dakar to attend a Colloquium on *Negritude*. The coloquium was in part a response to the festival held in Algiers which had provided a stage for confrontation between Eldridge Cleaver and Stokely Carmichael as well as a forum for the Guineans and others to attack Senghor under the guise of attacking *Negritude* in a mixture of pronouncements drawing from the presumed racelessness of Islam and Marxism. Hoyt had attended but did particularly enjoy the Algiers festival. He welcomed the opportunity to return to Dakar, though the possible use of the colloquium as a propaganda counterblast was clear to him.

In fact, the colloquium was most congenial, bringing a number of eloquent intellectuals, particularly from francophone Africa, to our attention. The United States delegation included E. A. Jones, Dorothy Porter, and Lillian Anthony. René Piquion was there from Haiti. Leon Damas, then in the process of settling in the United States, was also present, though his sudden hospitalization following an attack was a source of concern. Damas appeared, however, seemingly recovered, for the impressive closing ceremonies.

The most electrifying event in the Colloquium, however, was Senghor's announcement that, following an agreement with General Gowan, Nigeria, now recovering from its civil war, would host the Second Festival of Negro Arts in 1974. At the time of the 1966 festival, the then Nigerian government had agreed to receive the festival in 1970, thus establishing a quadrennial rhythm for this significant event. The civil war naturally frustrated any such project. Now there was a prospect of a festival taking place eight years later. This festival, ultimately to be known as Festac, actually took place in 1977, after two more governmental crises in Nigeria and the sacking of the first Nigerian festival commissioner, as well as the expulsion of Alioune Diop, the ultimate source of the festival idea, from his post as director of the secretariat.

Hoyt was determined that a cultural event as important as the forthcoming festival should reach as wide a Black constituency in the

United States as possible. As soon as the Nigerian government had appointed its Commissioner for the festival, Chief Anthony Enahoro, and a visit to the United States was arranged for him, Hoyt, with the cooperation of a group of conveners, called a "congress" at Chicago to set in motion the machinery for selecting a representative United States Committee. Out of this effort Ossie Davis was named chair, and Hoyt vice-chair.

In the early days of the committee's functioning there were inevitable conflicts and problems. Those with Chief Enahoro resulted in part from the fact that he was accustomed to dealing with government-appointed committees in most zones and with officials having governmental status. On the other hand, Ossie Davis, though committed to the festival idea, had too many projects afoot to coordinate so vast a *pro bono* effort. Eventually Ossie resigned from the chair and was succeeded by Jeff Donaldson who ultimately had to take leave from his position as chair of the Art Department of Howard University to bring the committee effort to completion. In all of this, Hoyt was always at the center, and the years of work on Festac '77 certainly drained him, as he struggled at the same time to keep *Negro Digest*, now named *Black World*, afloat. (The name was changed in May, 1970.)

While Hoyt had long talked of launching a literary magazine independent of Johnson Publications and of moving to Atlanta, these two possibilities became necessities when Johnson abruptly terminated the publication of *Black World*, after denying to Hoyt that rumors to that effect circulating among Johnson's staff were true. The story of the founding of *First World* belongs elsewhere, but Hoyt moved to Atlanta with a great deal of enthusiasm to begin the new venture.

During the early Seventies, with very little urging on my part, Hoyt accompanied me on several visits to the Caribbean, which he had not seen before. We went to Puerto Rico, on one occasion with Earl Clowney, where we saw Sylvia del Villard, whose aesthetic and whose politics—uniquely Black at that time in Puerto Rico—gratified Hoyt immensely. In Jamaica, I introduced him to Louise Bennett and to Rex Nettleford; they in turn presented him to a number of other Jamaican artists and intellectuals. We went to Haiti, where he already knew René Piquion. There he met Pierre Monosiet, then engaged in organizing the Museum of Haitian Art. One of our many visits to Haiti was on a study group of colleagues from Atlanta, including Lucy Grigsby, Gloria Blackwell, Edith and Hubert Ross, Dora McDonald, and Earle Clowney.

While Hoyt had, and indeed maintained, some residual lack of sympathy for aspects of the tone and attitude of Caribbean elites, the result clearly of a social formation which was different from ours, he developed as a result of these visits an enhanced sensitivity to the nuances of the Black world that he considered it his mission to connect up. Unfortunately, he went to Jamaica only after the death of Amy Jacques Garvey, thus failing to meet that dynamic woman whose critique of Jamaica and other parts of the Black world was always free from cant and illusion.

It was after Hoyt moved to Atlanta that I began to elaborate the idea of the New World Festival of the African Diaspora as a successor to the CAAS conferences which had in a sense run their course. Hoyt was a useful and enthusiastic member of the first advisory committee, which included Eugenia Collier, Eleanor Traylor, Margaret Burroughs, Fletcher Robinson, Helen Johnson, John H. Clarke and several others, most of whom were associated with CAAS, *First World* or both. He was a full participant in all aspects of the festivals held in Brazil in 1978 and in Haiti in 1979, and in some ways probably found his participation in these festivals, with the wide range of conviviality they provided, as relaxing as many experiences of the post-*Black World* era.

In Brazil, particularly, since it was his first visit there, he found a somewhat different Black experience that his encounters with Brazilians in the United States had only partially prepared him for. Along with several members of the festival advisory committee, he met both in Salvador and in Rio with a number of Black Brazilians struggling with the shape of racism in their society; the results of this experience were reflected in *First World*.

The festival in Haiti was also a source of satisfaction to him. Many of the veterans of Diaspora I returned, such as his friends Cledie Taylor and Henri Umbagi King, artists from Detroit. New to the Diaspora scene, but battle-scarred Festac veterans, were Jeff Donaldson, Abena Brown, and Samella Lewis. Most touching was the appearance of Sarah Webster Fabio, who had only a few more months to live, and was fully aware of it, but had come determined to see the friends she would find there. In contrast to what we had found in Brazil, the United States Embassy in Haiti was most helpful, headed as it was by Ambassador William Jones, with Millie McCoo as cultural affairs officer.

In the Spring of 1980, James Baldwin came to Atlanta as part of an extended tour he was doing through the South. Hoyt had many conversations with him and appears in the film made of Jimmy's visit by a British film crew. In the summer, Maya Angelou made her first visit to Atlanta to receive an honorary degree at Atlanta University—Baldwin had been awarded one in the Spring. I took Maya, Ella Yates, and Hoyt to dinner at Ivey's South. Afterwards, Hoyt had an involved discussion with Maya and Andrew Young, who had not by any means been given sympathetic treatment in *First World*, though Andy, typically, had exhibited Christian understanding in the matter.

In some ways, the distinct high point of Hoyt's Atlanta and *First World* years was the testimonial given at Ivey's South in November 1980. Arranged by Jan Douglass and Beni Ivey to fall during the Black South Conference organized by Sondra O'Neale, the occasion brought warm words from many people, including Hoyt's good friend Sterling Brown; Andrew Young spoke feelingly of *First World*'s mission. Oscar Brown, Jr. performed memorably. Dozens of Atlanta residents expressed support, surprising Hoyt more than it should have, but gratifying him fully. Jan and Beni had, of course, brought their well-honed activist and public service skills to the event. Neither they nor I had any suspicion that in six months the three of us would join together to plan a memorial program for Hoyt, dead at fifty-seven.

Consciously Hoyt: Colleague, Mentor, Friend

Carole A. Parks

October 30, 1979

Dear Carole:

I have a moment's breathing spell. . . . It occurred to me that in sending off that marathon letter I still had failed to make the final essential point that I intended—as explanation for my staying and trying to do the job:

There is a fundamental contradiction between seeking SECU-RITY and seeking measurable evolution and change within society.

My critics and those who "feel sorry" for me do not understand this, of course; but, then, how many of them are genuinely concerned with and involved in measurable CHANGE in this society?

That's all about that.

Have a good and happy life.

Love,
Hoyt

Hoyt Fuller was a brilliant man, an accomplished journalist, editor, critic, essayist, creative writer, speaker, teacher—a veritable fountain of wisdom on almost any subject. There are probably as many perspectives on why he was so magnetic as there are people who sought his counsel. He touched each of us differently, and each of us felt uniquely special in those eyes whose vision we respected beyond almost any other.

In retrospect, I believe that what we really appreciated was

Hoyt's simplicity. For despite his Renaissance Man achievements and the multi-layered personality that made him an enigma to even his closest friends, you always knew where Hoyt stood. He abhorred what he called "confusion." He could cut through waste, refine the complex and get right to the point with awe-inspiring precision. He rarely equivocated, never shuffled. He put one foot in front of the other with unmistakable direction, leaving clear prints for us to follow—if we wanted to. Now, there's no denying Hoyt's persuasiveness; you had to be pretty confident (or foolhardy) to challenge the forcefulness of his arguments. Yet Hoyt did not preoccupy himself with convincing others to walk in his steps; he devoted too much time to blazing his own path to worry about that. In fact, that's what impressed me most about Hoyt: that he lived so *consciously*.

Hoyt refused to abdicate control of his life, to be swept along by currents others acceded to. He eagerly absorbed knowledge, made it a kiln for forging his awareness into a weapon against ignorance. He knew full well that consciousness leads to understanding, that understanding carries responsibility, and that responsibility means accepting the consequences for what one does or does not do. Hoyt did not allow rationalizations from those who should know better. If you thought you did something unconsciously, he assumed you would learn why before you did it again. If you took an action consciously, he simply wanted you to own it. Of course, that could be pretty hard on those who intended to float through their existence attributing their lives to everyone else. Or to those who planned to watch life from the shorelines, identifying with whichever contestant appeared to be winning at the moment.

Hoyt seemed to approach his own life as a series of conscious decisions about who he would be and what actions would most unequivocally reflect that decision. Which brings me to the central point I'd like to make about Hoyt as an individual, a role model and an editor. And that is: Hoyt *chose* to be Black. "So what?", you ask. After all, physically, he couldn't have been mistaken for anything *but* Black. And during the late Sixties to mid-Seventies when his influence flourished, it was even rather fashionable to be *some* kind of Black. Indeed, several different viewpoints about Blackness competed with each other.

At one extreme were those who saw the focus on Blackness as contributing to hangups about race or color. It meant continued polarization, a dangerous form of self-imposed segregation that played right into the hands of those who wanted to deny our basic humanity. This group included many who considered themselves "universal"—not Black—writers. They rejected any labels they perceived to set limits on their ability to speak to all people. At the other extreme were those who wanted to strip themselves of European influences, who rejected "universal" work which described pastoral beauty rather than ghetto realities, which explored unrequited love instead of armed struggle. Some chose African names, dress and language. Others affected the talk, walk and look of urban "streetfolk" and revolutionaries. With good reason, they believed African peoples would not be able to dialogue profitably with whites until we had gotten ourselves together first.

Like the universalists, Hoyt never accepted limitations, but, then, he didn't see Blackness as any more limiting to us than was Shakespeare's concentration on a tiny segment of Elizabethan Englishmen. Hoyt felt the whole subject of Blackness went beyond superficialities or tactics. He saw the struggle as one over culture—over the identities, values and perspectives that determine our everyday decisions and actions. Had he so chosen, Hoyt could have moved quite comfortably among the universalists and their white brethren. He knew as much or more about European culture; had lived in the cultural meccas of France, Italy and Spain; routinely received invitations from the intelligentsia of Europe, Africa, the Caribbean, South America, and the U.S. The paternalistic literary establishment courted him determinedly, smuggly believing someone of his calibre would certainly gravitate to their ranks, realizing too late that he was a formidable foe who meant absolutely that we would determine the value of our own work.

Many in the Black bourgeoisie must have wondered when he would come to his senses. You could see it in their eyes: Here was such a fine specimen of the race. So patrician in his tall, stately bearing, so elegant in appearance and polished manners. He spoke with such commanding eloquence in perfectly modulated English (or French or Italian). He had virtually no rhythm, seemed incapable of swallowing the endings of words, and met references to the latest Black fad with a blank stare. Why, oh why, then, did he insist on cultivating bushy headed slang-slingers like those who wandered into his scruffy writers' workshop at Michigan Avenue and 35th Street?

For more reasons than his inability to execute the latest dance, Hoyt never took his Blackness for granted. Much to the chagrin of some "Blacker than thou" folks, Hoyt thought Black Consciousness meant just that: taking one's assumption of Blackness as a responsibility, not just an accident of birth. To him, the decision to be Black meant serious study of our heritage, awareness of the many forces that chip away at our cultural values, understanding of our role in a global context, the willingness to make sacrifices for future generations—and the honesty to admit that sometimes we act in conflict with the aggregate good because it seems easier or more advantageous for us as individuals.

He brought this same Blackconsciousness to *Negro Digest/Black World* and *First World*. Above all, Hoyt wanted the magazines to risk. He used them to encourage us—the young in particular—to study different ways for gaining more control over our lives, for participating in the world, for exploring and acting upon our imaginations. He gave writers a respected forum where they could experiment with old molds, fire and twist a cold language into new forms, turn traditional images upside down or inside out until we got the feel again of making something out of our selves.

Hoyt bore a lot of criticism for publishing the unknown, the untested, the rejects from mainstream journals. He could not have cared less. He wasn't interested in proving to whites our accomplished mimicry of what they'd already done and probably discarded. He saw only the

talent unbridaled all around him. He saw its need to be channelled pro-
ductively and to receive positive direction. His magazines would always be
a place where writers could kick off their shoes and feel at home—walk
around in their bare feet if they wanted to. Where a recently discovered
Sonia Sanchez or Haki Madhubuti could exchange ideas with each other,
then see what James Baldwin or Gwen Brooks had to say. Similarly, *Black
World* encouraged groundbreaking historical, social, political and economic analyses, the visual and theater arts. Its international perspective covered revolution in Southern Africa 10 years before the major media decided that the Black oppression there was news. *Black World* brought us
personal messages from the heads of state Hoyt visited in Senegal, Lagos
or Tanzania. It carried reports from the South Pacific, South America and
other places where Blacks wanted us to know they were alive and watching what their American brothers and sisters were doing.

Nowhere else could you see such a panorama, such a spectrum of
colors and emotions, from the past to the present, the rural to the urban,
our elders to our youth, east to west, tragedies to triumphs. No one
relished the magazines' offerings more than Hoyt. For while he liked
teaching, he loved to learn. We would plow with anticipation through the
stacks of manuscripts we received each day, knowing we'd find more
fresh, exciting thoughts than we had space to print. Hoyt cherished our
contributors. They were the ones who made each issue an adventure.
They were the ones who infused him with the inspiration to trumpet their
songs regardless of what the critics said.

In the last major speech he gave, in Chicago, Hoyt revealed that,
"(The) search I have been engaged in all the days of my life (is) a search
for nothing so mundane and banal as roots, but a search for a spiritual
essence that will enable me, at last, to find a kind of peace." Our world
traveler had not yet found a place to rest. Of America he asked, "Do we
want to be party to a conspiracy to control the world for the comfort of
stockholders in the suburbs—or even for Black men and women with
token jobs at powerful corporations? Will we, finally, be home in such a
place?" After numerous trips to the Motherland, he made the "devastating
discovery . . . that I also was not at home in Africa," for Africans there
suffered from the same deadly disease that turns Black people into white
parodies.

"The Black Consciousness Movement of the Sixties saved my
life," he said. "Africans in America, a significant number of them, for the
first effective time in our history—rejected the American, the Western,
ethic. We do not want to be white people in Black skins, the Movement
leaders said. We are an African people, and we want to rid ourselves of our
inbred allegiances to the European ethic and reclaim those spiritual values
which have sustained and guided our people for centuries." He continued, "Those who came here in chains brought with them a view of the
world and a deep connection with all living things that centuries of brutality and degradation have not erased. In reclaiming that legacy, we will do
ourselves a great honor and possibly contribute to the salvation of America. . . . There is a horror in the world," he concluded. "And there is

hope. But the hopeful can find no wholeness by accepting the horror. It is our duty to reject America's inclination toward the horrible. It is our task to transform America so that we can be at home here, at last."

A young woman who read part of my piece on Hoyt as it was being typed said, "This Hoyt Fuller sounds like he was quite a person, but I'm not sure I could live up to his standards." I smiled, reassuring her that *he* couldn't always do so, either. He would laugh along with us on those occasions when we'd gleefully point to a clay toe peeking out from beneath his royal robes. The point is that—from the boy forced to leave his native Atlanta for fighting with an insolent white streetcar conductor, to the young man who took refuge abroad because he came close to throttling another white man in New York, to the mature adult who realized dreams through *Black World* in Chicago and ultimately returned to Atlanta to shoulder *First World*—Hoyt never abandoned his soul.

Two years after our journey to Atlanta to launch *First World*, I finally admitted to myself that I could no longer withstand the various pressures we experienced publishing the new journal. I told Hoyt, "I think if I stay here, it will kill me." We both knew how hard it would be for him to carry on alone. But, as always, he understood and said simply that going on with the magazine was something *he* had to do. I took a long look at that bull-headed, vain, sometimes pompous man—my colleague, mentor and friend, for nearly 10 years—knowing I would never be honored by such magnificence again. His eyes revealed the soul of a man at peace with himself. A man who chose to die as he lived—fully conscious of what he was about. And perhaps if each of us he touched chooses to emulate his spirit however we can, we will, finally, give him the home he deserves—in our consciousness.

Index to
OBAC Writers

(Dates in parentheses indicate years as active OBAC member)

ALKALIMAT, ABDUL (GERALD MCWORTER) (c. 1967-1970): Founder of OBAC and People's College; former professor at the University of Illinois. Presently Executive Director of 21st Century Books; Chicago, Ill.
Essay: "OBAC Position Paper," 11 (reprinted from *NOMMO*, 1969)

AMINI-HUDSON, JOHARI M. (1967-1976): Author of five poetry volumes including *Images in Black* and *Let's Go Some Where*. Poems and essays published in *The Black Poets, The Poetry of Black America, Confirmation: An Anthology of African American Women*, and 14 other collections. Included in *Dictionary of Literary Biography, Black American Writers Past and Present* and *Contemporary Authors*. Chiropractor; Decatur, Ga.
Poetry: "A Hip Tale in The Death Style," 97 (originally published as Broadside No. 59 [Detroit: Broadside Press, 1972]); "Signals," 99 (reprinted from Woodie King, ed., *Black Spirits* [New York: Random House, 1972]; Untitled ["in commemoration of the Blk family"], 100 (from *Black Spirits*); "Story for The Remainder," 244 (reprinted from Amiri Baraka and Amina Baraka, *Confirmation: An Anthology of African-American Women* [New York: Quill, 1983]); Untitled ["before you"], 246.

ANDERSON, DEBRA (c. 1973-1976): Published in *Bicentennial Review*. Writes, teaches and works in theatre and film in New York City.
Poetry: Untitled ["i feel sorry for blk cats"], 86 (reprinted from *NOMMO*, 1975); "Gettin Back into That Swing," 242 (originally published in Obasong series, 1980)
Fiction: "The Gift of The Spirit," 187.

ARMSTEAD, COLLETTE (1983-present): Included in *DuSable Museum Seminar Anthology, Cumbaya, Divine Poetry in Chocolate, Forward Motion, Upfront: A Black Woman's Magazine*, and *Elancee*. Recipient of Ragdale Fellowship (1986), Northeastern University Talent Scholarship (1986), and winner of poetry contests at Olive-Harvey Community College. OBAC Program Director; Chicago, Ill.
Poetry: "dream/9139," 256; "On the Number 3," 257; Untitled ["God is so weird"], 257.
Fiction: "a lil dribble drabble," 164.

BARNES, S. BRANDI (1980-1985): Author of poetry collection, *Blackberries in the China-Cabinet*. Poetry included in *Essence, Black American Literature Forum, Black Collegian, Color-lines*, and *Seanna*. Recipient of Robert R. McCormick Fellowship (1986), Gwendolyn Brooks Award and Columbia College Literary Excellence Award. Freelance writer; Chicago, Ill.
Poetry: "Gentlemen at The Barber Shop," 259; "Prima Bopper," 260; "Sand Dance," 261 (all from S. Brandi Barnes, *Blackberries in the China-Cabinet* [Chicago: Kar-Mel Publishers, 1983]).
Essay: "Bag People," 45.

BLAKELY, NORA BROOKS (1975-1979): Author of *O.F.F.!: Overcoming Fat with Fun* and *Shani-On-The-Hill*. Articles and stories published in *Ebony Jr.!* Executive Director of Chocolate Chips Theatre Company; Chicago, Ill.
Poetry: "Negativism/Reconsideration," 115; "James T. Eldridge," 264.
Fiction: "The Saga of Sadfly," 161; "Why The Wind Moans," 162.

BOYKIN, RANDSON (c. 1967-1976): A poet/performance artist whose interest in African Diasporan culture has involved study and performances in the U.S. and Brazil. Founded the Katherine Dunham Foundation in mid-1970's and is presently Executive Director; Chicago, Ill.
Poetry, "Peace of Mind," 104.

BRADFORD, WALTER (1967-1971): Included in *Jump Bad: A Chicago Anthology*, *NOMMO*, *Journal of Black Poetry*, *Black World*, and *Heartland II*. Recipient of Gwendolyn Brooks Traveling and Writing Fellowship (1969), Chicago Community Trust Fellowship Award and Poetry on the Bus Award. Writer/Poet/Consultant; Chicago, Ill.
> Poetry: "Sermon for The Sake of My Children," 124 (reprinted from *NOMMO*, 1975); "As Woman," 262; "My Speech to A Casual Redeemer," 263.

BROWN, CECIL (c. 1967-1968): Author of the novels *The Life and Loves of Mr. Jiveass Nigger*, *Days Without Weather*, and screenplay "Which Way Is Up." Work included in *Evergreen Review*, *Negro Digest*, *Black Scholar*, *Yardbird Reader*. Recently returned to U.S. after doing film work in Germany for a number of years.
> Fiction: "The Doe," 136 (reprinted from *NOMMO*, 1969)

CHAMBERLAIN, CARL (c. 1973-1975): At last word, had returned to his native Missouri.
> Poetry: "Say It Ain't So," 111 (reprinted from *NOMMO*, 1975).

CHERRY, EILEEN C. (1969-1976): Included in *Toledo Blade*, *Black World*, *NOMMO*, *Spoon River Quarterly*, *Callaloo*, *Open Places*. Recipient of 1987 Illinois Arts Council Creative Arts Fellowship in Poetry and Fiction Writing. Academic Advisor, Columbia College; Chicago, Ill.
> Poetry: "fat legs," 127; "in the/groves," 129 (reprinted from *Black World*, 9/75); "garfield/55th," 277; "africans sleeping in the park at night," 278; "the mechanic," 279.
> Fiction: "The Butcher's Wife," 223.

CLARDY, DANIEL (c. 1973-1976): Published in *NOMMO* and *MOJO*. Studied film in Southern California, presently working on a collection of short stories. Admissions and Records Officer for the School of Architecture and Urban Planning, University of Illinois; Chicago, Ill.
> Fiction: "Open Grave," 266.

COCHRAN, BARBARA (1982-present): Included in *DuSable Museum Writers Anthology* and *Divine Poetry in Chocolate*. Copywriter; Chicago, Ill.
> Poetry: "Life Lines," 269; "Memories at Mayrinna," 270.
> Fiction: "The Phone," 213.

COLE-ONYANGO, PAULINE (c. 1969-1971): A teacher, left Chicago to live for a time in East Africa. At last word, working on a doctorate in psychology in Detroit, Mich.
> Poetry: "I Drink to The Glory of My God," 119 (reprinted from *NOMMO*, 1975).

COLLINS, ALFREDA (c. 1973-1976): Published in *NOMMO*, *Chicago Sun-Times*. Teacher of the hearing impaired; Chicago, Ill.
> Poetry: "Common Ground," 96 (reprinted from *NOMMO*, 1975).

COOK, SMALLEY M. (MIKE) (c. 1968-1972): Author of six play productions, including *Drums of the Night Gods* and *A Gift to the Galaxy*, and three radio productions. Fiction and poetry included in *Jump Bad: A Chicago Anthology*, *Black Expression*, *NOMMO*, *The Journal of Black Poetry*, and *Afrika Must Unite*. Winner of Gwendolyn Brooks Fiction Contest and New Screenwriters Award. Recipient of Theatre Grant, Chicago Office of Fine Arts. Producer/administrator/educator; Chicago, Ill.
> Poetry: "Mikado Quartet," 118.
> Drama: "Masque Etude," 176.

CUNNINGHAM, JIM (1967-1969): Author of *Blue Narrator*. Poems and essays included in *Jump Bad: A Chicago Anthology*, *Black World*, *Another Chicago Magazine*, *Black American Literature Forum*. Recipient of Florida Writing Fellow (1981-82), Purdue Black Cultural Center's Howard McCall Award (1987). Graduate student/freelance writer; West Lafayette, In.
> Poetry: "Music to accompany jack johnson," 106; "Damani on the Hudson," 252; "Man Wishing on A Moon," 254; "Laid Back Blues," 255.
> Fiction: "The Color Black," 217.

DAVIS, RONDA (c. 1967-1972): Work included in *Jump Bad*, *A Broadside Treasury*, *Black Spirits*, *Negro Digest*. Co-founder of *OBAC Newsletter* (now *Cumbaya*). Teacher; Bay Area of California.
> Poetry: "Towards A Black Aesthetic," 66, and "Wine-dipped Woman," 67 (both reprinted from *NOMMO*, 1975); "suhmtymz," 66 (reprinted from *Negro Digest*, 9/69).

DAWSON, JANICE (c. 1973-1975).
> Poetry: "Stop and Shop," 121 (reprinted from *NOMMO*, 1975)

DOOLEY, EBON (c. 1967-1969): Author of poetry volume, *Revolution*. Published in *Black World* and *Rhythm*. Co-founder and editor of a new literary magazine in Atlanta, Ga.
    Poetry: "The Mighty John Hancock Building. . . ," 80 (reprinted from *Negro Digest*, 9/69).

FAVORS, EUNICE (c. 1970-1974): Teacher; Chicago, Ill.
    Poetry: "Nature and Naturalness," 83 (reprinted from *NOMMO*, 1975).

FOULKS, WARREN (c. 1973-1976); Published in *Black World*. Died in 1980, survived by daughter, Serene.
    Poetry: "#5 The Courts," 87 (reprinted from *NOMMO*, 1975).

FULLER, HOYT W. (1967-1976): See "Hoyt W. Fuller—A Capsule," page 295 of this anthology.
    Essays: "Introduction Toward The Black Aesthetic," 15 (reprinted from *NOMMO*, 1972); "Foreword to *NOMMO*," 17 (reprinted from *NOMMO*, 1975); "The African Reunion: A Surpassing Urgency," 54.
    Poetry: "Twice Widowed," 126 (from *NOMMO*, 1975).
    Fiction: "A Plundered World," 148 (from *NOMMO*, 1975).

GREENLEE, SAM (c. 1968-1971): Author of the novels *The Spook Who Sat by The Door* and *Baghdad Blues*, the poetry volumes *Blues for An African Princess* and *Ammunition*, and the play "Southside Blues." Taught creative writing at the Marla Gibbs Arts Development Center in Los Angeles; presently living and working in Spain.
    Fiction: "Blues for Little Prez," 141 (reprinted from *Black World*, 8/73)

HIGGS, E. VAN (c. 1969-1972): Published in *Black World* and *Rhythm*. Teacher; Chicago, Ill.
    Poetry: "Bushwoman," 120 (reprinted from *NOMMO*, 1975).

JACKSON, ANGELA (1970-present): Author of the poetry volumes *Voodoo/Love Magic*, *The Greenville Club*, *Solo in The Boxcar Third Floor E*, and *The Man with The White Liver* and the plays "Witness! A Voice Anthology," "Shango Diaspora," and "Hillary Clay." Published in *Celebration*, *15 Chicago Poets*, *Mississippi Writers* Vol. 4, *The Writer and The World*. Recipient of numerous honors, including Before Columbus Foundation American Book Award, Illinois Arts Council Prize in Fiction (1986, 1980, 1977) and Poetry (1986), and Academy of American Poets College Prize. Presently a poetry instructor at Columbia College and teacher at St. Charles Lwanga School; Chicago, Ill.
    Poetry: "Second Meeting," 122; "in my fathers garden," 123 (both from *NOMMO*, 1975); "Arachnia: Her Side of the Story," 288 (reprinted from *13th Moon*, 1983); "In Her Solitude: The Inca Divining Spider," 290 (reprinted from *Open Places*, 1983); "Hattie," 291; "What I Said As A Child," 292 (reprinted from *First World*, 1977).
    Drama: "Shango Diaspora," 183.
    Essays: "Preface to *Cumbaya*, 24 (*Cumbaya*, 1976); "Why OBAC Is," 25 (*Cumbaya*, 1981).

JACKSON, MAGA (c. 1970-71): Author of *Poem Words for My Black Brothers and Sisters*. A psychiatrist living in Southern California.
    Poetry: "Change-Up," 88 (reprinted from *NOMMO*, 1975).

JACKSON-OPOKU, SANDRA (1972-present): Included in *Black World*, *First World*, *Africa Woman*, *Essence*, *Open Places*, *Heresies*, and *Black Enterprise*. Recipient of National Endowment for the Arts Fellowship, New York International Film and TV Festival Silver Medal Award, General Electric Foundation CCLM Award for Younger Writers, and DuSable Museum Writers Conference Hoyt W. Fuller Award. Freelance journalist/television scriptwriter; Chicago, Ill.
    Poetry: Untitled ["Here is my voice"], 71; "Ancestors," 72; "Black birds," 72 (reprinted from *NOMMO*, 1975); "To Be Awakened by Birds," 247.
    Fiction: "Mr. Gooden's House," 199.

JAMILA-RA (MAXINE HALL ELLISON) (1967-1972): Author of two poetry volumes, *The Good Book* and *The Look at Yourself Book*. Included in *Film Comment Magazine*, *Show*, *Continental*, *NOMMO*, *Negro Digest*, *To Gwen with Love* and *Afram Publications*. 1972 winner of the Chicago Poetry Festival and included in the Vivian G. Harsh Collection (1972, 1977). Writer; Chicago, Ill.
    Poetry: "Ode to Magus: Thou Art That," 101.

JOSEPH, OSCAR (1979-1981): Included in *AIM* and *Chicago Mahogany*. Caseworker; Chicago, Ill.
    Fiction: "Suite for Queen," 192.

KING, HELEN (c. 1967-1971): Author of children's books *Willie* and *The Soul of Christmas.* Published in *Ebony.* A journalist and creative writer; Chicago, Ill.
  Poetry: "To Be Here, Black," 90 (from *NOMMO,* 1975).

LEWIS, MELVIN E. (1976-1986): Published in *The Black Panther, Black Express, Obsidian, Urban Focus, Postal Life.* Recipient of Significant Illinois Poet Award (1987) and First Prize in Poetry from the Ernie Street Press (1982). Mail Processing Manager, U.S. Postal Service; Matteson, Ill.
  Poetry: "Seasons of Love and Juju," 108; "Campanera III," 250, and "Campanera IV," 250 (both from *Cumbaya,* 1981).

LOTT, JOHNNIE (c. 1971-1976): Published in *Black World.*
  Poetry: "Facing The Storm," 82 (reprinted from *NOMMO,* 1975)

LOVE, DENISE (c. 1971-1976): After working as an insurance underwriter in Chicago, married fellow OBAC member David Sims. They presently live in Iowa.
  Poetry: "The Zoo," 92 (reprinted from *NOMMO,* 1975)

LOWE, GEORGE LEON (1982-present): Freelance writer; Chicago, Ill.
  Fiction: "Mama Just Didn't Like Thunder," 209.

McCONNELL, ANTOINETTE (1984-present): University employee and student; Chicago, Ill.
  Poetry: "Brown Women and Sisterhood," 284; "Odessa Johnson," 285.

MADHUBUTI, HAKI R. (Don L. Lee) (c. 1967-1974): Author of 15 books, including *Don't Cry, Scream; Earthquakes and Sunrise Missions;* and *Killing Memory, Seeking Ancestors.* Poetry selections widely anthologized. Contributing editor to *Black Scholar.* Recipient of Illinois Arts Council completion grant, National Endowment Fellowship for poetry, Distinguished Writers Award from the Middle Atlantic Writers Association, the Robert and Hazel Ferguson Memorial Award for Poetry, Alain Locke Award for Literature. Director of Institute of Positive Education/Associate Professor of English at Chicago State University and Publisher of Third World Press (which is also celebrating 20 years); Chicago, Ill.
  Essays: "Black Poetics/for the many to come," 13 (from *NOMMO,* 1975); "Why Foreign Policy Is Foreign to Most African-Americans," 47.
  Poetry: "Communication in whi-te," 68; "But He Was Cool," 68; "Gwendolyn Brooks," 69 (all from Don L. Lee, *Don't Cry, Scream* [Detroit: Broadside Press, 1969]). "Luther," 236; "POET: Gwendolyn Brooks at 70," 237; "Always Remember Where You Are," 238; "The Great Wait," 239 (all from Haki R. Madhubuti, *Killing Memory, Seeking Ancestors* [Detroit: Lotus Press, 1987]).

MAHONE, BARBARA (c. 1968-1974): Author of poetry volume, *Sugarfields.* Published in *Black World* and *Black Culture.* Moved from Chicago to Atlanta in the mid-1970s.
  Poetry: "What Color Is Black?", 84 (reprinted from *Negro Digest,* 9/69); "A Sea of Brown Boys," 85 (reprinted from *Negro Digest,* 8/74)

MASSEY, JUDY B. (1983-present): Included in *American Poetry Anthology, Network Africa, Divine Poetry in Chocolate,* Winner of 1987 Hoyt W. Fuller Play Festival for *Shop Talk.* Advertising copywriter; Chicago, Ill.
  Fiction: "A Love Story Written in the Light," 165.
  Drama: "Shop Talk," 167.

PLUMPP, STERLING (c. 1968-1974): Author of *Black Rituals* and several poetry volumes, including *Portable Soul, Half Black/HalfBlacker* and *The Mojo Hands Call I Must Go.* Editor, *Somehow We Survive: An Anthology of South African Writing.* Included in *Black Culture, The Poetry of Black America, Celebrations, Nimrod: The New Black Writing, Mississippi Writers* Volumes 1-4. Recipient of Illinois Arts Council Literary Awards (1986, 1980, 1975); Carl Sandburg Award (1983); DuSable Museum Poetry Award (1983); Broadside Press First Publication award (1975). Associate Professor of Black Studies, University of Illinois-Chicago; Poetry Editor, *Black American Literature Forum;* Contributing Editor, *Another Chicago Magazine.*
  Commentary: "OBAC and Black Children," 21 (reprinted from *NOMMO,* 1972)
  Poetry: "Stand Up Stepping to Sounds of Coming Men," 78 (reprinted from *NOMMO,* 1975); "Speech," 271; "Alms," 272; "Big Maybelle," 272; "Official: for William Faulkner," 273.

RODGERS, CAROLYN (c. 1967-1971): Author of poetry volumes *Paper Soul, Songs of A Blackbird, How I Got Ovah, The Heart as Ever Green.* Included in *Sturdy Black Bridges, Jump Bad, To Gwen with Love, Black Women Writers at Work.* National Book Award nominee (1976) and recipient of National Endowment for the Arts Fellowship, Conrad Kent Rivers Memorial Award (*Black World*), Society of Midland Authors Poetry Prize. Profiled in *Dictionary of Literary Biographies*. Recently teaching at Chicago State University, alternating residence between Chicago and the Bay Area of California.

Commentary: "Black Poetry—Where It's At," 28 (reprinted from *Negro Digest*, 9/69).

Poetry: "how i got ovah," 73; "mo luv," 74; "For H. W. Fuller," 75 (all reprinted from Carolyn M. Rodgers, *how i got ovah* [New York: Doubleday, 1975]); "Touch (Poem 5)," 248; "wimmin," 249; "Aunt Dolly," 249 (all reprinted from Amiri Baraka and Amina Baraka, *Confirmation: An Anthology of African American Women* [New York: Quill, 1983]).

ROYSTER, PHILIP (c. 1970-1973): Author of the poetry volume, *The Back Door*. Published in *Black World, Obsidian, Black American Literature Forum*. At last word, Professor of English and Creative Writing, Kansas State University.

Poetry: "Intimacy," 116; "Truth . . . Honesty," 116; "Condemned," 117; "You've Got It Made," 265; "Enticement," 268.

ROYSTER, SANDRA (c. 1970-1973): Published in *Black World*. Winner of Gwendolyn Brooks Poetry Prize (*Black World*). Director Program, Chicago Office of Fine Arts; Chicago, Ill.

Poetry: "First Blues," 110 (reprinted from *NOMMO*, 1975); "Enchanted," 258.

RYAN, DON (1987-present): Included in *American College Poetry Anthology, Dollars and Sense*, and *Dawn*. Teacher; Chicago, Ill.

Poetry: "Negroes in the Middle Class Who Have No Class, But White Class," 280; "The Fear of AIDS," 281; "Bad Luck," 281.

SAFI, ADALISHA (c. 1967-1971): Los Angeles, Calif.

Untitled ["remember one early morning"], 114 (reprinted from *NOMMO*, 1975)

SHUAYB, OMAR (c. 1971-1977): Recipient of Illinois Arts Council Literary Prize (1976). Chicago, Ill.

Poetry: "John Henry Revisited," 79 (reprinted from *NOMMO*, 1975).

SIMS, DAVID (c. 1971-1976): Married to former OBAC member Denise Love and living in Iowa.

Poetry: "Midnight Blues Note," 112 (reprinted from *NOMMO*, 1975)

SMITH, D. L. CROCKETT (1976-1980): Author of numerous articles, reviews, and polemical writings published in *Ebony, Black Enterprise, Georgia Review, Dictionary of Literary Biography: Afro-American Writers After 1955, The Berkshire Eagle*, and *The Chicago Review*. Poetry included in *The Black Scholar, The Odessa Review, Open Places, The Minnesota Review, Cumbaya*, and *First World*. Winner of Bedford Prizes Competition, Sydney Smith Contest, John Billings Fiske Poetry Contest, and Massachusetts Arts Council Poetry Competition finalist. Associate Professor of English, Williams College; Berkshire, Mass.

Essay: "Angela Jackson," 38 (reprinted from *Dictionary of Literary Biographies*, 41).

Poetry: "Footnote to A GNP," 130 (reprinted from *Cumbaya*); "Spring Song," 131 (reprinted from *Open Places*); "December Requiem," 286; "Cowboy Eating His Children," 287 (reprinted from *Open Places*).

TIMBERLAKE, DETMER (1986-present): Published in *Chicago Fine Arts* and *Chicago Observer*. Has written for and performed with jazz bands around the country for more than 15 years. Chicago, Ill.

Poetry: "August Moon," 282; "Chicago," 283.

TOWNS, JEANNE (1982-present): Published in *Black American Literature Forum, Urban Focus, Chicago Observer, Catalyst*. Legal secretary; Chicago, Ill.

Poetry: "The Specter," 274; "When Morning Comes," 275.

WASAIAH, ANDREW (WHITFIELD) (c. 1971-1976): Published in *Black World*. Worked at a highway weigh station; left Chicago to attend college in the West.

Poetry: "cold ft," 95 (reprinted from *NOMMO*, 1975)

WASHINGTON, PATRICIA (c. 1973-1974): Left Chicago to attend a doctoral program in psychology.

Fiction: "The Face," 159 (reprinted from *NOMMO*, 1975)

WILLIAMS, BIRDIE (c. 1973-1974).

Poetry: "Roses, Love," 107 (reprinted from *NOMMO*, 1975)

WILLIAMS, TONY (c. 1971-1977): A graphic artist and poet; Chicago, Ill.
    Poetry: Untitled ["women, black/U a token"], 91 (reprinted from *NOMMO*, 1975)

WIMBERLI, KHARLOS (c. 1968-1971). Published one volume of poetry. Died in 1975.
    Poetry: "The Shadows of Your Smile," 76 (reprinted from *NOMMO*, 1975).

YAKUBU, YAKIE (c. 1968-1971): Published in *Black World*.
    Poetry: "Your Deal," 77; "Jagged Balagoon," 77 (both reprinted from *NOMMO*, 1975)

Guest Contributors

HOUSTON A. BAKER's prolific work in the area of Black literature includes his own *Long Black Song: Essays in Black American Literature* as well as *Twentieth Century Interpretations of Native Son* and *Black Literature in America*, which he edited. He has taught at the University of Pennsylvania, the University of Virginia (Charlottesville), and Yale University.

GWENDOLYN BROOKS, of course, is Gwendolyn Brooks. A Pulitzer Prize-winner, Poet Laureate of Illinois and former Poetry Consultant to the Library of Congress she has personally nurtured the careers of many writers, through several awards she funds, writers workshops, support of Black publishing companies, readings in the community, continuing to *live* in the community, and the sheer inspiration of her belief in the writers. Some of her later books include *Report from Part One, To Disembark, Blacks,* and *The Near Johannesburg Boy.*

PAMELA CASH-MENZIES is head librarian of Johnson Publishing Co.

EUGENIA COLLIER is presently a Professor of English at Coppin State College (Baltimore, Md.) and formerly taught at Howard University and several other institutions. A poet and fiction writer, she won the Middle Atlantic Writers Award (1984) for an excerpt from her novel-in-progress, *Cry from Infinity.*

MARI EVANS is a writer, educator and musician whose poetry appears in nearly every major anthology. Her three volumes of poetry are *Where Is All The Music, I Am A Black Woman* and *Nightstar;* she has also written plays, musicals, children's books, and several articles. She is at work on a novel.

ADDISON GAYLE, a Professor of English at Baruch College of the City University of New York, has contributed greatly to the development of relevant literary criticism. He edited *Black Expression* and *The Black Aesthetic* as well as authored *The Black Situation.*

ROBERT L. HARRIS, formerly a Professor of Afro-American History at Cornell University (Ithaca, N.Y.), recently became Director of Cornell's Africana Studies & Research Center.

The late **GEORGE E. KENT** stood, Hoyt Fuller once wrote, "in the top echelon of American writers of literary criticism." A longtime Professor of English at the University of Chicago, Brother Kent published his first book, *Blackness and The Adventure of Western Culture,* through Haki R. Madhubuti's Third World Press and also authored *William Faulkner and White Racial Consciousness.* He completed a study of one of his favorite authors, Gwendolyn Brooks, shortly before his death in 1982. He served as OBAC's advisor from 1978-80.

RICHARD A. LONG is internationally known as a scholar, writer, linguist, and *raconteur.* As Professor of English and Afro-American Studies, as well as Chairman of the Afro-American Studies Department, at Atlanta University, he was responsible for organizing important cultural exchanges between Africans in America, on the Continent, in the Caribbean and South America. He co-edited *Anthology of Afro-American Writing: Prose and Poetry* and is author of the pictorial *Black Americana* and *Ascending and Other Poems.*

MARIA K. MOOTRY has taught in the English Departments of Kennedy-King College (Chicago, Ill.), Northwestern University, and Southern Illinois University. Her poetry and essays have been published in *Open Places, Obsidian, The Massachusetts Review,* and *The College Language Association Journal.*

CAROLE A. PARKS was an editor with *Esquire* magazine and Anchor Books (Doubleday), as well as managing editor of *Black World* and *First World* magazines. She is presently a freelance writer and consultant in communications and human resource development.

KALAMU YA SALAAM (Val Ferdinand) is a writer and publisher who frequently coverd the New Orleans, La., theatre scene for *Negro Digest/Black World* magazine. His poetry/essay volumes include *Iron Flowers* and *Women Hold Up Half The Sky*. He moved into publishing with the launching of *Black Collegian* and *Black New Orleans* magazines.